The Real
Sinéad O'Connor

About the Author

Ariane Sherine is an author, journalist, scriptwriter and singer-songwriter who has been writing professionally for more than two decades.

She has previously authored, co-authored and edited four non-fiction books: *Talk Yourself Better* (Hachette); *How to Live to 100* and *The How of Happy* (both co-writes with David Conrad for Hachette); and *The Atheist's Guide to Christmas* (edited for HarperCollins).

As a journalist, she has written 75 opinion columns for the *Guardian*. She has also written travel features for the *Sunday Times*, features for the *Independent, Independent on Sunday* and *Esquire*, literary reviews for the *Observer*, celebrity interviews for *New Humanist* and album reviews for *NME*.

In addition, she has scripted and presented a video series about Twitter, *GNews140*, for the *Guardian*.

As a television comedy writer, she has written for BBC, ITV and Channel 4 shows. These include *My Family, Two Pints of Lager and a Packet of Crisps, Countdown, The Story of Tracy Beaker, The New Worst Witch* and *Space Pirates*.

Briefly famous in 2009 for creating the hugely successful Atheist Bus Campaign, which ran in 13 countries across the world including the US and Australia, she has appeared regularly on national and international television and radio.

A trained musician, she holds a BA in Commercial Music with First Class Honours. Her debut solo pop album *Better* is now available to buy and stream under the artist name Ariane X.

The Real Sinéad O'Connor

Ariane Sherine

WHITE OWL

AN IMPRINT OF PEN & SWORD BOOKS LTD
YORKSHIRE – PHILADELPHIA

First published in Great Britain in 2024 by
WHITE OWL
an imprint of Pen & Sword Books Ltd
Yorkshire – Philadelphia

Copyright © Ariane Sherine, 2024

ISBN 978-1-03610-823-6

The right of Ariane Sherine to be identified as the author of this work has been asserted by her in accordance with the Copyright, Designs and Patents Act 1988.

A CIP catalogue record for this book is available from the British Library.

All rights reserved. No part of this book may be reproduced or transmitted in any form or by any means, electronic or mechanical including photocopying, recording or by any information storage and retrieval system, without permission from the Publisher in writing.

Typeset by Concept, Huddersfield, West Yorkshire, HD4 5JL.
Printed and bound in England by CPI Group (UK) Ltd, Croydon CR0 4YY.

Pen & Sword Books Ltd incorporates the imprints of Aviation, Atlas, Family History, Fiction, Maritime, Military, Discovery, Politics, History, Archaeology, Select, Wharncliffe Local History, Wharncliffe True Crime, Military Classics, Wharncliffe Transport, Leo Cooper, The Praetorian Press, Remember When, White Owl, Seaforth Publishing and Frontline Books.

For a complete list of Pen & Sword titles please contact
PEN & SWORD BOOKS LTD
47 Church Street, Barnsley, South Yorkshire, S70 2AS, England
E-mail: enquiries@pen-and-sword.co.uk
Website: www.pen-and-sword.co.uk
or
PEN & SWORD BOOKS
1950 Lawrence Rd, Havertown, PA 19083, USA
E-mail: uspen-and-sword@casematepublishers.com
Website: www.penandswordbooks.com

Contents

Introduction	ix
1. Childhood (1966–1978)	1
2. Adolescence (1979–1985)	6
3. Starting Out (1985–1986)	13
4. Recording Her Debut (1986)	17
5. Affinity with Rastafari and Black Music (1986)	21
6. 'Heroine', and a Fight with U2 (1986)	23
7. First Child and First Marriage (1986–1987)	25
8. *The Lion and the Cobra* (1987)	26
9. Interviews (1987–1988)	29
10. Support for the IRA (1989)	37
11. *Hush-a-Bye-Baby* (1989)	38
12. 'Nothing Compares 2 U' (1990)	39
13. Finding a New Manager	43
14. *I Do Not Want What I Haven't Got* (1990)	44
15. Commemorating the Fall of the Berlin Wall (1990)	46
16. A Run-In with Madonna (1990)	46
17. Affair with Hugh Harris (1990)	46
18. Refusing the US National Anthem (1990)	47
19. On Abortion (1990)	49
20. Breaking a Mic (1991)	50
21. A Tribute to Elton John (1991)	50
22. A Fist Fight with Prince (1991)	51
23. Boycotting the Grammys (1991)	54
24. Saddam Hussein Incident on MTV (1991)	56
25. *Am I Not Your Girl?* (1992)	56

26. Ripping Up the Pope (1992) 57
27. The Bob Dylan 30th Anniversary Concert (1992) 61
28. Supporting Peter Gabriel (1993) 64
29. Advert in *Irish Times* (1993) 65
30. *Universal Mother* (1994) 65
31. Reconciling with U2 (1994) 67
32. A Second Child (1995) 67
33. Guesting on *Broken China* (1996) 67
34. Represented by O'Ceallaigh a Second Time 68
35. *Gospel Oak* (1997) 68
36. *So Far. . . the Best Of* (1997) 69
37. Changing Record Label (1998) 70
38. Her First Suicide Attempt (1999) 70
39. Being Ordained as a Priest (1999) 70
40. Dating Dermott Hayes (1999) 71
41. *Faith and Courage* (2000) 72
42. Saving Shane MacGowan (2000) 73
43. Coming Out. . . And Coming Back In (2000) 74
44. Nursing Steve Fargnoli (2001) 75
45. Getting Married Again (2001) 76
46. *Sean-Nós Nua* (2002) 77
47. *She Who Dwells in the Secret Place of the Most High Shall Abide Under the Shadow of the Almighty* (2003) 78
48. Early Retirement. . . But Not for Long (2003) 78
49. A Third Child (2004) 78
50. Advert in *Irish Examiner* (2004) 78
51. *Collaborations* (2005) 79
52. *Throw Down Your Arms* (2005) 79
53. A Love Rivalry and Fourth Child (2006) 80
54. *Theology* (2007) 82
55. *Live at the Sugar Club* (2008) 83
56. Represented by O'Ceallaigh Again (2008) 83

57. Collaboration with Mary J. Blige (2009) 83
58. Song Used Without Permission on Real IRA Website (2009) . 84
59. A Third Marriage (2010) 84
60. Vindication (2010) 85
61. Looking for Love on Twitter (2011) 88
62. A Cry for Help (2011) 89
63. A Fourth Marriage (2011) 90
64. *How About I Be Me (and You Be You)?* (2012) 92
65. Splitting with O'Ceallaigh for the Second Time (2012) 96
66. A Very Candid Interview on Mental Health (2012) 96
67. An Argument with Miley Cyrus (2013) 103
68. Getting Face Tattoos (2013) 106
69. Recognition of Misdiagnosis of Bipolar (2013) 107
70. *I'm Not Bossy, I'm the Boss* (2014) 108
71. A Second Neil McCormick Interview (2014) 110
72. Interest in Sinn Féin (2014) 113
73. Blasting *Rolling Stone* and Reality Shows (2015) 113
74. Becoming a Grandmother (2015) 114
75. Being Shafted by Her Agent (2015) 114
76. A Radical Hysterectomy (2015) 114
77. Suicide Attempt (2015) 115
78. Letters to Her Family (2016) 115
79. Surgery and Complications (2016) 116
80. Dispute with Arsenio Hall (2017) 116
81. Sued by O'Ceallaigh (2017) 118
82. Charity and Trans Rights (2017) 118
83. Breakdown in Motel (2017) 118
84. Dr. Phil Interview (2017) 119
85. Change of Name (2017) 120
86. Conversion to Islam (2018) 120
87. One More Yard (2018) 123
88. Performing Live Again (2019) 123

vii

89. Studying Healthcare (2020)	124
90. 'Trouble of the World' (2020)	124
91. *Rememberings* (2021)	125
92. A Retirement Announcement and Retraction (2021)	126
93. Putting Her Own Stamp on the World (2021)	127
94. Shane (2022)	127
95. *Nothing Compares* (2022)	129
96. Choice Music Prize (2023)	130
97. Struggling with Grief (2023)	130
98. Death (2023)	130
99. Tributes (2023)	131
100. Pushback to Tributes (2023)	134
101. Pushback to Obituary (2023)	135
102. Funeral and Further Tributes (2023)	138
103. Family Statement (2023)	139
104. Legacy (2023)	139
Author's Note	148
Bibliography	151

Introduction

This book is called *The Real Sinéad O'Connor*, as it is one of '*The Real ...*' series of books from publisher Pen & Sword, each revealing the truth about a different public figure from history.

'Real' is also the perfect description of O'Connor. She was one of the world's most emotionally honest and open public figures, though she preferred to be known as a protest singer rather than a pop star or celebrity.

O'Connor lived her truth and wore her heart on her sleeve, a character trait which would cause her great pain during her life, but also allow her to be fully herself. She refused to conform to society's demands, whether in terms of her appearance, behaviour or beliefs, and was accordingly unfairly vilified by many.

I hope this book will document how courageous, genuine, resilient and revolutionary she was, as an abuse survivor, recording artist and a woman of her time.

1. Childhood (1966–1978)

"Child abuse casts a shadow the length of a lifetime," wrote the sculptor and artist Herbert Ward. At the end of her 2021 memoir *Rememberings*, Sinéad O'Connor reassured her parents that they hadn't contributed to her mental health problems, saying in typical endearing fashion that she was "born bonkers" and "would have been as nutty as a fuckin' fruitcake and as crazy as a loon even if [I'd] had Saint Joseph and the Virgin Mary for parents"[1]. Yet it would be surprising if her abusive upbringing hadn't affected her greatly.

She was born Sinéad Marie Bernadette O'Connor on 8 December 1966, at the Cascia House Nursing Home in Glenageary, Dublin. Named Sinéad after the mother of Éamon de Valera Junior, the doctor who supervised her delivery, her namesake Sinéad de Valera was the wife of the then-president of Ireland, Éamon de Valera. O'Connor was given her second middle name, Bernadette, after Saint Bernadette of Lourdes.

She was the second-youngest of four children from the marriage between her father John Oliver 'Seán' O'Connor and mother Johanna 'Marie' O'Grady: in order, Marie gave birth to Joseph, Eimear, Sinéad and John. Both well-off middle-class practising Catholics, Seán and Marie married young – Marie was barely 21 – in 1960 at the Church of Our Lady of Good Counsel in Drimnagh, a suburb of Dublin.

In 1966, the year of O'Connor's birth, Ireland was fiercely Roman Catholic, conservative and hugely in thrall to the church. Women were not allowed to have abortions, access contraception or have children out of wedlock, and they had to stop work as soon as they married. Same-sex relationships were not an option for either men or women, and had to be kept secret.

Women were expected to be submissive housewives and devote themselves to pleasing their husbands and raising their children. Magdalene Laundries still existed, institutions where 'fallen women' were locked up – often for their whole lives – if they became pregnant outside of marriage or failed to conform to conservative society in a way it deemed unacceptable.

Sinéad O'Connor would grow up to shine a light on these injustices.

While she was young and her parents were still together, O'Connor became enchanted with the piano at her paternal grandfather's house. She would talk to it, asking it questions, and imagining it asked her to play it.

Her father also had musical talent: "My father understands about songs making me cry," she wrote in her memoir. "He sings me 'Scarlet Ribbons' … His voice sounds very sad." She said that Seán often felt very melancholy, the same way that she did. She was stunned by the song, but didn't want actual scarlet ribbons. Instead, she just wanted to escape into music, because her home life was so bleak: "I don't like reality."[2]

The family dynamic was extremely dysfunctional. O'Connor would later say that she felt furious and neglected by her family, as no one discussed what was happening within the family or asked how she was dealing with it.

O'Connor would grow up to record a haunting *sean-nós* version of 'Scarlet Ribbons' for her third studio album. Backed only by tin whistle, the song would end with a coda on traditional Irish uilleann pipes.

Aged 19, O'Connor would tell *Hot Press*, "My father has a really great tenor voice and I think always wished he'd been a singer. He's from Crumlin and had a lot of old-fashioned Irish songs which he used to teach us, then we'd sing into a little dictaphone machine. He still has the tapes!"[3]

Seán had the dictaphone for business purposes. He taped his daughter's sweet, pure voice and kept the recordings as they were so beautiful.

O'Connor's parents separated in 1975. Seán wanted to divorce Marie, but divorce was illegal in Ireland. The first divorce in Ireland would only be granted in 1997, after a 1995 referendum on the issue showed that 50.3% of respondents thought divorce should be legal. In a 1986 referendum on the question, only 36.5% had said yes.

When O'Connor's father Seán left, the four children cried because they missed him. In fury, their mother Marie locked the children out of the house, putting them in a hut Seán had built them in the garden. She said if the children loved their father so much, they could go and live in the hut.

In response, O'Connor crouched on the ground in front of the back wall of the house when dusk fell, and called up to her mother to let the children back in. But Marie didn't reply – she simply turned out her bedroom light, pitching the garden into darkness and causing O'Connor to have a major panic attack. The experience would later become a song, 'Troy', on O'Connor's debut album.

O'Connor described blanking out the trauma, saying the next thing she could recall was being talked to by the judge of her parents' custody case in his garden, her hand in his. She was scared of revealing what her mother had done, in case Marie took retribution on her.

The incident made her agoraphobic, she told the *Guardian*'s Simon Hattenstone: "I find it difficult being outside. I don't mind when it turns into black night, but once the hours of dusk come, I get very anxious."[4]

Seán was finally awarded custody of the children as a result of the incident. He was only the second father in the country to be given sole custody. A structural engineer by profession, his struggles to gain custody and divorce his wife prompted Seán to qualify as a barrister.

Brendan O'Connor wrote in the *Irish Independent*, "[Sinéad's] father's efforts to secure custody of his children, in a country which routinely gave custody to the mother and prohibited divorce, caused him to become chairman of the Divorce Action Group and a prominent public spokesman ... He even debated his own wife on the subject on a radio show."[5]

The incident happened on the current affairs programme when, unknown to Seán, a fundamentalist group opposed to divorce put forward a 'Mrs O'Connor' to debate him. Seán didn't reveal that he knew he was actually debating Marie.[6]

Though they were safe while living with Seán, O'Connor and her younger brother John missed Marie deeply. O'Connor was affected by Marie's weeping when their father drove away with them, and by her mother's crying on each occasion she saw her.

As a result, while living at her father's house, O'Connor would lie under her brother's bed and wail loudly all day. After six months of listening to her keening, their father sent her and John back to live with Marie. O'Connor stayed there for four years, until she was 13.

During those four years, Marie repeatedly violently and sexually abused O'Connor, forcing her to lie on the floor naked with her legs and arms open before hitting her between her legs with a carpet sweeper, making her repeat the phrase "I am nothing" over and over. O'Connor suspected her mother wanted to damage her private parts, telling Hattenstone: "She had a thing about wanting me to be a boy."[7]

In 1991, O'Connor told *SPIN* magazine that she "was beaten up very severely with every kind of implement you can imagine yourself being beaten with." She added that she had no food for long periods and would be locked in her room, naked.[8]

She thought her mother abused her because she closely resembled her in looks.

As well as beating her reproductive parts, Marie drove her knee into O'Connor's stomach when she was standing against a wall, gave her a black eye and left her with welts on her legs. O'Connor won a prize at school for her ability to curl up into the tiniest ball, because she would have to do so when being punished by Marie. No one realised why she could curl herself up so compactly.

When questioned by a concerned teacher as to whether her injuries were due to abuse by her mother, the young O'Connor denied it, due to fear that Marie would kill her when she found out. She felt guilty for lying to her kindly teacher, and wished that she were the teacher's daughter instead of Marie's.

"[Child abuse] affects you in the now, all your relationships for the rest of your life," O'Connor would go on to say on a 1995 episode of *After Dark*. "And that is, to me, against God. God gave us life so that we could feel alive and good and love each other." But, she said, that was impossible if the 'Christ figures' [authority figures] in your life hadn't shown you love as a child.[9]

O'Connor attended Dominican College Sion Hill in Blackrock, County Dublin, and described being jealous watching her classmates walking down the street after school with their mothers' arms around their shoulders. She was envious because she spent the last day of each term petrified of her own mother's wrath. She would claim to Marie that she'd lost her hockey stick, for Marie would beat her with it throughout the holidays if she brought it back home.

As well as being physically and sexually abused, O'Connor was forced to steal by Marie. She told Hattenstone that her mother was a kleptomaniac who would steal from the church collection plate and view houses up for sale so she could nick items from them. During a hospital stay, Marie stole the crucifix from the wall, and sent O'Connor home concealing the hospital weighing scales under her school uniform.

This was despite both her parents being comfortable financially, she continued. She said her father was relatively wealthy. As for her mother, the family discovered after her death that she had been sitting on €250,000, despite having stopped paying her utility bills.

O'Connor became addicted to stealing, thieving peanut butter sandwiches from the other girls at school, money from teachers' handbags in the staff room and dresses from shops. Along with her mother, she would rattle charity tins in front of the general public and her mother would keep the donations.

"I was trying to make my mother happy by getting money for her," O'Connor told *SPIN* magazine in 1990. "Between the ages of 9 and 13 I must have been dragged to police stations about eight or nine times, but I never got charged with anything because I used to put on the waterworks." O'Connor would tell the police that Marie would literally kill her if they told her.[10]

In numerous interviews after Marie's death, O'Connor described her mother as a "beast" and a "devil", and said that she was only able to calm her mother's anger by singing to her, lulling her to sleep.

When she got confirmed into the Catholic church – undertaking a religious ceremony meant to confer the gifts of the Holy Spirit onto the confirmed person – O'Connor asked to visit the holy town of Lourdes in France for her confirmation present.

Her rationale was that she might be able to get a priest stationed there to fix her mother, given that pilgrims went to Lourdes to be healed. She didn't explain that this was why she was desperate to visit the holy place, and family members put her interest down to her being fascinated with the concept of a town where one could be healed.

O'Connor first heard about Lourdes because her birthday, 8 December, was a holy day. It was when the Pope had stated that the Immaculate Conception meant the Virgin Mary was free of Original Sin. Her grandmother explained this to her, and also told her about Saint Bernadette, after whom O'Connor had been given a middle name. A peasant girl named Bernadette Soubirous, she had claimed to have seen apparitions of the Virgin Mary on her visit to Lourdes in 1858, and had been canonized by the Catholic church as a result.

However, the visit to Lourdes didn't seem to have fixed her mother's mental illness. On the day before they were due to leave, O'Connor made the excuse that she wanted an ice cream, then went out alone searching for a priest, and found one casually reading a newspaper in the sunlight. In her memoir, she says she literally dragged the priest back to the hotel.

The priest went up to Marie's room, as O'Connor waited in the lobby. When he returned, he told her there was nothing he could do for her mother, and that she was to pray until she was an adult and was able to leave home – unless she could leave sooner.

O'Connor was dismayed and presumed the priest incompetent.

In Lourdes, O'Connor also fell in love with a tour guide, so decided to ask him to marry her. She wrote him a love letter and walked the two miles to his travel agency, her heart beating with great trepidation. When she saw him speaking on the phone, she suddenly realised that he might have a wife and the call might be to her.

When he hung up, O'Connor asked if she could speak to him in private, so he took her to the agency's kitchen and she handed him her love letter. He read the letter, finding it adorable and amusing, and thanked her for it. However, he said he was far too old to marry her, and he was gay in any case. He asked her not to tell anyone that he preferred men, because some people weren't OK with it, even though they were wrong and didn't understand that his sexuality was fine in the eyes of God.

He also told her not to tell any other adult men that she was in love with them, because adults shouldn't love children in that way, and not all adult men were as safe as he was. But he stressed that she was courageous in having told him that she loved him, and that she should always be fearless like that.

So she was pleased, and felt proud of herself for having had so much courage. Even though she had to return to Ireland without marrying him, and without getting her mother fixed.

2. Adolescence (1979–1985)

Eventually, at the age of 13, O'Connor escaped from her mother and chose to live with her father again, though her younger brother John remained with Marie.

The incident which prompted her escape happened in response to her brother Joseph telling her mother he wasn't ever coming home to her. Marie told Joseph that, if that was the case, she would strap O'Connor into the front of the car and deliberately crash it.

When Joseph refused to take her seriously, Marie acted out her threat: she strapped O'Connor into the passenger seat of the car and drove it into a car heading towards them. They both survived, but O'Connor understandably shrieked at her mother. When the pair arrived home, O'Connor called her mother's doctor, who put Marie in the hospital for the children's safety. After that, O'Connor and her older siblings weren't allowed to see her mother.

Her father Seán was an unhappy man. He would get depressed, O'Connor said, though he didn't want his children witnessing this and would regularly retire to bed after lunch. By this point he had remarried a gentle and good-natured woman called Viola Margaret Suiter (*née* Cook). The pair had wed in 1976 in the US, so the marriage wouldn't be legally recognised in Ireland.

The couple cared for a combined seven children. These comprised three daughters from Viola's first marriage – Jane, Lisa and Kate – and also the children from Seán and Marie's marriage, excluding John, as well as their son together, Eoin (O'Connor's half-brother).

Out of all O'Connor's seven siblings and step-siblings, only her eldest brother Joseph followed her into the public eye, and only he commented to the press about their childhood, corroborating her account. Now a successful author of several bestselling novels, in 2016 he told the *Irish Sun* that listening to his sister's music about their abusive upbringing was too traumatic.

He also suggested the dysfunctional dynamic and cultural richness of their childhood could be responsible for his and his sister's creativity. He explained that the siblings grew up in a house filled with literature and music.

"It was a very destructive place," he said, which was potent, "if you want your kids to be creative."

He and O'Connor "unconsciously encouraged each other" as children, he revealed: "You realise these sort of things are possible, so why [not] give it a shot, don't be scared."

He agreed with O'Connor's claims about their mother, describing Marie as "a deeply unhappy and disturbed person" who perpetrated "extreme and violent abuse, both emotional and physical."[1]

Joseph was responsible for introducing O'Connor to Bob Dylan's music, having brought home the album *Slow Train Coming* on its release in 1979. O'Connor was 12 years old and was completely enraptured by the record, playing it over and over. Fittingly, given O'Connor's own fixation with religion, it was Dylan's first album after he converted to Christianity, and the tracks are all about Christian scriptures and his own personal faith in Jesus.

O'Connor was also obsessed by John Lennon, and wept when he was assassinated on 8 December 1980 – her 14th birthday.

Alongside her interest in white artists, she also became very interested in black culture. Tara Joshi wrote in the *Guardian* after O'Connor's death: "As a child she was obsessed with Muhammad Ali, moved by the slavery drama series *Roots* (which would later inspire the title for her song Mandinka), and fell in love with reggae songs she heard on TV."[2]

Throughout O'Connor's time at her father's house, he would drop her at the front gate of her school and she would walk straight out of the back gate and play truant.

When asked if she was lonely as a child in a 1991 interview with *SPIN* magazine, O'Connor replied, "Yeah, I would say that I was."

She added: "If a child is being abused it will react in different ways ... I went into myself. I couldn't communicate with anybody, I couldn't study ... I couldn't get out of my own head."[3]

Seán mostly left Viola to deal with the children, described by O'Connor as "savages", though she exempted Eoin, her youngest stepsister and her sister Eimear from this description, including her father instead. Viola was peaceful and loving, and O'Connor ran rings around her, knowing Viola was too soft to punish her. She recalled how Viola would feign slapping her hand to reprimand her, but so softly O'Connor couldn't even feel it.

One of O'Connor's earliest television interviews was on RTÉ's *The Late Late Show*. After castigating her good-humouredly for shaving her head, host Gay Byrne accused her of being a "difficult child ... you went through a lot of schools, did you not?"

O'Connor, smiling shyly and awkwardly, replied that her father had paid for five or six.

Byrne then asked Seán, who was sitting in the front row of the audience, how many schools O'Connor had gone through. He echoed his daughter's response, smiling.[4]

There was no mention of the family dysfunction that had likely caused O'Connor to act out as a teenager, such as her mother forcing her to steal, setting her on this path.

O'Connor continued misbehaving, stealing sweets and clothes. When she was thrown out of three schools over the course of nine months for thieving, Viola called in a social worker, Irene, in response to O'Connor being discovered thieving a pair of gold shoes for a pal to wear to a Pretenders gig.

Irene advised Seán and Viola to send O'Connor to reform school, and she was duly sent to An Grianán ('the sunrise') Training Centre in Drumcondra. It was an institution of the Catholic monastic Order of Our Lady of Charity which had originally been one of Dublin's grim church-sponsored Magdalene Laundries. A large L-shaped grey building featuring a huge statue of Jesus, a garden and a church, O'Connor described it as a melancholy place full of out of control children, where she was forced to wash priests' clothes on an unpaid basis.

Run by nuns, it was both a school for excluded and misbehaving girls and, in a different part of the building, an asylum for mentally ill elderly ladies. Sent up to the asylum once to sleep there as a punishment, O'Connor was horrified and vowed never to end up there as an adult. She decided to start behaving better, as she had previously run away.

One of the girls at An Grianán fell pregnant by a local boy and gave birth to a tiny baby boy. The girl fussed over her newborn son, delighted and totally in love with him, and was utterly heartbroken and despondent when the nuns took him away from her, refusing to say where he had been sent. O'Connor explained that in Ireland, at that time, you weren't allowed to keep your baby if you were under eighteen and unmarried.

One of the nuns, Sister Margaret, discovered O'Connor had musical talent and bought her a guitar and a 'punk rock parka', and O'Connor began taking guitar lessons with a teacher called Jeanette Byrne. O'Connor later described Jeanette in the 2022 documentary *Nothing Compares* as "the loveliest woman alive, who I still know ... If not for her, I wouldn't have made it through that place."[5]

Byrne said in the same documentary that she encouraged O'Connor to sing a song on the first night Byrne worked at the residential school.

"And I won't forget it for as long as I live. Because we were just stunned."[6] Byrne resolved to nurture her talent.

She was so taken by O'Connor's voice that she asked her to sing 'Evergreen' by Barbra Streisand at her wedding.

While singing, O'Connor was spotted by Jeanette's brother Paul, of the band In Tua Nua. He asked her if she would be willing to record vocals and write lyrics for a piece of music which they had recorded, as they were looking for a singer. O'Connor wrote lyrics on the subject of death, creating a song called 'Take My Hand', which would eventually become the first release on U2's label Mother Records. Sister Margaret allowed O'Connor to leave An Grianán on a few Sundays to record the song's vocals at a local recording studio.

O'Connor had never recorded with headphones and reverb before, and was delighted with the reverb, as the echoey effect reminded her of singing in church. She was crushed when the band deemed her too young to be their singer.

I interviewed the *Telegraph*'s rock critic Neil McCormick in person at his North London home about meeting O'Connor early on, when he was also the vocalist and songwriter in an unsigned Dublin band, Yeah! Yeah! Did he anticipate even when O'Connor was recording for In Tua Nua that she'd become a global success?

"No, we weren't really thinking in those terms," McCormick replied. "I mean, In Tua Nua was formed by our roadie Ivan O'Shea, and Paul Byrne and bassist Jack Dublin. We all lived in Howth. Paul Byrne was a really good drummer, and would sometimes play with our band, and he always made us say that he wasn't a member when we played. He thought we were too punky – he was a bit of a heavy rock guy at that time, but a really good drummer. And so Ivan O'Shea had an idea of fusing folk music with New Wave stuff and combining instruments in interesting ways. In Tua Nua had a strange little rehearsal space where we sometimes hung out together. It was a cottage on a cliff which had a cave underneath it – really quite a dangerous place.

"I know that Paul's sister taught Sinéad guitar, and then Sinéad sang at her wedding. There were always lots of things going on – there were lots of bands. It was an exciting period in Dublin, the late 70s, early 80s. Paul was transfixed by Sinéad I think, and In Tua Nua didn't have a singer and they got Sinéad to come and sing with them.

"So that was it, really – she was just somebody sort of floating around the edges of that scene. She was very pretty – she had hair in those days – and she was a few years younger than me. You don't really think that much about it. I knew she could sing, that was obvious, and it was obvious to

9

everybody that she had a compelling way with her voice, but In Tua Nua didn't even ask her to join the band. She seemed young and a little bit out of her depth, that's all, so there was no strong impression of somebody who's going to be a star. She was very soft-spoken and very young.

McCormick said in his bestselling book *Killing Bono* that he knew that she had something special, I reminded him.

"Well, she could sing, you know, that's something special always," McCormick said. "Most people can't, and they don't have interesting voices, and she had an interesting voice. And that presence when she sang was there, that was obvious."

During the 18 months when O'Connor lived at An Grianán, Sister Margaret also allowed her to attend the school across the road – Maryfield College – to study for her Inter Certificate. After leaving An Grianán she attended another boarding school, Newtown School in Waterford, but left before sitting her Leaving Certificate.

O'Connor said that in Ireland in that era, it was common to have a job from the age of 11. One of her first jobs was working in a pizza place. She was also famously a kissogram girl aged 16. "I was a terrible kissogram because I was very shy," she would tell the breakfast show *Good Morning Britain* years later, saying her costume of choice was "the naughty nun. It was a full length nun's outfit, at the back it was all cut away. You'd have to read a terrible poem in a French accent then put a pair of knickers on the fella's head."[6]

She also spoke about driving around a cemetery searching for her mother's headstone in the kissogram vehicle. The kissogram firm she worked for had the name Hot Lips, so the vehicle was red and had a large pair of red lips on the roof.

There is a much-publicised photo of a 16-year-old O'Connor wearing a French maid's outfit next to kissogram regular Ken Ferrell in a caveman costume.

In 2023, *Hot Press* editor Niall Stokes reminisced about the first time O'Connor appeared in the iconic Irish magazine, of her hundreds of appearances: she "appeared in a story we did on the new – and thankfully brief – phenomenon of the kissogram. In what would later be seen as her typical couldn't-give-a-fuck style, [she] was doing the gig as a way of earning a few quid." In her inaugural *Hot Press* photoshoot, the first of at least ten, O'Connor posed "not as an artist, but dressed up as a French maid".[7]

In 1984, aged 17, O'Connor placed an advert for musicians in the Irish music and politics magazine *Hot Press*, and received a call from the Dublin musician, composer and music producer Columb Farrelly, who was seeking a female vocalist. In his 1991 book about O'Connor, *So Different*, Dermott Hayes quoted Farrelly saying that he'd swung a crystal over the 'Musicians Wanted' section and it had pointed him towards O'Connor's ad.

"The thing was spinning on an ad that read something like … 'FEMALE SINGER seeks band, Call Sinéad. No messers.'"[8]

When Farrelly called the number, he discovered that *Hot Press* had printed it wrongly. He had to call the magazine and get them to look up the correct number from O'Connor's original form. However, when he'd finally achieved this and O'Connor answered the phone, she casually said she'd had lots of other calls.

On meeting her, Farrelly was immediately sure that she had "the combination of a star on her forehead and a fire in her belly to make it."[9] Both were interested in the spiritual world: Farrelly was intrigued by world music, witchcraft, voodoo and anything mystical, which chimed with O'Connor's interest in spirituality.

Together, the pair formed a band called Ton Ton Macoute – an unwise choice of name. It was based on Farrelly's interest in mysticism, but brought to mind Haiti's barbaric warlord 'Papa Doc' Duvalier and his reign of terror with his much-feared secret police, the Tonton Macoutes.

Farrelly recalled that O'Connor's voice was "one of those 'this-thing-is-bigger-than-both-of-us' feelings."[10] He and O'Connor recruited other band members, and the band settled in Waterford for a while to allow O'Connor to attend school; eventually, she left. She then returned home and informed her father that she intended to become a singer. He duly sent her to Dublin College of Music to study singing and piano.

Ton Ton Macoute began gigging in Dublin in the evenings while O'Connor studied music in the day.

"I came over to London around that time, but I was aware of Ton Ton Macoute," Neil McCormick told me. "You'd go back [to Dublin] and there were bands on the scene, and [O'Connor] was striking, always. Obviously there's lots of bands and nobody is really thinking anybody else is going to be a star, you're only thinking that *you're* going to be a star.

"So I'd just say that her presence on the scene was known. Ton Ton Macoute were doing interesting things, she looked great, and she had a voice that cut through. It had some Irish folk in it but fit into this electronic and rock soundscape. That's all.

"She'd float in and out of the *Hot Press* offices, and I would float in and out of the *Hot Press* offices. I used to go back and work there and she was one of the musicians who would float in and out. Niall, the editor, really liked her and kind of took her under his wing a bit."

11

Ton Ton Macoute spent a year together, writing, rehearsing and gigging. However, their relationship grew increasingly acrimonious.

The band came to the attention of Ensign Records at a gig, and a showcase was quickly arranged; however, Ensign boss Nigel Grainge only wanted to sign O'Connor, not the rest of the band.

* * *

At the age of 18, on 10 February 1985, O'Connor saw her stepmother's car driving down the road and knew that her mother must have died. The previous night, coincidentally, she had been talking to her ex-boyfriend about how they would react if either of their parents died.

Marie had skidded on black ice while driving to Mass in Ballybrack, losing control of the vehicle and colliding with a bus. She was 45. Her son John, the only one of O'Connor's siblings still been living with Marie, had been a passenger in the back of the car, but had thankfully survived without physical injuries, as had the man in the passenger seat. John had, however, been knocked unconscious and had woken up in hospital.

Sinéad and her siblings ran to Marie's house, looked through her belongings and burnt a biscuit tin full of her Valium in the garden. Sinéad also ensured she took a photograph of Pope John Paul II down from her mother's wall, one of only two possessions she collected from the house (the other being a recipe book).

The young adults then bought a dress for their mother to wear at her funeral from the shop Dunnes, having been given fifty pounds by Seán and Viola and told to buy a dress that buttoned at the neck. The siblings couldn't stop laughing hysterically during the shopping trip, knowing the helpful sales girl was unaware that the dress they were searching for was to be used to bury their mother in.

When people came to shake her and her siblings' hands in the church, O'Connor felt furious that they'd known what Marie was like and yet hadn't rescued the children from her. And now here they were, standing in front of O'Connor, saying they were sorry for her loss.

Afterwards, O'Connor cursed God, calling Him every name she could think of, until she threw up. It felt awful and wrong to her to curse Him, but it wasn't the first time.

She was also filled with rage at the sight of her father weeping over her mother's body at the funeral home, telling her mother he was sorry. She wondered why Seán hadn't said sorry to Marie while she was still alive, and why neither of them had ever said sorry to their children. She sprinted away in a rage, down through the suburb of Glasthule into Dún Laoghaire.

The next day, while sitting in her father's house, waiting for the cars to drive them to Marie's funeral, O'Connor decided to become a lifelong smoker and smoke as many cigarettes as were necessary for her to end up in heaven with her mother. She looked downwards the whole way through the funeral, crying.

3: Starting Out (1985–1986)

O'Connor left Ton Ton Macoute, moved to London in 1985 to start a new life, and signed as a solo artist with the record label Ensign. It was named after founder Nigel Grainge, who had started it in 1976, with its name meaning 'N-sign'. However, in 1984, just before O'Connor signed to the label, Ensign were bought by Chrysalis – which would later be taken over by EMI.

In 1986, before her debut album was released, she would sign up to be managed by Fachtna O'Ceallaigh, who had previously managed the Boomtown Rats and Bananarama.

I asked Neil McCormick if it was a surprise when O'Connor signed to Ensign.

"It wasn't a surprise, because there was some buzz building around her," McCormick replied. "Fachtna was managing her, who had been running Mother Records, so he would have met In Tua Nua ... [McCormick's band] were supposed to be the first single on Mother Records. I may have even given Bono the In Tua Nua tape. They became the first single. Fachtna was running the record label. Fachtna had been [managing] the Boomtown Rats and he took [O'Connor] under his wing.

"So she was one of the people things were building around."

A former Evening Press journalist, Fachtna O'Ceallaigh started at U2's own record label Mother Records just before the label's second single release, 'Love Don't Work This Way' by Hothouse Flowers (In Tua Nua's 'Coming Thru' was the label's first release).

However, O'Ceallaigh soon came to loathe U2. He felt they were pompous, and their denial of and negativity towards the Irish republican resistance was anathema to him, as he was a staunch republican. His views would rub off on O'Connor.

O'Ceallaigh fell out with the band after criticising them in an interview, at which point they let him go from the label. He moved to London in 1985. Soon after this, he received a call from U2's accountant Ossie Kilkenny, telling him a girl from Dublin called Sinéad O'Connor had been signed by Ensign. She'd been put in a flat way out in Rotherhithe in East London's Docklands, and didn't know anyone in London. Would he give her a call and keep an eye on her?

The pair became close friends, and O'Ceallaigh soon became O'Connor's first manager, working with her between 1986 and late 1989. She called him early on in their partnership and told him, "Nigel and Chris [Hall, Grainge's Ensign business partner] want me to wear dresses and grow my hair. What should I do?"

O'Ceallaigh asked if she wanted to do that. O'Connor replied that she didn't. "Shave your head then," O'Ceallaigh replied.

His inspiration for the idea came from a woman named Scarlett, whom he had first seen working in a small shop called World, near Cambridge Circus. The shop was owned by Michael Costiff who, along with his partner Gerlinda, ran an irregular club night called Kinky Gerlinky. The club was frequented by the then small coterie of tastemakers in the intersection between the fashion, gay and music worlds – people such as Leigh Bowery, Stephen Jones, Stephen Linard, John Maybury, Kim Bowen, Kate Garner, Marco Pirroni, Leslie Winer – and others who were just as creative, if less acclaimed.

At the time, O'Ceallaigh was DJing at an Old Compton Street Sunday night comedown gathering called Black Thrash, where he encountered some of the same crowd.

O'Connor took his advice and had her head shaved. It represented a kind of liberation to her, and to all who saw her. O'Connor's hair would remain shaved or cropped at all times throughout her career.

In a 2014 interview with Oprah Winfrey for her *Where Are They Now?* series, O'Connor said that men in the music industry could be a bit predatory, and that she wanted to protect herself from them. She called the record executives, "a bit frisky ... you'd be better to have a bag on your head, really."[1]

O'Connor also told Winfrey that it was a rejection of record company expectations of her. "They wanted me to grow my hair really long and wear miniskirts, because they reckoned I'd look much prettier," she disclosed. "So I went straight around to the barber and shaved the rest of my hair off."[2]

O'Connor said she told the record executives that they were trying to make her look like their mistresses.

I interviewed ex-Japan guitarist Robert Dean, now a bird illustrator living in Costa Rica. He had a different recollection of how she initially ended up with shaved hair.

"We were in a demo studio in Kilburn or Willesden, somewhere like that," he told me. "There was some downtime, I think the machine had to be fixed or something. So I said to Sinéad, 'I think I'm going to go and get a haircut.' She said, 'I want my hair cut too, I want a flat top.'

"So we went out onto the street, and we went to a men's barber, to cut both our hair. But they refused to cut her hair because she was a woman!

"So I had my hair cut, and we went down the street and she went to another hairdressers. She said to the woman, 'Can you do a flat top?' and the woman said, 'Yes, I can do a flat top.'

"So she sat her in the chair, and she basically butchered [O'Connor's] hair! It was shaved very short at the sides and was about three inches high on top. But it didn't have any taper to it – it went from nothing to three inches. The sides would flop down, so she had to spray it all the time to keep it standing up.

"It wasn't a flat top at all, it was more like a sort of really bad Mohawk. And the next time we saw her, she'd shaved it off!"

So you think her shaved head came from having a really rubbish haircut, I asked Dean?

"Well, that's what I thought," he said. "But it probably sounds better the way she tells it. But that's how I remember it. Because I can distinctly remember the haircut, and it was pretty damn bad!"

The truth is probably that O'Connor's Mohawk did look bad. But also that, as O'Connor wrote in *Rememberings*, O'Ceallaigh suggested that she shave it off.

O'Connor's iconic look would help her become far more famous and successful than if she hadn't shaved her head. It helped her career by setting her apart from everyone else.

But she was still beautiful, I remarked to Simon Hattenstone, a long-time *Guardian* journalist who interviewed O'Connor twice for the newspaper.

"She was more beautiful for it, probably," Hattenstone replied.

"She looked like what a pop star could look like in the future, instead of what a pop star looked like in the past. She kind of created a new pop star look, but that was in revolt against what she'd been told to do."

Subsequently to O'Connor shaving her head, Kim Bowen, O'Ceallaigh's girlfriend at the time, captured the starlet's essence and beauty by dressing her in her iconic leather jacket, tutu and boots, along with other stylish garments. Bowen's role in shaping O'Connor's image has gone thus far unheralded.

Bowen was the person who brought O'Ceallaigh into the world of St Martin's creatives, where he would meet John Maybury and his partner Baillie Walsh, as well as PR person Patrick Lilley (who represented O'Connor in those early days). Lilley also ran club night High on Hope with Norman Jay, and started the club Queer Nation.

This small 'outsider' group played an essential if subconscious role in bringing O'Connor and her music into their community as early, crucial followers.

*   *   *

O'Connor's first ever television appearance was, fittingly, as a trailblazer: at the age of 19, she starred in a mock-up ad for a fictional brand of condoms, 'Prophyltex', in a two-part BBC documentary called *AIDS: The Last Chance*. It was screened when condom advertising was illegal in the UK – and when condoms themselves had been illegal until a year previously in Ireland without a doctor's prescription.

The ad showed O'Connor with her skinhead, looking cool in a black bomber jacket and studded jeans, along with images of condoms in foil. One poked out of her jacket sleeve pocket, as a voiceover recited: "Scarlet insists her friends wear the strong protector, Prophyltex, the strong one."[3]

Decades later, O'Connor told Irish tabloid *Sunday World* that she'd been cast in the ad because of her androgynous look.

"There had never been an ad on TV up to then for condoms. I'm really proud to have taken part in that advert . . . I was thrilled to see it resurface recently. I remember it being filmed, I hope it saved lives."

O'Connor said the Catholic church and the Irish government had "cost lives" by banning condoms and the Pill until 1980 in Ireland.

She told the tabloid that Irish teenagers would be stunned when they learned about the country's former prohibition on condoms. She recalled that Virgin founder Richard Branson would bring condoms into Virgin Megastore in Ireland, and that U2 would place them in HMV.

Dublin's Virgin Megastore offered condoms for sale to customers in 1988, only for the Irish government to launch legal action against it as it wasn't a pharmacy or approved seller.

O'Connor thought that the Irish campaigner Nell McCafferty and her friends were the first to distribute the barrier contraceptive: they would travel by train around the country and toss condoms out of the carriage windows. O'Connor reminded *Sunday World* that the contraceptive pill wasn't available either.

"Remember Ann Lovett [a 15-year-old girl who tragically died in 1984 while she was trying to give birth in a Granard cave after being refused an abortion]? That's my mantra about all of this." O'Connor spoke movingly about the incident, stating that the system in Ireland was still messed up.[4]

Condom manufacturer Durex finally screened the UK's inaugural condom ad later in 1986. However, it received a surfeit of complaints and was threatened with lawsuits by pressure groups such as the Mary Whitehouse-run National Viewers' and Listeners' Association.

* * *

In O'Connor's first interview with the *Irish Times*, aged 19, she spoke to journalist Kate Holmquist.

Holmquist wrote, "Sinéad is somewhat starry-eyed and breathless in the way she describes her next break, the offer of a contract in 1985: 'It was surprising. I was just kind of having a laugh. I wasn't looking for a record deal.'"

Holmquist reported that Ossie Kilkenny, the accountant for U2, assisted O'Connor when he found out she'd been offered a contract by her record company. He spoke to her father Seán about it and, O'Connor says, he was instrumental in ensuring the deal was safe for her legally. It was through Kilkenny that O'Connor first met Bono. O'Connor said the pair had a heart to heart.

Later in the *Irish Times* interview, O'Connor stated that she didn't wear makeup, but refuted Holmquist's suggestion that feminism could be behind this. She would deny being a feminist throughout her career: "It's just my personality."[5]

In another 1986 interview in *Hot Press*, O'Connor was sweet and guileless, open to answering any and all questions: "'I love attention,' bubbles Sinéad, as if admitting a sin. 'When I came over here I was totally green. I'd only ever been singing for fun.'"[6]

She described how she was recording her first album with an all-male band of five older musicians: John Reynolds on drums, Japan's Robert Dean on guitar, Michael Clowes on keyboards, Rick Finley on percussion and Spike Holifield on bass.

O'Connor and Reynolds would soon start a relationship and O'Connor would fall pregnant with his baby.

4: Recording Her Debut (1986)

Robert Dean spoke to me over the phone about how he came to record O'Connor's debut album with her.

"I was working with a band in the West Country and I wasn't having a particularly good time," Dean explained. "It was winter, maybe 1986, and I bumped into Tim Butler from the Psychedelic Furs. He asked if

I wanted to play guitar for their upcoming tour. I said, 'Well I can't, because I'm working with this band, and I feel as though I have a commitment there.' So I turned it down.

"In the meantime, I went back to London one weekend and met up with my friend Ali McMordie, the bass player in Stiff Little Fingers. He said, 'I'm working with this really great singer called Sinéad O'Connor', and he played me some of their demos. And I said, 'Wow, that's really great, that's something I'd really like to work on.' He said, 'Well, we have a guitarist at the moment, but if anything happens, I'll let you know.'

"And within a week, it turned out that their guitarist got the job with the Psychedelic Furs that I'd turned down! So Ali contacted me and said, 'Are you still interested in working with Sinéad?', and I said, 'Yes, definitely!' So that's how it happened. It's just one of those weird things.

"So we met up in a café on the South Bank with Sinéad and the band. Ali wasn't working with her anymore at that point – Spike Holifield was the bass player. We rehearsed a lot, working on stuff for the first album. We had Nomis Studios booked out for months at a time, working on getting the songs together."

I asked Dean what his first impressions of O'Connor were.

"'My God, you're beautiful!' She had the most amazing eyes. Everybody knows that, but when you saw her in person, it was pretty stunning really. She oozed star quality. It was sort of unmistakable. It was unmistakable in her voice, in the demos I'd heard, and in her personality. She was still a teenager at that time – 19, maybe – and all the band were like her sort of brothers, really. Looking after her, taking care of her. We felt that sort of responsibility towards her."

I asked Dean what the process of recording O'Connor's debut album had been like.

"We did a few sets of demos in small demo studios, and then Ensign decided that Mick Glossop was going to produce the album," he told me. "He'd worked with The Waterboys, who were also on their label, so it seemed pretty logical that he would be the producer. So we went in the studio with Mick, and his technique for recording was quite old-fashioned. We would play mostly live in the studio, which was very antiquated [as a process] and wasn't really what I was used to from my days with Japan. You'd normally put down the bass and drums first, and use rough guitar tracks and rough vocals to get it all together.

"But Mick's process was a very sort of organic one, which I think worked against us, because there were situations where we wanted to do overdubs, and he wasn't keen on doing that. At one stage I said, 'I'd like to redo that guitar track', and he basically said, 'Well you've made your bed, you're gonna have to lie in it.' Rather than trying to get a better take – stuff like that.

"Also, there were projections from Ensign that we would need to do 12-inch mixes of some songs if they were going to be singles. So Mick Glossop's way of dealing with that was to have us jam on the tracks for ten minutes. We weren't using click tracks, we were just doing everything organically. What it actually meant was that when Ensign took the recordings to other producers or remixers, they said, 'This is unremixable as there are no click tracks and nothing to adhere to [in order] to keep the mix on track.'

"Some of the recordings we did with Mick Glossop were actually really pretty good, but it was a totally different feel to what the record company wanted, I think. And we recorded some songs which still haven't been heard today – we did a version of 'The Crystal Ship' by The Doors which I particularly liked.

"And we did a version of 'Troy' which was like a big band version, with horns and guitar solos. It was very, very epic – full band, drums, everything, which I still have a copy of. I think I might have the only copy! There was talk of doing a deluxe edition of *The Lion and the Cobra* a few years ago, and so all the multi-tracks were located, and that wasn't among them. So it doesn't seem like that's ever going to show up.

"Some of the songs were totally different to what they turned out to be later on. 'Jackie' was totally different. It was kind of like a folk-rock song. But basically, some of the recordings were a bit of a mess, to be honest. Which was a shame. But the idea from Ensign was that we re-record the entire thing. So the only thing that was kept from those original recordings, I think, was the orchestra in 'Troy'."

So then Sinéad produced it, I asked?

"Yes, she co-produced it with the engineer, Kevin Moloney," said Dean. "The idea was that everything was much more stripped down, not too much heavy instrumentation. There was a track called 'What Do You Want?' which was actually released as a B-side. It's a Gaelic song. That was the original recording from the Mick Glossop sessions, as far as I can remember – I think it was exactly the same. It was probably remixed, or something. That's more of the feel of what the first recording of the album was.

"So anyway, it was recorded relatively quickly and was relatively simple. Personally, I think some things work really well and I like some elements of the original recordings. But I totally understand where the record company were coming from and what they wanted for Sinéad. It was less of a band recording and more of her solo record, which is what it should have been. It's still a very good album and I'm very proud of it."

Dean co-wrote the track 'I Want Your (Hands On Me)'. I asked him how that came about.

"Oh, we just jammed," he replied. "That's basically what we did. When we were in the rehearsal studio, we just jammed on everything, and just came up with it from a riff, I think. I can't really remember. It was a very long time ago. But a lot of the things we jammed on for hours, sometimes. That's what you do when you're trying to create some music. You just go over and over and over it until it becomes something. Or doesn't, as the case may be!"

I asked Dean what O'Connor was like to work with.

"She was a real joy to work with," he answered. "I have nothing but positive thoughts about the time recording with Sinéad. She was always very open to our ideas. I mean, she was strong-minded, but that's the Irishness in her! But she rarely got angry. She was always the sweetest thing.

"There was one time when we were in the studio and I wasn't feeling very well – I think I was coming down with flu or something – and she went out and bought me a toy robot to cheer me up! That was the sort of thing she did. She was very generous and just a joy, really. I don't think any of us would have anything negative to say about that time."

What was it like to watch her become a global superstar?

"I wasn't living in England at the time," Dean explained. "I was living and working in Melbourne, Australia by that point. After we recorded the album, Sinéad was pregnant, so it was decided to delay everything until she had the baby. During that time, we weren't working much at all, and so I got offered a gig in Australia and went there, which evolved into me having my own band and recording an album there.

"So I was sort of apart from all that."

So he didn't stay in touch or see her again after the album recording process had finished?

"I went to see the band live. I was back in England when she was on tour and I went to see her at the Dominion Theatre, in London. That might have been the last time I spoke to her, I don't know. But it was weird, because I was so separated from it all at that point.

"While we were recording with Sinéad, my old band Japan had a fan club get together, which they did every year at the 100 Club in London. The fan club was called Bamboo, so it was called a Bamboo party, and I persuaded Sinéad to come with me and play some songs. That basically was her first gig [in London], as far as I know. We played four songs:

'Jackie', a Velvet Underground cover called 'All Tomorrow's Parties, a Patsy Cline song called 'I Fall to Pieces', and we did one other *Lion and the Cobra* song.

I'm amazed you can remember the set list, I told Dean. It's so long ago.

"It keeps getting posted up on the Japan fan pages on Facebook. It went down really well, everybody was amazed by her, because nobody knew her at all, of course. So it was a nice little intro."

I had read an interview of Dean's where he said he got into things not 100%, but 200%. Does he think the same was true for Sinéad and her commitment to what she believed in?

"Oh for sure, yeah, absolutely. Even more, in Sinéad's case! She was very, very dedicated to what she believed in, always. The documentary [*Nothing Compares*, released in 2022] I thought was fantastic, it showed her in the absolute right light, and also showed how right she was."

5. Affinity with Rastafari and Black Music (1986)

Music journalist Neil Perry would interview O'Connor for *Sounds* when her first album came out. He told me,

"In the interview she said, 'I'd never heard of Aretha Franklin or Prince until I came to London. I never used to *listen* to anybody else, which is why I can unashamedly say I don't sound like anybody else.'

"Which I always thought was a great quote, and the mention of Prince there, no one could have guessed what was coming down the line in just a few years with 'Nothing Compares 2 U'."

Living in ethnically diverse, multicultural London was an eye-opener for O'Connor. She'd never heard much black music before, except for reggae songs on television as a child, but on visits to Notting Hill she heard wall-to-wall roots reggae and rap. She was also introduced to a lot of black music by her manager Fachtna O'Ceallaigh.

He was devouring hip hop at that time, just as he had done with all sorts of reggae since the mid-1970s. O'Ceallaigh was also, separately, best friends with George Anderson, aka Daddy Lepke, who had set up the first black pirate radio station, Dread Broadcasting Corporation, DBC, a few years previously.

O'Ceallaigh met Anderson when the station's transmitter was seized by the DTI and he paid for a new one. Anderson had a stall on Portobello Road where he sold DBC t-shirts and revolutionary mix tapes, and this is where O'Connor first experienced MCs live on the mic. O'Ceallaigh also brought her to the Dub Vendor shack on Ladbroke Grove a few times when he was buying 7″ records from Jamaica.

21

O'Ceallaigh fed O'Connor with his own mixtapes of all sorts of music, not just hip hop and reggae. Via those tapes, O'Connor first heard 'I Am Stretched On Your Grave', which she would go on to record. She also heard MC Lyte's first single 'I Cram to Understand U'. O'Ceallaigh later persuaded Lyte to rap on the 12″ mix of 'I Want Your Hands on Me', produced by hip hop legends Audio Two. Most importantly, O'Ceallaigh also played O'Connor the original version of 'Nothing Compares 2 U'.

Throughout her musical career, O'Connor would experiment with rap and even record a whole reggae album. She saw the similarities between black and white music where other less enlightened artists of her era didn't, and on many of her tracks she created a fusion between them.

On the 20th anniversary of John Lennon's death, O'Connor told the *Guardian*: "He would probably love the rap movement. In a lot of ways, rap is where his voice can still be heard. People underestimate the subliminal impact of not just his music but the things he was doing publicly, like the shit-stirring. All of that had a huge influence on rap."[1]

Tara Joshi wrote in the *Guardian* that O'Connor "visited record stores at Portobello Road market run by Rastafarian elders."[2]

O'Connor would fall in love with Rasta culture, though she would correct interviewers who described it as 'Rastafarianism', saying that it was in fact 'Rastafari'. She also insisted that it wasn't a religion, but instead a movement – which explains why she never converted to it.

A big Bob Marley fan, O'Connor was serious enough about her love of Rastafari to get his lyric 'The Lion of Judah shall break every chain' tattooed on her hand during later life – just one of a series of religious inkings alongside Catholic, Jewish and Islamic tattoos.

"And the new tattoo isn't the only Rastafarian reference Sinéad has on her body," the *Daily Mail* would report in 2013. "She also has the words: 'King of kings, Lord of Lords, Earth's rightful ruler', etched on her left arm – a reference to His Majesty Ras Tafari."[3]

O'Connor would also go on to express "gratitude to the Rasta people, because I am one of those human beings who would not be alive today if it was not for the teachings of Rastafari," she would tell the *Associated Press*.[4]

She felt a deep spiritual connection to Rasta music, telling *NPR* later on that Rasta was "the religious aspect of reggae music … they use music to reassure people that God is actually with them and watches them, can be called upon. They're a kind of prophetic movement in that way, and they use music as the vehicle … When you're around those people, you can taste God."[5]

Later on, in 1989, the Grammy awards Recording Academy, which was nearly all-white, introduced the category of Best Rap Performance.

Before, they had neglected the genre. But they didn't think the category was worthy of televising, and plenty of artists chose to boycott the ceremony as a result. Wanting to show solidarity, O'Connor decided to shave the Public Enemy logo featuring gun crosshairs into the side of her closely-cropped hair.

A year later, she would stand up for black hip hop group 2 Live Crew, who were banned in Florida due to purported obscenity, saying that their censorship was racism – and she refused to attend any awards ceremonies at all in 1991 in protest.

Having experienced being marginalised and disenfranchised, especially as a child, O'Connor always stood up for those who were discriminated against.

In 1999, she had the honour of presenting Nina Simone with the Lifetime Achievement Award at the *Hot Press* Music Awards in Dublin. Singer Gary Lightbody, whose band Snow Patrol won Best New Band at the same awards, said, "It was an extraordinary moment that I remember well. They were from different generations and sides of the Atlantic, but had the same fighting spirit and determination to stand up for what they believed to be right – regardless of what the cost might have been personally or career-wise."[6]

6. 'Heroine', and a Fight with U2 (1986)

The Edge (real name David Howell Evans), U2's guitarist, recorded his first and only solo album in 1986 – and became, to date, the only member of U2 ever to record a solo album. The record was the soundtrack to a film called *Captive*. An Anglo-French cinema release based on the life of Patty Hearst, an heiress who was forced to join the Symbionese Liberation Army, the soundtrack was the most notable thing about the film.

The Edge enlisted Michael Brook, inventor of the guitar he used, to co-produce the album. For the main theme, he chose a new female vocalist just beginning to make a name for herself: Sinéad O'Connor. The pair co-wrote the song's lyrics, the Edge provided the music, and U2's Larry Mullen Jr. played drums.

O'Connor sang the praises of the Edge and his wife in *Melody Maker*, and lauded The Edge's musicianship.

She also said to Molly McAnailly Burke in *Hot Press* that she wanted to help other artists one day, in the same way that she was given a leg-up by U2.

However, O'Connor then signed up to be managed by expert music manager Fachtna O'Ceallaigh, who had had a big falling out with U2.

They had fought partly because O'Ceallaigh wanted disruptive, subversive bands on the label, and U2 weren't signing any.

The band's fan website U2 Songs said U2 chose the phrase 'incompatible temperaments' to explain the reasoning behind their decision.

O'Connor soon became very loyal to O'Ceallaigh – the pair were extremely close and would eventually become lovers – and she took his side in his battle against U2.

The band, she would tell *i-D* magazine a year later, were "bombastic".[1] Another year went by, and *NME* put O'Connor on the cover with the headline, "Fighting Talk: Sinéad O'Connor vs U2." However, the Edge apparently found the whole thing amusing.

I asked Irish music journalist Stuart Bailie, former Assistant Editor at *NME* from 1988–96, what the whole feud was about.

"Fachtna O'Ceallaigh had managed the Boomtown Rats and Bob Geldof," he explained. "And then he worked with Mother Records, which was U2's record label, and they had a very nasty falling out – I don't know quite what it was about. It was about control, artistic control and other things.

"And Fachtna had a lot to do with how Bob Geldof embraced punk and kind of fed him musically. So he's a very savvy music mind. And I think he probably had a bit of import on Sinéad's music tastes as well. And I could be wrong, but I think he was the guy who heard 'Nothing Compares to You' first, and then suggested that Sinéad do it.

"And then, as with many relationships, they had a fallout and he was history.

"But he loathed U2, and a lot of the early Sinéad interviews were about how shit U2 were! She had a badge saying 'Bono has short legs', didn't she?

"I think every Irish act, certainly out of Dublin, had this thing of you were either mates with U2 or you had to almost fight them, you know? Because that was the first question of every interview. 'Do you like U2?'

"For a lot of artists it was almost like a ritual patricide. You had to kill U2 to move on with your creative life! There was a band called Power of Dreams who had a song called 'Never Been to Texas' which was [kind of a response to U2, like] 'I don't give a fuck about America, I don't want to write about touring America.'

"And in response, U2 just love-bombed everyone. Bombs of love were dropped on everybody. And it was almost their style to absorb all the blows and to befriend everybody and take away the enmity.

"But the Fachtna O'Ceallaigh thing certainly added to the enmity.

"Around the time of *Rattle and Hum* [1988], we set up 'Sinéad hates U2' as a cover story. The previous week we'd had U2 on the cover talking about *Rattle and Hum*, and the next week was Sinéad saying 'U2 are shit!' As a music paper, that's fantastic fun, having sparring matches between people.

"There was another band called That Petrol Emotion and they hated U2, and I think they more or less said U2 had bought *Hot Press* and *Hot Press* only wrote nice things about them. And I think the *NME* were threatened with a lawsuit.

"So there was stuff going on but U2 weathered it out. And Sinéad probably got a bit of mileage out of it! 'Sinéad hates U2' and everybody goes 'Oh, right?!'"

However, the two acts would reconcile by 1994.

7. First Child and First Marriage (1986–1987)

O'Connor fell pregnant by music producer and drummer John Reynolds in September 1986. She'd first met him in 1985, at the London flat belonging to Stiff Little Fingers bass player Ali McMordie.

"Sinéad and I got on great from the start, because we were both just mad into music," Reynolds would tell *Hot Press* after O'Connor's death. The pair got together "around a year after we first met. It was quite soon after that that she was pregnant with Jake. She fought for herself, and for us, to keep Jake."[1]

Reynolds was referencing the fact that O'Connor's record company sent her to their doctor as a result of the pregnancy, who informed her that, as Ensign had spent £100,000 on her album, she had a duty to them to terminate the pregnancy. O'Connor refused, and gave birth to her first son, Jake Reynolds, on 16 June 1987.

Reynolds described that period where the three were a little family as "a really good time."[2]

Her debut album was released less than four months later. After being introduced to John Maybury by Kim Bowen, Fachtna O'Ceallaigh had persuaded Ensign to shell out £20,000 for the filmmaker to shoot a ten-minute promotional video of O'Connor in Ireland, featuring the seven-minute song 'Troy'. This became her first hit, reaching number 3 in The Netherlands. Maybury also shot the videos for 'Mandinka', 'I Want Your Hands on Me' and 'Jump In the River', assisted by talented set designer Alan McDonald, who was also part of furniture-makers Frick and Frack.

In the publicity shots for the album, taken just before the birth, the record company instructed photographer Kate Garner, ex-singer in Haysi

Fantayzee, to only shoot O'Connor from the chest up so that her pregnant belly wouldn't be seen.

They shot different covers for the UK and US markets. Both featured a shaven-headed O'Connor in a bright sky blue vest, her pale hands curled into fists crossed over her chest, but the UK cover featured O'Connor appearing to scream; in fact, she was singing. The record company felt the US market, being more conservative, wouldn't appreciate this image and might feel it was too aggressive, so a shot of O'Connor looking down pensively was chosen instead.

Garner recalled in *Nothing Compares* that after the album photos were in the can, the pair had fun taking different photos, and she snapped O'Connor wearing a t-shirt saying 'Wear a Condom', cropped to display her large baby bump.

O'Connor told *Record Mirror*'s Stuart Bailie in his interview with her, months after the birth, that motherhood was "the best thing that ever happened to me, in that it has completely banished any self-doubt or embarrassment. But it hasn't changed me . . . I'm 20 and I don't feel like a baby machine. It's actually made me wilder; I think, I can do anything because I have this wonderful child."[3]

O'Connor and Reynolds wed in March 1989 at Westminster Registry Office. They stopped being a couple in mid-1989 and publicly announced their intention to divorce in November 1991, having lived separately for a while. However, the pair remained friends, and Reynolds went on to co-produce or produce several albums for O'Connor, among them 1994's *Universal Mother* (for which the Q Awards nominated him as Producer of the Year), *How About I Be Me (and You Be You)?* and her last studio album, 2014's *I'm Not Bossy, I'm the Boss*.

After O'Connor and Reynolds split, she started a romance with Fachtna O'Ceallaigh.

8. *The Lion and the Cobra* (1987)

O'Connor's debut record, recorded in Oasis Studios in Camden and released in November 1987 on Ensign/Chrysalis, was comparatively short. As with many successful 1980s albums – Michael Jackson's *Thriller* and Prince's *Purple Rain* among them – there were only nine tracks, but they ranged from Irish folk and mysticism to disco. O'Connor wrote five of them all by herself; the rest were co-writes.

O'Connor described the album as "schizoid", listing the number of different styles of music, including waltz, disco, hard rock and traditional Irish music. She said in interviews that her influences were Bob Dylan, Siouxsie and the Banshees, The Pretenders, David Bowie and Bob Marley.

The album features O'Connor's fellow Irish female singer Enya speaking aloud a passage from the Bible in Gaelic. She recites the 91st Psalm, including the line, "You shall tread upon the lion and the cobra, the young lion and the serpent you shall trample underfoot" (Psalm 91:13).

The opener is the haunting 'Jackie', O'Connor's pure soprano voice contrasting with muddy electric guitar, with no other instrumentation. The lyrics tell the story of a love lost at sea.

Ross Horton, writing in *music OMH*, said of Jackie, "Sinéad's voice immediately conjures a world of pure imagination. With a storm-clad voice – a child of both Kate Bush and Bob Dylan – she unveils her innermost struggles and triumphs like a lone lighthouse guiding ships through treacherous waters."[1]

This is followed by the lively, jangling, poppy 'Mandinka', with its catchy swooping chorus, one of only five of O'Connor's songs to chart in the UK Top 40. The album sold 2.5 million copies largely because of the track's success.

Listing 'Mandinka' as one of O'Connor's 10 greatest songs, Annie Zaleski wrote in the *Guardian* that it was "her electrifying, rock-oriented second single" and that "thrilling fearlessness permeates the studio version of the song... [O'Connor playing guitar properly for the first time was] a leap forward matched by strident vocals full of acrobatic howls and coos."[2]

Rolling Stone's Anthony DeCurtis wrote, "The shift from a folkloric world of love beyond the grave to a contemporary setting of pop hooks and fetching emotional hesitancy ... is a bracing tour de force."[3]

Speaking to magazine *The Tech* in April 1988, O'Connor explained its title: "Mandinkas are an African tribe. They're mentioned in a book called *Roots* by Alex Haley, which is what the song is about. In order to understand it you must read the book."[4]

Next up is the upbeat and rocky 'Jerusalem', with its cryptic religious references. "'Jerusalem' soars into an exultant, semimystical chorus" wrote Anthony DeCurtis in the 4* *Rolling Stone* review.[5]

Sam Sodomsky of *Pitchfork* wrote, "In songs like 'Mandinka' and 'Jerusalem', the magic is in the interplay between O'Connor's voice and the bed of cavernous rock music: how she stretches the titles into one-word choruses, weaving the syllables through their knotty arrangements."[6]

'Just Like U Said It Would B', the album's fourth track, features a beautiful and intricate instrumental arrangement in 6/8 time, accompanying O'Connor's increasingly abrasive vocal.

Terry Nelson of *Albumism* reckoned, "'Just Like U Said It Would B' illustrates O'Connor's versatility as a songwriter. It starts off like an Irish folk song with only her voice and a guitar and the other instruments enter this conversation one by one."[7]

'Never Get Old' is the track with the Biblical spoken-word intro and outro by Enya, interspersed with O'Connor's angelic Arabic-influenced vocal. *Pitchfork* described its sound as "old-Irish mysticism",[8] while the *Guardian* said it was "extraordinary: alien and bewitching."[9]

'Troy', O'Connor's first ever single release, is reminiscent of Kate Bush, yet didn't chart except for in the Netherlands, where it reached number 8.

The *Genius* explanation says, "The song uses the story of the ancient city of Troy as a metaphor. The lyric 'Being what you are, there is no other Troy for you to burn' is a reference to the poem 'No Second Troy' by William Butler Yeats ('Was there another Troy for her to burn?')."

First on her list of O'Connor's ten best tracks, Annie Zaleski wrote in the *Guardian* that the song is "intensely personal. Its lyrics weave together depictions of private traumas and the struggle between resilience and self-destruction, anchored by pointed references to Helen of Troy."[11]

A review in the *New York Review of Books* said, "Her most spectacular early achievement is the song 'Troy' from her debut album, *The Lion and the Cobra* (1987). Its searing string-driven climax climbs from a strident accusation to a desperate shriek: 'You should have left the light on! You should have left the light on!'"[12]

The seventh track on the album, 'I Want Your (Hands on Me)', the co-write with Robert Dean, is unlike most O'Connor tracks: it has a strong hip-hop groove and very straightforward, mildly sexual lyrics, though quite a discordant melody. With a guest appearance from rapper MC Lyte on the remix, the track was played over a death scene in the film *A Nightmare on Elm Street 4: The Dream Master*.

Stephen Thomas Erlewine of the *Los Angeles Times* wrote, "O'Connor's music burns so brightly in its intensity that the playfulness of 'I Want Your (Hands on Me)' remains startling. Setting the song to a bright, bustling drum loop, O'Connor sings over a hip-hop beat, her longing serving as a tantalising contrast to the colourful rhythms."[13]

Including the track in their rundown of O'Connor's finest musical moments, *Variety* writer A.D. Amorosi wrote, "Commandingly sexual and breathy, O'Connor ... pinned her cooing vocal and icy, sensual lyrics to a clunky programmed pulse."[14]

The impassioned anthem 'Drink Before the War' is next, with O'Connor castigating her antagonist for not seeing the truth.

Rolling Stone included the track in its list of 10 Essential Songs by O'Connor, explaining that she "was 15 and full of teenage angst when she wrote this eviscerating dirge about a man — the headmaster of her

Catholic school, it turns out — determined to smother creativity ... the vulnerable defiance of the lyrics ... built towards a cathartic purging."[15]

Sputnik Music's Dave de Sylvia focused on O'Connor's extraordinary vocal, writing, "'Drink Before The War' sees Sinéad hold a single note for extended periods without a variation in pitch (barring the odd glitch), yet the very fact she's less than perfectly trained (in essence, human) makes it sound pained, almost primal."[16]

Lastly, on 'Just Call Me Joe', heavy electric guitar contrasts with O'Connor's soft vocal.

Billboard's Ron Hart wrote, "The album's epic closer 'Just Call Me Joe' is a tour-de-force. Described by renowned *Rolling Stone* critic Anthony DeCurtis as 'a droning, hypnotic guitar dirge straight out of the Velvet Underground and Jesus and Mary Chain songbooks' that highlights the potency of Sinéad's crack studio band.'"[17]

Writing in *NME* after O'Connor's death, Mark Beaumont said of the album: "Inspired by Dylan, Bowie, Bob Marley, Siouxsie And The Banshees and The Pretenders, the record weaved together pop and dance elements, Irish folk, pre-shoegaze atmospherics and cathartic personal and political fervour and stood as testament to O'Connor's uncompromising determination to be in charge of her own life and career."[18]

Most critics agreed that it was an astounding debut from a new artist, even before taking into account O'Connor's tender years. The album saw O'Connor awarded a Grammy nomination for Best Female Rock Vocal Performance, which was won by Melissa Etheridge.

9. Interviews (1987–1988)

Early on, O'Connor was described by those who knew her as very shy, diffident and awkward – an embryonic rock star in the making. She didn't seem entirely comfortable with publicity, and would later say that she always felt like an impostor.

Telegraph rock critic Neil McCormick interviewed O'Connor when she was promoting her debut album and told me the amusing story of when he first interviewed her.

"When it came out, 'Mandinka' and that *Lion and the Cobra* album was extraordinary," McCormick began. "It was obviously extraordinary. And with the shaved head, she looked absolutely amazing and she sounded absolutely amazing. And it was only at that point that you kind of go, 'Wow, that's little Sinéad,' you know, for us.

"She hadn't been a big part of the [Dublin] music scene but she ripped right through, to my ears, and I think a lot of other people I knew were very, very taken with her. With her sweet and sour, her fierceness that came through, and the fragility as well in her voice. At that point, it's game on – obviously she had so much going for her, she was generally just considered a talent.

"I interviewed her when the second album came out, and that was my disastrous interview."

It was funny though, I said.

"It is funny, but it wasn't funny at the time," said McCormick. "Because I was in a place where my band had broken up and I needed to work, I needed to find something. Sinéad was literally the coming thing and I knew somebody at *The Times* and I told them I could get an interview. I just thought, 'Well, I know Fachtna and I'll just make a phone call', which is what I did, and I set up an interview with a feature story for *The Sunday Times* magazine. It was my first big British publication story.

"Then I trotted along. I'd done a lot of journalism but all for *Hot Press*. So I went along to Chrysalis Records – it was just off Oxford Street at that time – you went up some stairs, I was led upstairs into this room, and it just went disastrously wrong from the first moment.

"First of all, she didn't even act as if she knew me. Maybe she didn't – I'd just be a guy around the Dublin scene – so it wasn't, 'Oh hi, how are you?'

"She just sat there eating a curry, kind of staring at me with her big eyes. So I sat down and I put my tape recorder on the table. It was odd, because she was eating the whole time, but I started to ask her questions. There was no small talk because she just wasn't opening up.

"It was one of those absolutely disastrous interviews where the subject doesn't open up and I was probably quite inexperienced – I'd done it quite a bit before but maybe I was nervous because it was *The Times*. And we were kind of rattling through these questions, and she was just saying 'yes' or 'no' to things. And so in literally about 15 minutes, I had asked everything I could think of to ask, and got nothing that I could use. We had a minor squabble about reincarnation."

Oh, I asked, because you asked the question about her mum and that upset her?

"I can't remember . . . it was this idea that she had that we choose where we're born."

In McCormick's 2004 book *Killing Bono*, I reminded him, he'd said something like, 'You didn't get on with your mum, so why didn't you choose a better mum?'

The actual paragraph from the book reads: "Drawing on something she once said about how we choose our own parents before we are born, I asked her why, since she was always complaining about her mum, she didn't choose a better one. She became incensed and announced that our meeting was over."[1]

Back in 2023, in McCormick's living room in North London, he had understandably forgotten this quote from 19 years previously. He told me, "You've done your research. I couldn't even remember that, but you know, it was just awful and so then I just said, 'You know this is terrible, you know, this is rubbish – why don't I go out and you can finish your meal and I'll come back and we can start again as if nothing has happened?' Hard reset, which I thought was the only way to salvage anything.

"And she said, 'No. This isn't like an interview, this is like a conversation on a bus.' Very, very cutting, I'll never forget that.

"And so I said, 'Right, well I'm gonna go then.'"

And she wanted the tape recorder.

"She wanted the tape recorder. I literally said, 'You can't take that.' She said, 'Well, give me the tape. You're just going to make a fool of me.' And I said, 'You're doing a very good job of that yourself.'

"So then she just got up and ran out of the room and then I was left on my own. So I was like, 'Right, OK.' So I started to leave, I got as far as the top of the stairs, and the press officer was a woman – I can't remember her name – and was very embarrassedly saying, 'Neil, I have to ask for that tape,' and I was like, 'I don't work for you.'

"And then I realised that Sinéad was behind her, sort of pushing her at me. And we had an argument at the top of the stairs, and then I left this record company, holding my hand up in the air so that they couldn't reach the tape – they were both much shorter than me!"

That's so funny, I said. And you had to tell *The Sunday Times* that you didn't get the interview?

"Well, I didn't tell *The Sunday Times*," confessed McCormick. "That's the other thing is that if that happened to me now I'd be thinking, 'This is gold.'"

You'd just write it up.

"Yeah, but at that point I was really wanting to get work with *The Sunday Times*, and so I just puffed it. You know what you do when you get a terrible interview, you just write around the interview, and so use whatever stray bits of quotes you can find to puff it up.

"So that was it. Only that from then on I had no interest in [interviewing her] ... So that's that – I used to see her playing live and on the fringes of the Irish music scene, that was it. I didn't talk to her, and my own experience had been very bruising."

Describing O'Connor as "polarising", McCormick said she had both great defenders and detractors. "And I was more on the 'she's crazy, I don't need to have anything to do with her' side of the fence, except that I liked her records.

"And I would go and see her live, as my job is to write about music."

But McCormick would eventually interview O'Connor again, many years later.

Irish music journalist and author Stuart Bailie had a much better experience with O'Connor. A former Assistant Editor of *NME*, where he worked on the staff from 1988–96, Bailie met O'Connor several times over 35 years, from 1987 until close to the end of her life. He now lives in Belfast, so I interviewed him over the phone.

In a 1987 interview with Sinéad in *Record Mirror*, Bailie understandably seemed very impressed and awed by her. Was this because, unlike many interviewees, she was very unguarded and spoke her mind, I asked?

"Yes," Bailie replied. "And also – I'm a bit embarrassed reading it again, because it sounds a little bit condescending, but I didn't mean to be. She was just full on, you know, and *Record Mirror* would be between *Smash Hits* and *NME*. It wanted to be more than a pop paper, but it wasn't quite sure what it was. So it was always quite hard to get the tone when you were writing for *Record Mirror*.

"Sinéad's publicist at the time was a guy called Patrick Lilley. He would have been more of a club PR person but he would have been part of the original squat round Warren Street with Boy George and Marilyn and John Maybury, and all those people. I think he had come to Sinéad through John Maybury, the film-maker.

"And for months before the record was coming out, Patrick was going, 'It's coming out, it won't be long now', and also giving me a running commentary on the pregnancy and birth of Jake. He was very canny, probably, in a way, but he got me very engaged in the story of this person called Sinéad.

"Then he said, 'Come round and hear the record', and I went in and he played 'Troy' and a couple of other tracks, and I was astounded. I just thought, 'My goodness! This is one of those very unique individuals that doesn't really sound like anything else.'

"So a few weeks later, I interviewed her and there was no small talk, no airs, no graces, and you're just straight into this whole thing. And I can't quite remember what the quotes were about, but she talked about her mother, she talked about pregnancy. She talked about not giving a fuck, and not being musical in a muso sense. And that was just great.

"And I think quite soon after that I said, well, we really should put her on the cover. And I think it was a shared cover about 3–4 months later. It was two or three artists on the cover, for possibly the January issue, I can't remember. But it was very evident from the very start that she was a major talent."

Bailie said in his *Record Mirror* write-up that *The Lion and the Cobra* was one of the most superbly unusual records in years. In his view, how did it compare to her later releases?

"Well, it was very primitive and she says, 'Oh, there's only two chords in "Troy"' and I think there's actually three! But for the most part, the song is just the rise and fall of those three chords.

"And I think at the time she said it was inspired by WB Yeats and the poem 'No Second Troy', and in her memoir she talks about Yeats in a slightly mocking tone because Yeats was obsessed with Maud Gonne, the Irish revolutionary, and he compared her to Helen of Troy and sent all these people out to their destination, all the rest of it. Helen's beauty reportedly sparked off the Trojan War, and I think Yeats felt Maud's beauty and personality was part of the Irish independence movement.

"So, even the fact that that was going on was amazing. I didn't quite understand what the lyrics were about and then later on it transpires that the song 'Troy' is almost a conversation between Sinéad and her mother. I think the voice changes between the two people, and at least half the song is written by this frightened child, who's been locked away in the dark. You think, 'Bloody hell, what a thing to write a song about!'

"I think at the time, I mentioned 'Wuthering Heights', in that there'd been nothing like it before or since, it just arrived like a thunderbolt. The rest of that first album's really good, there are loads of really good characters in there. She just said exactly what she wanted to say."

And at such a young age as well, I said.

"Yeah, yeah. The idea of the legacy of punk and then the post-punk [movement] afterwards was that you're your own artist, you don't have to be beholden [to anyone]. And she absolutely took that up.

"I remember saying to her, 'What was "Jackie" about?', and she said, 'Well, I saw a play, it was about this grieving Irish woman and she started keening.' That's the Irish voice for funerals – you have this keening sound. I could be wrong, but there's a play called *Riders to the Sea* by Synge, and that's about a woman in Galway who starts howling in that very primeval Irish way.

"And although Sinéad was very new in a way and embraced hip-hop and other things, she had that Irish thing as well. She was drinking from that very deep well of Irish unaccompanied singing – that sean-nós tradition, as on 'I Am Stretched on Your Grave', albeit with the James Brown sample."

If you could go back and meet her for the first time again in 1987, I asked Bailie, is there anything in particular you'd say to her, any advice that you would give her? Or was she always going to blaze her own trail whatever?

He laughed. "I don't think I could have advised her! She was an absolute artist, you know? And that was so important. Maybe with the gift of hindsight I would say, 'You need to see a really good therapist and get all the stuff about your mother [resolved].'

"Maybe she *was* seeing a therapist at that time, I don't know. But her mother, the behaviour of her mother ... I had a pretty happy childhood, I can't comprehend what that would have been like. And it created great art, but if you're suddenly pushed into a major level of success and a public profile, that's not going to be good for you down the road."

Journalist Neil Perry also told me over email that he had a good experience when he interviewed O'Connor for *Sounds* in 1987.

"The *Sounds* interview actually took place around October–November 1987, when the first album was released, but *Sounds* held it over until January 1988 for some reason," he explained.

"It seems crazy now, but of course no one knew who she was, so it wasn't a priority. The fact I interviewed her at all was quite strange – I was one of *Sounds*' resident metalheads, at that time pretty much all I wrote about and listened to was thrash metal, punk, heavy rock, anything noisy.

"That was mostly my thing – but I also loved to listen to female singers. A beautiful voice could always stop me in my tracks. Next to all my hardcore metal albums I had quite a Dolly Parton collection.

"It must have been luck that I got to hear the album before it was released, as I don't think most record labels and PRs had me down as someone who would be into that sort of thing, so it wouldn't have been sent to me. I just remember hearing that voice on the first single, 'Mandinka', and thinking, who and what the fuck is this? An amazing voice, simple spiky/punky indie rock, it didn't sound like anyone or anything else.

"I told the editor I wanted to do the interview, and luckily got in first.

"The interview was in a loft space in an office near Camden Tube, her PR's office I think. She was so softly-spoken that I had to ask her to hold my tape recorder, as I was worried there would be nothing on the tape.

"The crazy thing about it when I think of it now is that I was 22 and she was 21, we were so young ... except I had all the emotional maturity of a teenage boy and she was talking about having given birth to her first kid –

which happened about 5 or 6 months before this interview – and then writing and recording her first album, and fighting off all manner of vile music business misogyny along the way.

"I don't think I fully understood then what she had already achieved. And I didn't know about the shittier aspects of her childhood of course, her mother, the abuse. I just thought she was cool, sweet, tough, seemed like she had her head screwed on right. But there was a diamond-hard edge to her, for sure. I hoped she was going to do well ... I obviously had no idea she was going to swiftly become globally famous.

"I don't think she liked talking about herself, to be honest, but she warmed up as the interview progressed. It was a very peaceful hour or so, she would mostly sit very still, talking in that very soft voice, with the floaty Irish accent. It was quite hypnotic.

"The funny thing was, before the interview, my friends Ann and Mary Scanlon (sisters, who worked for *Sounds*, Ann was a writer and Mary a photographer) had dared me, being single at the time, to ask her out for a drink, and during the interview this ridiculous thought popped into my head, should I ask her out for a drink? She was probably the most beautiful woman I'd ever met, so that's very intimidating for a not-overly-confident young man.

"I also risked coming across as one of the oily music biz types she'd been ranting to me about. I didn't know anything about her situation, although her mentioning a baby was a bit of a giveaway. Obviously, I didn't ask her out for a drink! My friends called me a wimp afterwards ...

"About six months after that interview, she appeared on the David Letterman show for the first time, and 'Mandinka' had become a hit in the US. She was nominated for a Grammy and then performed at the Grammys ... she became famous so quickly.

"I never met with or spoke with Sinéad again. She became such hot property so quickly that when interviews were up for grabs, every journalist on the paper wanted to do it. So I was at the back of the queue, having already done one. I would have loved to have met up a few years later and compared the two Sinéads, as it were, the 1987 version and the 1992 version, but it wasn't to be.

"Watching someone live out their life in a very public way was always fascinating when you had met them. Funnily enough, I had a friend/ colleague who was married to Sinéad's step-sister, so I used to get insider updates on her progress every now and then.

"My friend Ann was very plugged in to the Irish music scene, she was good friends with Shane MacGowan and The Pogues, and you would hear Sinéad gossip/stories buzzing around all the time – nothing bad,

I hasten to add. I think every Irish musician was happy to see a compatriot doing well."

I asked Perry, who had seemed impressed by O'Connor in his *Sounds* write-up, if he had been taken aback by her openness and honesty, in comparison to other acts?

"She was no more or less honest than many people I'd interviewed," he replied. "I was impressed by her because I was used to carrying out interviews in greasy dressing rooms and tour vans and squalid venues with groups of young men. And it was, in those days certainly, pretty much *always* men, if you wrote about rock (and/or pop).

"The number of women I'd interviewed by that time in late 1987 – I started writing in mid-1985 – you could count on one hand. So I was relieved and fascinated in equal measure to get a different perspective from a female musician. And, for once, not having to sit in a greasy dressing room or grimy tour van. Bands I'd interviewed might have gone on about what a tough time they'd had in their early days – no money, struggling to get gigs, etc – but that was all part of the rock'n'roll adventure for a bunch of lads trying to form a band.

"It was nothing compared to the sort of crap Sinéad (or, as I was then realising, any woman) had already put up with at this early stage of her career. So I was impressed by her resolve – she had got over the giant hump of getting her first record out sounding how she wanted. All while battling an entire industry that wanted her to shut up and look pretty. Things might be better now for female artists, I'm hoping, but in the 1980s they were still shit. It was an eye-opener."

I asked Perry if he could go back in time and relive the 1987 interview, was there was anything in particular he'd say to O'Connor, or any advice he'd offer.

"No," he replied. "She was an artist, she had to do what she had to do. Her demonic side was going to come out, as much as her angelic side. Some people are not cut out for fame, and I think Sinéad was one of those people, but at the same time she used her fame to make some amazing statements. She was never going to be a Beyoncé/Taylor Swift type, a stadium-filling superstar, although I'm sure in the early 1990s that's the masterplan that her record company was working on. She was unique in that way, no record company or manager was going to package her and sell her."

I also asked Perry about his favourite O'Connor records.

"*The Lion and the Cobra* is a perfect debut LP. Some bands build up to releasing something great, others do it straight away. It appeared seemingly perfectly formed. An interesting clutch of musicians on it too, people from Adam and the Ants, Irish punk band Stiff Little Fingers, the band Japan. If the album were released today it would have the same effect – it is both a moment in time, but also timeless. With Sinéad's stunning voice and the originality and diversity of the songs, to me it still sounds like it could be *right now*, even though I've been listening to it for 35 years.

"Plus those songs were everything to her, songs she had been working on for years, some she wrote as a teenager. Sometimes bands or artists never better their debut records. I think Sinéad went on to write better songs – every record of hers has at least two or three stone cold classics – but I'm not sure if any of her albums matched this one for flow or immediacy.

"My favourite song of hers is 'The Emperor's New Clothes', on *I Do Not Want What I Haven't Got*. It is as great a personal statement as John Lydon/Johnny Rotten made with the song 'Public Image' 11 years earlier. And the music is punchy and tight, of a style she would gradually move away from (which was a shame). She talks about her pregnancy, relationships, fame. And the video, the knowingly goofy dancing, totally unsexualised in a way that few female performers were then, the words delivered straight to camera with that confident gaze.

"It is a bittersweet feeling, of course, to watch that now, but it represents a moment in time when I think she was as happy and confident as she'd ever been.

"*Universal Mother* and *Faith and Courage* both had superb songs but for me are pick and skip albums. My favourite album of latter-era Sinéad is the album of reggae covers, *Throw Down Your Arms*. Just superb, and so rare to hear a beautiful female voice on some heavy-duty roots reggae classics."

10. Support for the IRA (1989)

In 1989, O'Connor came out in support of the IRA (Irish Republican Army), a paramilitary group who wanted to end British rule in Northern Ireland. The IRA was labelled a terrorist organisation by the UK and an unlawful organisation in the Republic of Ireland, so O'Connor's statement was very controversial. It is possible that she made it after chatting with Sinn Féin leader Gerry Adams at a 1989 gathering.

However, in 1990, she rescinded her declaration, saying that she was too young to properly grasp the situation in Northern Ireland. And in 1993, she joined protests after the Warrington IRA bombing which resulted in the deaths of two children.

A clearly embarrassed O'Connor described her early comments supporting the IRA as "really shit, really awful," reported the *Irish Examiner* in 2005. "I was very, very young and I didn't know what I was talking about. Obviously one has compassion and understanding of the circumstances that drive people to violence. But y'know, especially for someone like me who'd come from violence, to talk like that was bollocks."[1]

11. *Hush-a-Bye-Baby* (1989)

O'Connor's first speaking role as an actor was in the Northern Irish TV film *Hush-a-Bye-Baby*. Funded by Channel 4 and RTÉ and directed by Irish filmmaker Margo Harkin, it was the story of a 15-year-old Catholic teenager trying to hide her pregnancy during the Troubles. The plot was inspired by three tragic events: the 1984 case of Ann Lovett; the abandoned baby found in the grotto of Derry's Long Tower church; and the 1984 Kerry Babies case in which two newborn infants were discovered dead in County Kerry.

Harkin first approached O'Connor to produce the music for the film, but O'Connor loved the script and asked for an acting role too. She was originally cast as a nun, but ultimately decided on the small part of the eponymous 'Sinéad'. O'Connor said she was taken with the film, as she too had personal experience of the protagonist's situation.

The main music theme was an instrumental remix of O'Connor's song 'Three Babies', about three miscarriages she had experienced, while the remix with vocals on played over the end credits.

As well as acting in her music videos and narrating the 2022 documentary about her, *Nothing Compares*, O'Connor would go on to star in three more films: *The Ghosts of Oxford Street*, *Emily Brontë's Wuthering Heights*, and Neil Jordan's 1997 family drama *The Butcher Boy*.

The latter was the story of an orphaned boy, Francie, who goes off the rails after his mother commits suicide and his father drinks himself to death. It starred O'Connor in the part of Colleen/Our Lady, playing the Blessed Virgin Mary – a role which contained the line, "For fuck's sake, Francie!"[1]

Jordan became friends with O'Connor, and would go on to become godfather to her youngest son, Yeshua. He told the *Guardian* after O'Connor's death, "I had known her on and off since the '80s, relished a friendship with her that thankfully never went offside. She was always devastatingly beautiful and terrifyingly provocative, a combination that some found hard to deal with. When [I asked] Sinéad to play the role ... she said yes immediately."[2]

12. 'Nothing Compares 2 U' (1990)

O'Connor's first album had fared relatively well, reaching number 27 in the UK charts. However, its singles 'Mandinka', 'Troy' and 'I Want Your (Hands On Me)' had peaked at numbers 17, 48 and 77 respectively. Her fourth single, 'Jump In The River', which would be the first from her sophomore album *I Do Not Want What I Haven't Got*, only reached number 134. O'Connor was still slightly under the radar as far as the general public were concerned.

All this changed with the release of 'Nothing Compares 2 U' on 8 January 1990, the second single from her yet-to-be-released second album. A cover originally written by US superstar Prince, 'Nothing Compares 2 U' was a virtually unknown album track released without note in 1985 by Prince's band The Family. The lyrics describe the agony, loss and abandonment felt after a breakup.

The song had been chosen for O'Connor by her talented manager Fachtna O'Ceallaigh, a huge music fan who was always listening to obscure releases in a wide variety of genres.

The Prince original of 'Nothing Compares 2 U', though still heartfelt, is less commercial and immediate and is considered by most to be unexceptional. It is sung in the key of C, in a soul-R&B style.

O'Connor's cover is a heartbreaking pop ballad, her voice full of wistfulness and sadness. The pronouns are changed from male to female (and vice versa for her love interest).

Along with the rest of the album, the track was co-produced by Wild Bunch alumnus Nellee Hooper, who would go on to produce Bjork's *Debut* and U2's *How to Dismantle an Atomic Bomb*. During the recording, however, Hooper was fired. O'Connor and O'Ceallaigh moved to Eden Studios in Chiswick; O'Ceallaigh produced the vocal recording and mixed the record with Chris Birkett, a brilliant and experienced engineer.

Instead of the organ, female harmonies, saxophone and occasionally a cappella production of The Family's version, O'Connor's version – transposed into the key of F – favours a more straightforward and commercial production. It features heavy synth strings (by Japanese musician Gota) and vocal to start, followed by drums kicking in on the fourth line of the first verse, and backing vocals starting on the second verse.

Synth strings play throughout the 16-bar bridge, followed by the impassioned third verse. The song showcases O'Connor's vocal range, reaching a peak of high F and low of A below middle C (nearly two octaves).

The song was always destined to be a worldwide hit, and the video complemented it perfectly.

Again, it was directed by John Maybury, who had previously directed music videos for Boy George and Neneh Cherry. Shot near Paris, it featured footage of religious statues in a park, Parc de Saint-Cloud, in Hauts-de-Seine, Île-de-France – along with shots of O'Connor wearing a long black coat, walking through the park.

However, a close-up of her face lip syncing emotively to the track in a studio comprised the majority of the video, her expressions conveying pain, wistfulness and anger at different times. Her hair halfway between a short crop and being totally shaved, she wore makeup including eye-shadow, her face pale. As she mouthed the lyric about her willingness to enter the relationship again, a single tear rolled from each eye down her cheeks.

O'Connor later revealed that when the song reached the line featuring the word 'Mama', she started recalling her own mother, who had died just five years beforehand, and this caused the tears to flow.

She had also split up with Fachtna O'Ceallaigh just 48 hours previously, ending their managerial relationship as well as their romance, and revealed later: "My life was really falling apart. Also, it's a pretty heavy song. 'Don't Worry Be Happy' it isn't, you know?"[1]

"Fachtna was the first big love of Sinéad's life," an anonymous source told the *Sunday Tribune*, "and she was very affected by the split ... [her split with Fachtna as well as her recalling her mother contributed to] why she was so emotional."[2]

It was this strong performance and evident emotion that won O'Connor Best Video for 'Nothing Compares 2 U' at that year's MTV Video Music Awards, making it the first ever video by a female singer to win the category. In addition, it scooped the awards for Best Female Video and Best Post-Modern Video; altogether, O'Connor collected three 'Moon-men' statues.

The 1990 VMAs host Arsenio Hall introduced Don Henley to present the Best Female Video award, which was the very first MTV award of the decade.

The 'Nothing Compares 2 U' video beat the videos for Madonna's 'Vogue', Paula Abdul's 'Opposites Attract', Alannah Myles' 'Black Velvet' and Michelle Shocked's 'On the Greener Side'.

O'Connor, aged 23, looked completely stunned at winning, cupping her hand over her mouth and laughing. She came up on stage with John Maybury to collect the award, wearing round John Lennon-style sunglasses on her shaved head and a long-sleeved loose-fitting white dress.

She said shyly that she didn't know what to say, eventually holding up two fingers in a peace sign and walking off the stage.

The Best Post-Modern Video award was presented to O'Connor by Sherilyn Fenn and Michael Ontkean from David Lynch's cult TV series *Twin Peaks*.

The other nominees for the award were Depeche Mode's 'Personal Jesus', Red Hot Chili Peppers' 'Higher Ground' and Tears for Fears' 'Sowing the Seeds of Love'.

This time, O'Connor seemed less shocked, though equally pleased. Sweetly, she asked the award presenters if she could keep the envelope they'd opened with her name in. She let John Maybury accept the award this time, and he thanked everyone involved in the making of the video.

The pair also won Best Video, presented by Cher, beating the videos for Madonna's 'Vogue', Aerosmith's 'Janey's Got a Gun' and Don Henley's 'The End of the Innocence'.

In addition to the above three awards, the video was nominated for the Best Breakthrough, Viewer's Choice and International Viewer's Choice awards.

The song also led to O'Connor being presented with *Rolling Stone*'s Artist of the Year award for 1991, as well as Best Album and Best Female Singer – all voted for by readers.

The 'Nothing Compares 2 U' video became so well-known, it was parodied by US comedian Sam Kinison the same year in the video for his single 'Mississippi Queen'.

It was also parodied by singer Gina Riley on Australian TV sketch show *Fast Forward* in a version called 'Nothing Is There', poking fun at O'Connor's shaved head, with comedy lyrics.

The single shifted a million copies in its first month. Two months later, its album *I Do Not Want What I Haven't Got* came out, and would go on to sell over 7 million copies worldwide, fast achieving multi-platinum status.

At the end of the year, *Billboard* held its first *Billboard* Music Awards ceremony and gave 'Nothing Compares 2 U' the accolade of '#1 World Single' of 1990. Legendary artist Joni Mitchell presented the award with a very complimentary and considered intro.

Dressed all in black, O'Connor walked onstage smiling, and this time a piece of paper was clutched in her hand.

"The success of this record has exposed me to more happiness and more pain than I've ever imagined existed," she said, explaining that the happiness came from creating music which connected with others and helped them.

"The pain comes from the fact that as a result of being famous, I'm constantly struggling to be recognised and accepted and understood and loved as an ordinary human being."[4]

She reminded the audience that she was only 23 years old. She then thanked a host of people, and God, before performing Cole Porter's 'You Do Something To Me' with a jazz ensemble.

She had recorded the track for the 1990 compilation album *Red Hot + Blue*, one of the music industry's first benefits for AIDS victims. The 20-track album, which also included Porter cover songs from artists such as Debbie Harry, Iggy Pop, U2, Neneh Cherry and David Byrne, raised nearly $1m for the activist organisation ACT UP.

O'Connor's version of 'Nothing Compares 2 U' was a hit around the globe, reaching number 1 in Ireland, the UK, the US, Australia, Canada, Austria, Denmark, Germany, Mexico, the Netherlands, New Zealand, Norway and Sweden. Ironically, the only major place where it didn't reach number 1 was France, where its video had been filmed, where it peaked at number 5. It achieved platinum status in the UK, America and Austria, and gold in Germany and Sweden.

In America, it stayed at the number 1 spot on the *Billboard* Hot 100 chart for four weeks, and also reached number 1 on the *Billboard* Alternative Songs chart and number 2 on the *Billboard* Adult Contemporary chart. This meant that, out of every song in the whole year in 1990, it reached number 3 overall. In 2019, it would achieve number 97 in a 60th anniversary Hot 100 list spanning the years 1958 to 2018.

In terms of the single's UK performance, it achieved number 2 overall for 1990, but was held off the number 1 spot by the Righteous Brothers' 'Unchained Melody'. The response from the music press to the song was overwhelmingly favourable, and has been ever since.

Rob Harvilla wrote in *The Ringer*, "This is a hostile takeover. Sinéad embodies this song on a molecular level. She changes the fundamental meaning of this song. She owns this song. She steals this song. Just the audacity of that. The greatness and the fearlessness required of her to do that."[5]

Writing after O'Connor's death in *The New Republic*, Daphne Merkin praised O'Connor for the track: "She seemed to have a visceral understanding of when to push her voice to something close to a yell or scream and when to pull it back into a more intimate, whispery timbre. Her performance seemed both effortless and ardent, imbuing the song with wistfulness at one moment and anger the next."[6]

In 2014, O'Connor joked, "Well, lucky it's a good song. Jesus, can you imagine if it was 'The Birdie Song'?"[7] This was a reference to the 1981 novelty hit by The Tweets, which reached number 2 in the UK charts. A 2000 poll commissioned by music website Dotmusic saw the bird-song-featuring instrumental voted the most annoying song of all time.

Stuart Bailie described the reaction from the music press: "Much as she was liked, there were always people going, 'Oh not her again, she's tiresome!' And I think it was a thing at the *NME* where Danny Kelly banned Sinéad from the paper. So basically, some of the people at the *NME* were going, 'No, she gets us into bother'.

"And then James Brown and a few other people had heard 'Nothing Compares 2 U' and were going, 'This is just incredible! This is way beyond everything else.' And so she was re-established at the *NME* and everywhere else. I think we all thought it was great. She was obviously humongously successful. And everyone was delighted."

Simon Hattenstone thought the runaway success of the track wasn't something O'Connor had ever anticipated or wanted: "I remember she said that when she found that she was number one with 'Nothing Compares 2 U', she burst out crying and it wasn't out of happiness but distress. So I don't think it was her ambition to be a great pop star."

Is that because fame was scary, I asked him, or because she didn't like it and she didn't want it, or because it was an incredibly big commercial song that didn't really encapsulate what her music was about?

"I don't know," Hattenstone replied, "but I think it wasn't what she'd planned or dreamed of, though I'm sure there was a bit of her which really liked it as well."

13. Finding a New Manager (1990)

O'Connor first met her second manager Steve Fargnoli at a Prince gig at the Camden Palace, shortly after the release of *The Lion and the Cobra*. She'd met him at several events by the time he took on the role of managing her.

She told *Hot Press* after his death, which came after he'd managed her for 11 years, that she'd learned a lot from the Rhode Island-born Fargnoli as he was "a real veteran of the business."[1] Fargnoli's first role as a teenager had been at the Newport Jazz Festival, where he'd had to rap on the door of Ella Fitzgerald's dressing room to announce it was showtime.

One of the most famous artist managers in the music world, with a career spanning almost four decades, Fargnoli had managed 1970s legends Earth, Wind and Fire and Sly Stone, as well as J. Geils Band, The Emotions, Karl Wallinger and nu-metal band Godsmack – though,

43

of course, his superstar charge had been Prince. His relationship with the latter had ended acrimoniously by the time he began managing O'Connor.

Under the name Steven Fargnoli, he had also produced four films for Prince including *Purple Rain*, and he produced a 1990 live concert documentary called *The Year of the Horse* for O'Connor of her performing a 12-song set. With an 8.2 average rating on iMDB, it received a 1992 Grammy nomination for Best Music Video (Long Form).

14. *I Do Not Want What I Haven't Got* (1990)

O'Connor's most commercially successful album by far, her sophomore effort – traditionally a difficult release for any artist who found success with their debut – was released on 12 March 1990 on Ensign/Chrysalis. Produced by O'Connor and Nellee Hooper and recorded in STS Studios in Dublin, it featured playing from musicians including The Smiths' Andy Rourke and Adam and the Ants' Marco Pirroni. O'Connor wrote six of the ten tracks solo. The album achieved multi-platinum status, largely because of 'Nothing Compares 2 U'.

The single's huge success meant *I Do Not Want What I Haven't Got* reached number 1 in all major territories except France again, where it climbed to number 4.

The album met with almost universally positive reviews. *NME* rated it the second-best album of the year, after the Happy Mondays' *Pills 'n' Thrills and Bellyaches*. US rock critic Robert Christgau wrote, "Not since Patti Smith has anybody had a better chance of defining rock-not-pop in a specifically female way – she's just the right mess of emotion and savvy, crudity and sophistication, fury and independence and love."[1]

"I bought it. I spun it. I was hooked," wrote *Diffuser*'s James Stafford retrospectively, saying the record "wasn't so much a collection of ten songs as an open wound spinning at 33⅓. That was its magic. The album felt like a Malkovich-like portal into O'Connor's head, even when she was singing someone else's song."[2]

The introductory track, 'Feel So Different', begins with O'Connor reciting the Serenity Prayer, before launching into the dramatic six-minute ballad full of live strings. The lyrics allude to being betrayed by friends and strangers, yet state that O'Connor has no bitterness towards them.

The opener is followed by 'I Am Stretched On Your Grave', in which O'Connor sets a translation of an anonymous 17th-century poem, 'Taim Sinte ar do Thuamba', to an Irish-influenced sean-nós-style track. It features fast-paced violins and an up-tempo groove.

Third track 'Three Babies' clearly meant a lot to O'Connor, with its passionate vocal and lyrics referring to her three miscarriages.

In contrast to the preceding track's softness and sweetness, 'The Emperor's New Clothes' is a jaunty and upbeat song about having the courage of your convictions in an oppressive world, with its lyric '*I will live by my own policies/I will sleep with a clear conscience*'. The single was remixed by Public Enemy producer Hank Shocklee, and reached number 31 in the UK charts.

In a later review, Matthew Hocter of *Albumism* wrote that the track "shows a conviction that is part anger and part middle finger to the never-ending judgement the singer faced at the time with her star sky-rocketing, scrutiny around her Catholic faith, and her role as a newly single mother."[3]

The tragic and melancholy 'Black Boys on Mopeds' is a protest song about the killings of two 21-year-old black British youths: Colin Roach, who died in police custody in suspicious circumstances in 1983, and Nicholas Bramble, who died in 1989 after being arrested by racist Met police, who falsely accused him of stealing his own moped.

While the lyrics don't directly reference Bramble or Roach, *I Do Not Want What I Haven't Got* is effectively dedicated to Roach's family, with the inlay sleeve featuring a picture of his depressed parents on a rainy day, standing in front of a poster of Roach. Text below the photo states: "God's place is the world; but the world is not God's place."

On 'Nothing Compares 2 U', the synths and pared-back production coupled with O'Connor's beautifully emotive voice allow the melody and lyrics to shine more brightly than in the Prince version.

'Jump In The River', a co-write with Marco Pirroni, is a chugging guitar-heavy track, seemingly about being so deeply in love that you'd do whatever the other person said. It featured on the soundtrack of the 1988 film *Married to the Mob*.

'You Cause As Much Sorrow' is a heartfelt acoustic lament about O'Connor's mother's actions still affecting the singer after her death. *Q*'s Robert Sandall thought the track was reminiscent of Carly Simon.

Penultimate song 'Last Day of Our Acquaintance' is a slower acoustic ballad about a lover falling out of love with O'Connor. The gentle, melancholy vocal and guitar gradually give way to a louder, more raucous sound.

Final song 'I Do Not Want What I Haven't Got' is a hymn-like a cappella track, O'Connor's powerful and pure voice reverberating down the mic.

Slant's Sal Cinquemani wrote, "The disc ends even more sparely than it begins; the a cappella title track brings the singer back to a place of prayer and hopeful redemption, but whether it's God or a lover she seeks on her 'journey', this is clearly the voice of someone who will never stop searching."[4]

Around the time of the album's release, O'Connor moved to Los Angeles.

15. Commemorating the Fall of the Berlin Wall (1990)

On 21 July 1990, O'Connor was one of many luminaries who took part in Pink Floyd co-founder Roger Waters' Berlin concert to commemorate the fall of the Berlin Wall, which had happened eight months previously. The concert was a live performance of *The Wall*, the eleventh Pink Floyd studio album, which was released in 1979.

O'Connor joined guest artists including Joni Mitchell, Van Morrison, Bryan Adams, Marianne Faithfull and Cyndi Lauper. She performed the track 'Mother', accompanied by a band.

16. A Run-In with Madonna (1990)

In her 1991 *SPIN* magazine interview, O'Connor lambasted Madonna for allegedly making cruel comments about her appearance. She claimed Madonna had suggested that O'Connor was unsexy and unattractive, with the *Like a Prayer* singer comparing O'Connor to a Venetian blind and joking that she looked like she'd been attacked by a lawnmower.

O'Connor added in a 2019 interview with the *Belfast Telegraph*, "She was raging after 'Vogue' was beaten by 'Nothing Compares'" [at the 1990 MTV Video Music Awards, in the categories of Best Video and Best Female Video]. O'Connor then told the *Belfast Telegraph* that Madonna confessed she had told her protégé Alanis Morissette to copy O'Connor's distinctive vocal style for her debut *Jagged Little Pill*, which went on to sell millions.

"I got even, though," O'Connor promised the newspaper. "I can't tell you how, though!"[1]

17. Affair with Hugh Harris (1990)

After splitting with Fachtna O'Ceallaigh, O'Connor started dating her support act, the singer Hugh Harris, who was black. In 1990, when things weren't as progressive as they are now, an inter-racial relationship between famous people was a huge story – especially as O'Connor was still technically married to John Reynolds.

There were numerous headlines about the romance, with a tabloid even paying O'Connor's nanny for information on the couple. The pair split acrimoniously, and O'Connor dropped Harris from the second leg of her tour.

"It's nobody's business," O'Connor told *Rolling Stone* at the time. "Why should I discuss what I've gone through with millions of people? I go through a lot of pain and a lot of really hurtful things, and if I talk about them in public, it causes me a great deal more pain."[1]

She also quipped that the Irish press considered her a "disgraceful adulteress" because of the relationship.[2]

18. Refusing the US National Anthem (1990)

On 24 August 1990, O'Connor was due to gig in New Jersey at the Garden State Arts Center. She recounted in *Rememberings* that a man and woman came to her dressing room before the show and suggested they play the US national anthem 'The Star-Spangled Banner' over the speakers before she went on, wanting to know her thoughts.

O'Connor thought they meant she had a choice as to whether to play the anthem or not, and that if she said no, they'd be fine with that. She thought that anthems were desperately uncool. So she told the strangers that, if it were up to her, she'd rather the anthem not be played.

She described the event as a set-up, explaining that while she was on stage, the man and woman phoned a local TV station and lied that *she'd* approached *them* and insisted that 'The Star-Spangled Banner' wasn't played. They also alleged that she'd refused to go on if the anthem was broadcast, a choice which, she pointed out, her tour insurance wouldn't cover.

As a result of this, at the peak of the tour, O'Connor was branded 'anti-American'. US radio stations refused to play her music and switchboards in New York and New Jersey were besieged with angry callers. The rapper MC Hammer publicly mailed her a cheque telling her he'd cover her First Class airfare back to Ireland.

Frank Sinatra, O'Connor's father Seán's favourite singer, was playing his own New Jersey tour date at the same venue the following night. Sinatra ranted to the audience, "This must be one stupid broad. I'd kick her ass if she were a guy. She must beat her kids to stay in shape."[1]

In response, Seán replied that the 74-year-old Sinatra was so old, he wouldn't be able to lift his leg high enough to administer the kick. O'Connor herself joked that she was checking her bed for horse heads.

On morning drive time shows a day later, DJs destroyed O'Connor's albums on the airwaves.

The *Washington Post* reported that Mike Opelka, the morning show producer at WHTZ in Newark, informed them his station received roughly 1,200 unsolicited calls during the three-hour slot. Callers demanded O'Connor not be played by a ratio of 30 to 1.

However, program director Steve Kingston told the *Post* the ban wouldn't last long.

"Tomorrow, when people forget about it, we'll probably go back to playing her record," he said.[2]

And Armed Forces Radio, reported the *Post*, kept playing O'Connor's songs, with spokesperson Jim Kout saying: "If a song is popular and goes up the charts with various audiences in the US [we play it]. We don't ban artists. The only time we wouldn't carry a song would be when a judge declared it obscene."[3]

Nicholas Spano, a New York state senator and Westchester County Republican, didn't take the same view. He encouraged music-lovers to boycott O'Connor's upcoming New York tour date in Saratoga Springs.

O'Connor's publicist, Elaine Schock, branded him "pathetic", saying he should be ashamed, and expressing amazement that the senator was in favour of censorship, considering Americans' professed love of freedom of speech.

The most dramatic incident took place at a store called Mrs. Gooch's Natural Food Market in Beverley Hills. The *Los Angeles Times* reported that O'Connor was shopping there when a meat clerk called Mike Rechtien clocked her, noticing her shaved head. "I have a song for you," he told her, and proceeded to loudly sing 'The Star-Spangled Banner', to a mixed reception from customers.

O'Connor complained, but didn't want Rechtien to be sacked. However, the store promptly fired Rechtien due to his poor customer service, while adding that "no company is more patriotic than Mrs. Gooch's."[4]

Their former employee was unapologetic. "I believe [O'Connor] practises censorship of our anthem in our country by not allowing it to be played," he said. "I sang in protest of her censorship. She's insulted us and I don't think we should take it lying down."[5]

There were also tiny protests outside O'Connor's next gigs after her refusal to have the national anthem played made the news. The *Sydney Morning Herald* reported, "Not without a sense of humour, she dressed up in a wig and hat to 'protest' outside one of her own shows soon after; she said there were just 'two old guys there ... mad-looking blokes with the thick glasses and the foam on their lips.'"[6]

At the end of the year, O'Connor told the *Los Angeles Times*, "On every level – emotionally, musically, intellectually – it was the busiest year of my life." She said she was happy that people had enjoyed her second album.

She added, however, that 1990 had been "very painful ... awful things happened to me ... The good thing was I could go on stage and scream my heart out when I needed to ... if I hadn't had that, I would have gone mad."[7]

19. On Abortion (1990)

O'Connor wrote the poignant song 'My Special Child' about her first abortion, which took place in 1990. The song's eponymous 4-track EP was released in 1991 to raise funds for the International Red Cross Kurdish Relief program, and the track also appeared on *I Do Not Want What I Haven't Got.*

In her 1991 *SPIN* magazine interview, O'Connor explained that the track was about her termination the previous year, and how she'd suffered emotional pain, because she hadn't wanted to have an abortion. She confessed that she'd been in love with the father, but that he hadn't wanted the child and would have been an absent father.

She added that she'd had three miscarriages in the past, and was anxious about whether she would be able to carry the pregnancy, but it looked as though it would be possible. She then made the very difficult choice of giving up the pregnancy.[1]

On the 1992 RTÉ show *Marian Finucane In Conversation with Sinéad O'Connor*, O'Connor appeared in a brown wig and black dress for a long interview with the Irish presenter.

After talking about the Catholic church and divorce, Finucane asked O'Connor about her views on abortion.

O'Connor told the Irish host that it was a very difficult subject. That the Catholic church thought abortion was murder, but in her view, it was murder to give birth to a baby that you didn't want, because it was ruining the baby's life. She said the child abuse statistics for Ireland were among the highest in the continent.

This, she said, showed that terminations were essential for women carrying a foetus against their wishes. "There's no point in having children that you don't want – you are murdering them by doing that, because they're just sitting there being neglected or being abused, they're being treated like shit, they're being put into care, they're being given away ... it's a terrible thing for a woman."[2]

She said that extricating herself from a toxic environment was something she was fine with, and if that meant having a termination or divorcing a husband, then that was OK. She emphasised the importance of responsibility, and admitted she had been careless when it came to using contraception.

O'Connor said she felt it would have been irresponsible to go ahead with the two pregnancies she had terminated, the second of which was by a man who had a wife – a fact she only discovered after falling pregnant by him.

She espoused feminist views in Ireland well ahead of her time. However, when asked by the *Guardian* in 2014 how she thought the latest feminist movement had changed the pop industry, O'Connor was adamant that she didn't see herself as a feminist, telling Tim Jonze: "I don't think of myself as being a feminist, so I don't really think about feminism a lot.

"I wouldn't label myself anything, certainly not something with an 'ism' or an 'ist' at the end of it. I'm not interested in anything that is in any way excluding of men."[3]

When Jonze told her this wasn't an accurate description of feminism, and that many people would absolutely consider O'Connor a feminist, she retorted that she didn't care what people might want her to be.

20. Breaking a Mic (1991)

In 1991, O'Connor sang backing vocals for cult musician Jah Wobble *aka* John Wardle, friend of the Sex Pistols, on a dubby, Indian-influenced indie track, 'Visions of You' (released as Jah Wobble's Invaders of the Heart).

In September 2023, Wobble did an interview with Scotland's *Herald* newspaper, calling O'Connor, "very present, very real, very funny. She had a very mischievous sense of humour. But when she clicked into performance mode and she felt it, she was unstoppable."[1]

And he described how, for O'Connor's first studio take, he was "so excited to hear the power of her voice ... And in the first note sung in earnest she actually blew the mic."[2]

21. A Tribute to Elton John (1991)

Another guest appearance in 1991 was O'Connor's track on the tribute album *Two Rooms: Celebrating the Songs of Elton John & Bernie Taupin*. Her version of the chart-topping Elton John smash hit 'Sacrifice' was considered one of the album's highlights, though it received mixed reviews overall. Other songs which were lauded included Kate Bush's 'Rocket Man', a reggae cover which won the *Observer* award for all-time Greatest

Cover, and Tina Turner's 'The Bitch Is Back', which was nominated for a Grammy.

Other artists on the all-star line-up included Sting, The Who, Eric Clapton, The Beach Boys, Wilson Phillips, Joe Cocker, Jon Bon Jovi, Rod Stewart, Phil Collins and George Michael.

22. A Fist Fight with Prince (1991)

For years, O'Connor alluded obliquely to the fact that she'd met Prince and that the encounter turned nasty, telling Arsenio Hall in 1991 that the pop superstar got "vicious". She also told *Uncut* in January 2013 that the pair detested each other. She explained to the music magazine, "It got violent too, which is why I can't go into it, but it is a very funny story. I'll tell it when I'm an old lady and I write my book."[1]

In 2018, after Prince's death, *TMZ* reported that O'Connor had been interviewed over the phone by investigators from Carver County. They released audio of the call, in which she told them Prince "used hard drugs. I know this because I spent time with the man." She also said that Prince "had been violent to a number of women in his life", some of whom needed hospitalisation. And she revealed that Prince had told her that he'd refused to put out his *Black Album* because he'd hallucinated that he'd seen God while on drugs, and God had ordered him not to release the record.[2]

The claims were refuted by Prince's ex-wife Mayte Garcia.

When asked in 2019 by Piers Morgan on *Good Morning Britain* if she'd ever met Prince, O'Connor replied with a shaky smile, "We did meet once but we didn't get on very well ... he tried to beat me up and I was defending myself."

When questioned by co-host Susanna Reid as to whether she was joking, she replied, "It's not a joke at all. It was a very frightening experience, actually."[3]

Two years after her *Good Morning Britain* appearance, O'Connor recounted the full story in *Rememberings*. She described how Prince had phoned her up soon after the release of 'Nothing Compares 2 U', asking in his Minneapolis accent, "Is this Shine-head O'Kahn-er?"

Not recognising his voice, she answered, "No, this is Sinéad O'Connor" to rile the caller, before asking his name.

He replied that it was Prince, and that he intended to send a car to collect her so they could meet at his house in Los Angeles. O'Connor had met him briefly once before in 1987, around the time that her debut album was released, but said they just listened to music together in a club and didn't chat.

With no involvement at all in the recording or release of her version of his song, it was the first time the two had been in touch since their brief meeting.

O'Connor told her friends she was going to meet the diminutive singer, and they fantasised that she would become romantically involved with him. Failing that, they hoped the artists would click and start a friendship, as Prince's ex-manager Steve Fargnoli was now O'Connor's manager.

They imagined that Prince's intention was to celebrate 'Nothing Compares 2 U' hitting number 1 across the globe.

They couldn't have been more wrong.

At nine o'clock that evening, the limousine Prince had sent pulled up outside O'Connor's. She chatted to the driver, asking what Prince and his house were like, but received only silence and frightened looks in return.

O'Connor rode in the limousine for a long time before it stopped at the top of a hill, where a huge, badly-lit house stood. The driver nodded at the door to suggest that O'Connor should press the doorbell.

Eventually the door creaked open, and Prince's assistant opened it with a submissive, drooping air. He was silent too, and led O'Connor through two huge dimly-lit living rooms. Affixed to each of the enormous windows were several layers of silver foil.

When asked why, O'Connor received the answer that Prince wasn't a fan of light.

Eventually, O'Connor found herself in a tiny kitchen, and the assistant vanished.

After several minutes, Prince appeared. He smelt strongly of perfume and was absolutely covered in makeup. He asked O'Connor if she wanted a drink, and she replied that she'd like something non-alcoholic, as she had a low alcohol tolerance.

Prince smashed a glass down in front of her and snapped, "Get it yourself!"

O'Connor's senses sprang into high alert, as she realised that she could be in for the same kind of abuse she suffered as a child. She was instantly heightened to Prince's every movement, and began trying to work out how she could escape from the house.

She was suddenly aware that she didn't know her location, as she hadn't requested Prince's address before getting in the car. Nor did she know where the front door was, or where to hail a taxi. This was in the days before mobile phones.

All she knew was that she was up in some hills, ages away from the main road. She was in fact in Beverley Hills, in an Italian-style gated compound.

Prince started walking up and down the kitchen, folding his arms and scratching his chin. He regarded O'Connor with a look of utter disdain, and she thought he might be trying to work out where to punch her in order to cause the most harm.

He then yelled at O'Connor that he didn't like that she cursed in newspaper and magazine interviews – a strange opinion for a man about to release the extremely rude and sweary song 'Sexy M.F.' from his upcoming *Love Symbol* album.

Perhaps he just didn't like women swearing?

O'Connor deftly replied that if Prince didn't like it, he could fuck himself.

Prince summoned his assistant, who turned out to be called Duane, and demanded soup. Asked if she wanted any, O'Connor replied that she wasn't hungry.

Duane soon brought in two bowls of soup, trembling. Prince introduced him to O'Connor as his brother, sneering. O'Connor reiterated that she didn't want any soup. She couldn't believe how badly Prince was treating Duane.

After this, Prince suggested he and O'Connor have a pillow fight. But when she agreed, she discovered this was no ordinary pillow fight: Prince had stuffed a hard object into his pillow and was trying to cause her pain.

More odd behaviour ensued from Prince, until O'Connor escaped from the house and was pursued by the superstar.

She said it was early in the morning by this point. The two tiny pop stars were racing around Prince's car. O'Connor was spitting at him and he was attempting to punch her.

O'Connor finally escaped the ordeal when she rang a stranger's doorbell and Prince decided to leave in a sulk, clearly not wanting the fight to be witnessed.

O'Connor later found out that Prince and Steve Fargnoli, her manager, were suing each other. Fargnoli hypothesised that this was a revenge attack on O'Connor.

Though it's also possible that Prince was jealous, as O'Connor's cover of his song was superior to the original and had become the definitive version.

In addition, Prince didn't seem to like other artists recording covers of his songs. While not mentioning the O'Connor cover, in 2013 he objected to Maroon 5 re-recording his 1986 global number 1 hit 'Kiss'.

"I do pay performance royalties on others' songs I perform live, but I'm not recording these songs and putting them up for sale," he informed *Billboard*.

"Why do we need to hear another cover? Art is about building a new foundation, not just laying something on top of what's already there."[4]

However, the two versions of 'Nothing Compares 2 U' are markedly different.

O'Connor spoke to *People* magazine in 2021 about her experience with Prince. "It certainly didn't change my opinion of him as an artist, which was the only opinion I could have had. I never knew him otherwise," she said.

She also referred to Prince as a "devil" and an "awful monster of a man", and said that recording the audiobook chapter of *Rememberings* involving her altercation with him was traumatic. She said it was the most distressing chapter and she'd had to lie in bed for a few days afterwards.

However, O'Connor also said news of Prince's death, where he died alone in a lift, led her to cry when she learned of it. "The price you pay for being so successful is an awful, aching loneliness, and I think he was terribly lonely, terribly vulnerable."[5]

When the *New York Times* interviewed O'Connor, also in 2021, she called Prince a "violent abuser of women." When the interviewer asked whether it bothered her that her most famous song was written by him, O'Connor replied, "As far as I'm concerned, it's my song!"[6]

Sadly the copyright resided with Prince. When O'Connor film-maker Kathryn Ferguson asked to licence the song for the 2022 documentary about O'Connor titled *Nothing Compares*, Prince's estate banned them from using it in an act of revenge.

Prince's half-sister Sharon Nelson told *Billboard* in a statement, "I didn't feel [O'Connor] deserved to use the song my brother wrote in her documentary, so we declined. His version is the best."

Prince had released the live version of 'Nothing Compares 2 U' with Gaines in 1993. His album *The Hits 1* peaked at number 4 in the UK.

Ferguson explained to *Billboard* that Prince's estate's decision had the right to revoke the song as they held the licensing, and it meant the crew had to think of other ways to soundtrack the film.

"In the end we were very happy with that section of the film," she revealed. "It meant the focus remained on Sinéad's words, and on her own songwriting."[7]

23. Boycotting the Grammys (1991)

In 1991, though nominated for four awards including Record of the Year, O'Connor declined to attend the 33rd Annual Grammy Awards. She explained to comedian Arsenio Hall beforehand on his show that she wouldn't be attending the Brit Awards either, and explained: "The reason

I wanted to pull out was because I believe very much that the music industry as a whole is concerned mainly with material success, and a lot of artists are responsible for encouraging the belief among people that material success will make them happy."[1] She wrote the Recording Academy a letter to this effect.

O'Connor told Hall that awards ceremonies were just the music industry's way of trying to generate more commercial and material success, and she thought that artists should be rewarded for honesty or being inspiring, not merely for achieving record sales.

Hall suggested that Jimi Hendrix and Bob Dylan never received Grammys. [Hendrix did, but only post-humously, and was only nominated for one during his lifetime. Dylan has been nominated for 38 and won 10, though the first came in 1973, 11 years after he started his recording career.]

O'Connor joked that Dylan received a Grammy for Best Rock Vocal Performance in 1979 when he couldn't sing. She argued that he should instead be awarded Grammys for fighting for causes he believed in.

When Hall questioned why O'Connor had attended the AMAs [American Music Awards], she said she'd gone to see if any artists would speak out about the Gulf War, and they hadn't, which informed her decision not to attend any future awards ceremonies. She then stressed that she wasn't anti-American, and that she wouldn't live in America if she were.

Hall asked what she thought of the music industry's charity initiatives, such as We Are the World and Live Aid.

O'Connor said the initiatives themselves were laudable, but that the record companies were using them to make money for themselves.

In a review of the 33rd Annual Grammy Awards, *Variety* magazine called the ceremony "one of the most unmemorable in memory" and opined that "this year's telecast was doomed from the moment Sinéad O'Connor, the artist behind the year's most compelling record, announced that she would boycott the show because the awards celebrate commercialism."[2]

O'Connor won the Grammy for Best Alternative Music Album but wasn't there to accept the award.

She also won Best International Female at the Brit Awards, over Mariah Carey, Janet Jackson, Neneh Cherry, Whitney Houston, Tina Turner and Madonna. Paul Jones, ex-lead singer of Manfred Mann, presented the award. A video voiceover then said, "Unfortunately, Sinéad can't be with us. She's in America. So here's our tribute to her and to that wonderful country, from a fellow nominee."[3]

They then played a clip of Whitney Houston singing 'The Star-Spangled Banner'. This was clearly a dig at O'Connor, given the furore over her reluctance to have the US national anthem piped through the speakers before a New Jersey show the year before.

24. Saddam Hussein Incident on MTV (1991)

According to a *Sunday Tribune* article published in 2008, O'Connor "declared on MTV that the US and England had a history of terrorism 'no better than Saddam Hussein'. She then denounced MTV as well."[1] This incident presumably took place during the Gulf War.

25. *Am I Not Your Girl?* (1992)

O'Connor's third studio effort, released on 14 September 1992 on Ensign/Chrysalis, was a covers album of jazz standards written between 1936 and 1978, backed by orchestral arrangements. It was produced by O'Connor and Phil Ramone. O'Connor's smooth, expressive voice lent itself well to the songs, which she described in the booklet as the songs she'd grown up listening to which had made her want to become a singer.

Am I Not Your Girl received mixed reviews and fared comparatively poorly in the charts, achieving only Gold status. This is most likely because O'Connor's fans were into alternative indie rock songs and not jazz, and favoured her original compositions.

Rolling Stone's Elysa Gardner only gave the album two stars, saying that her performance was "all whispers and sighs, tries too hard for demure understatement ... she flirts relentlessly with the melodies but is loath to caress them. Her coyness grows cloying; moreover, it suggests that the singer is substituting affectation for technique ... she has yet to display the emotional authority required of a great chanteuse."[1]

SPIN's Jonathan Bernstein gave it a mixed review, saying, "O'Connor hits waif overload. This is not just music: this is her life and her blood. Even with the luxury of a fully appointed big band to bask in, O'Connor doesn't exactly lighten up, kick back, and swing." However, he added, "*Am I Not Your Girl?* isn't the karaoke nightmare it might've been."[2]

Greg Sandow of *Entertainment Weekly* gave it a rating of A-, saying, "Love this or hate it – O'Connor can sing these songs. She seizes them with force and finesse, her voice breathing a thousand shades of longing, lust, and despair. And her conscious or unconscious agenda soon becomes clear. She's going to deconstruct Tin Pan Alley, exposing hidden layers of unending pain."[3]

The choice to record a covers album in a less commercial style may have been intentional on O'Connor's part, to take down her profile after the extreme and overwhelming fame she had experienced since 'Nothing Compares 2 U'.

The album's singles were 'Success Has Made a Failure of Our Home', which reached number 18 in the UK charts, and 'Don't Cry for Me Argentina', which reached number 53. However, promotion of the album was stymied due to O'Connor's iconoclastic appearance on *Saturday Night Live*.

26. Ripping Up the Pope (1992)

O'Connor made headlines across the globe during a 1992 appearance on the popular NBC entertainment show *Saturday Night Live*, aged 25. For it was then that she decided to use the photo of Pope John Paul II which she had taken from her mother's house after her death seven years earlier.

She had initially refused to appear on *SNL* two years previously, on 12 May 1990, because comedian Andrew Dice Clay was hosting the episode, and she found him offensively misogynistic.

"It would be nonsensical of *Saturday Night Live* to expect a woman to perform songs about a woman's experience after a monologue by Andrew Dice Clay," she declared in writing. "I feel it shows disrespect to women that *Saturday Night Live* expected me to perform on the same show as Andrew Dice Clay."[1]

However, O'Connor did perform on the show in 1990, on 29 September instead, singing 'Three Babies' and 'The Last Day of Our Acquaintance'. She was well-known enough in America for *SNL* regular Jan Hooks to impersonate her in a sketch called 'The Sinatra Group' the following January.

But it was the 3 October 1992 performance that would completely alter the course of her career. O'Connor had decided to perform two cover songs from her latest album *Am I Not Your Girl?*: 'Success Has Made a Failure of Our Home', originally sung by Loretta Lynn, to be followed by an unaccompanied cover of Bob Marley's 'War'.

The rehearsal had gone to plan, with O'Connor telling the producers she wanted to hold up a photo of a refugee child during the second song, then doing so. Accordingly, the cameramen were poised to close up on the photo.

As the cameras rolled in Studio 8H of the Comcast Building at number 30 Rockefeller Plaza, known colloquially as '30 Rock', O'Connor performed 'War' without any backing, in her pure and clear voice. In her version of the song, she had changed the lyrics towards the end to advocate for sufferers of child abuse.

Confident, angry and defiantly staring into the camera lens, she wore a long-sleeved white lace top and gold necklace.

As planned, at the end of the song, O'Connor held up a photo. But instead of holding up the photo of the refugee child, she held up the photo of the Pope. In it, he was standing smiling beatifically on a balcony, hands raised, wearing red and white robes and a large gold cross.

Carefully and deliberately, O'Connor tore the photo three times into several pieces, ripping it down the middle first, then into quarters and eighths.

"Fight the real enemy!" she shouted, still making eye contact, throwing the torn fragments of photo straight ahead at the camera.

The audience sat in shocked silence. There was no applause, for the sign for the audience to applaud was not held up.

O'Connor's publicist at the time, Elaine Schock, said in the documentary *Nothing Compares*: "My blood ran cold."[2]

As Jack Whatley described the scene in *Far Out* magazine, "Following the sudden switch, NBC Vice-President of Late Night, Rick Ludwin, stated that after seeing the religious protest from the singer, he 'literally jumped out of [his] chair', and the crew scrambled while the production team contemplated cutting the feed."[3]

Despite the audience being stunned, show creator Lorne Michaels let O'Connor appear on stage as the episode finished, in order to wave goodnight.

He told the press O'Connor's stunt had been "the bravest possible thing she could do. To her, the church symbolised everything that was bad about growing up in Ireland the way she grew up in Ireland, and so she was making a strong political statement."[4]

NBC received an unprecedented 4,400 complaints in the aftermath of the incident, and banned O'Connor from the network.

As Emma Specter would write in *Vogue* after O'Connor's death, "[Her] allusion to the Catholic Church's widespread abuses of power would later be confirmed many times over ... But from that moment on, O'Connor became low-hanging fruit for disdain and moral panic, with *Saturday Night Live* quickly banning her from the programme."[5]

O'Connor's manager Claire Lewis received sacks of letters containing death threats, both to O'Connor, the team and her personally.

Madonna, a lapsed Catholic, said afterwards of O'Connor, "I think there's a better way to present her ideas rather than ripping up an image that means a lot to other people."[6]

Hosting the next episode of *Saturday Night Live*, the Italian-American actor Joe Pesci said he was angry at what had happened, and held up the restored picture of Pope John Paul II, which he'd asked someone to paste together.

"It wasn't my show, it was Tim Robbins's show," Pesci said. "But I tell you one thing, she was lucky it wasn't my show. 'Cause if it was my show, I would have gave her such a smack. I would have grabbed her by her – her eyebrows."

The audience broke into applause. Pesci proceeded to talk about the incident for another minute, describing O'Connor as "just a kid."[7]

A week later, the National Ethnic Coalition of Organizations hired a steamroller to crush more than 200 copies of O'Connor's albums in front of the Chrysalis offices in New York. "A feeble cheer went up from a few of the approximately 100 people who had gathered, in addition to members of the media, to watch the protest, across the street from the offices of Chrysalis Records, 1290 Sixth Ave," reported UPI.[8]

Three months after the *SNL* incident, Madonna mocked O'Connor when appearing on *Saturday Night Live* herself. She quipped "Fight the real enemy!" and ripped up a large photo of sex offender Joey Buttafuoco.

A commenter called @EmlynBoyle posted recently beneath the Madonna clip on YouTube: "It's ironic that Madonna courted controversy with the Catholic church, with her 'Like A Prayer' video, years earlier ... but then [mocked] Sinéad O' Connor for actually, genuinely having something to say about that institution's cover-up of abuse, etc. That's the difference between the two – Madonna was just doing it to boost her career, Sinéad actually meant it. R.I.P. Sinéad ... while Madonna continues to become a parody of herself."[9]

Self-proclaimed feminist Camille Paglia had one of the nastiest reactions to O'Connor in an interview shortly after the incident. She said O'Connor's name and pretended to retch, then opined, "Sinéad O'Connor is completely a robot brain, she's like a Victorian. She has messages which she slaps onto art like labels ... In the case of Sinéad O'Connor, child abuse was justified."[10]

TIME magazine labelled O'Connor the Most Influential Woman of 1992 for her performance, but it's unclear whether they intended this as a compliment to her.

As the *Big Issue* reported after O'Connor's death: "The front page of the *New York Daily News* branded her a 'Holy Terror'.

"Catholic organisations pressured record stores to pull her albums from their shelves. Public figures competed for the most repulsive ways to denigrate her. O'Connor and her team received bags of death threats. Her career never really recovered."[11]

The *SNL* incident effectively derailed O'Connor's career, though she always maintained she didn't see it that way.

"I'm not sorry I did it. It was brilliant," she would later tell the *New York Times*. "But it was very traumatising. It was open season on treating me like a crazy bitch."[12]

"I'm an intelligent woman, I knew there would be an aftermath," she told the BBC in 2010, when the Catholic church finally apologised for the abuse scandal. "I didn't expect that I was going to be carried around on a chair and have champagne poured all over me ... What we knew in Ireland was ten years before anyone in America and Canada knew."[13]

However, despite O'Connor's action and fury over the scandal in the church, she would never lose her love of or fascination with Catholicism. In 2010, she would tell Catholic weekly *The Tablet* that the leaders "who are running the business of Catholicism don't actually seem to appreciate true Catholicism. The love and curiosity I have about religion, and the passionate love I have for the Holy Spirit, come from Catholicism. I'm interested in the idea of the saints, everything about it. I mean, it's beautiful."[14]

Irish Fiction Laureate Colm Tóibín reflected on the incident after O'Connor's death in 2023, explaining to Radio 4 that Pope John Paul II was cherished by millions, with massive crowds flocking to catch a glimpse of him when he travelled to Ireland in 1979.

Tóibín said he thought O'Connor ripping up the Pope's photo was a seminal incident, displaying her willingness to flout conventional wisdom to bring to light the Catholic church's child abuse scandal.

"I think for all of us, we all felt, certainly if you're gay in Ireland as I was, that the first thing we had to remove was the power of the church, and the power of the church was insidious and the power of the church would not go willingly," Tóibín explained.[15]

Claims of physical and sexual abuse started to come out in the late 1980s. But it was only in 2010 that O'Connor would be proved right on a worldwide scale by Pope Francis's apology.

"In hindsight, everyone now is going 'Oh, she was right', which is all well and good but it's also a bit late," O'Connor's producer David Holmes said after her death, saying that her "legacy should be to treat people better. Listen to them and don't just fob them off as being in inverted commas 'mental' because she was far from it."[16]

Journalist Neil Perry told me, "The Pope photo incident was one of the greater moments of public rock 'n' roll rebellion carried out by a star in the late 20th century. And she was right, wasn't she? Considering what unfolded in the years afterwards, the history of abuse against children carried out by priests and nuns in Ireland. I cheered her on. She knew she was going to cop a shitstorm but she did it anyway. It was incredibly brave to put her career on the line like that. It was very punk rock."

Robert Dean said, "It was certainly positive for her, because it was something she truly believed in and she was right to do it. I knew it wasn't a great career move, but it was her career and not mine. But I didn't realise until the documentary [*Nothing Compares*] that there was so much more to it. Like there was that thing in America when she refused to let them play [the national anthem] before she went on stage ... that lit the touch paper, that set it on fire. And the Pope thing was just adding fuel to the flames. But I didn't even know about that thing with the [national anthem].

"And then of course there was the Bob Dylan show, which amazes me. Because Bob Dylan was a political artist and his fans should have realised that the *Saturday Night Live* thing had to be done. But that's America for you!"

I asked Simon Hattenstone if he thought O'Connor ever set out to shock people, or whether it all came from a very organic, natural place.

"I don't think she did, really. She did shock people, and I'm sure she was aware of the impact and the effect ... She was like the ultimate rock 'n' roll person. But she was also the ultimate anti-rock 'n' roll person!

"With most people who've really shocked in rock 'n' roll, it's been incredibly planned. It's been organised with Svengalis and managers, [suggesting] biting the heads off birds and snakes. Bashing guitars or throwing TVs out of hotel windows, or the Sex Pistols telling the guy on telly to fuck off. Stuff like that was all incredibly planned.

"Whereas I don't think anyone would or could tell [Sinéad what to do] and it came from the heart.

"With lots of people [it was contrived]. Malcolm McLaren was a mega-capitalist and a marketing man, so it was marketed scandal and controversy. I don't think hers was. Because if you look at the Pope [incident], it did its best to destroy her career. It wasn't like, 'Wow, she threw a telly out of the window, buy a few more albums!'"

27. The Bob Dylan 30th Anniversary Concert (1992)

"All right, I gotta tell ya, I'm real proud to introduce this next artist, whose name's become synonymous with courage and integrity. Ladies and gentlemen, Sinéad O'Connor!"[1]

This is how US country star Kris Kristofferson introduced the 25-year-old O'Connor to the crowd at the Bob Dylan 30th Anniversary Concert in

Madison Square Garden, which took place on Saturday 16 October 1992. O'Connor was due to sing 'I Believe In You', Dylan's 1979 anthem.

It was to be one of dozens of Dylan songs sung by more than twenty famous artists that night to commemorate Bob Dylan's 30th anniversary as a recording artist – including three songs performed by Dylan himself. Other major artists paying homage included Lou Reed, Neil Young, George Harrison, Stevie Wonder, Tracy Chapman, Eddie Vedder, Ronnie Wood and Eric Clapton.

Clearly, it would have been an honour and a very special night for O'Connor, as she had been a huge Dylan fan since the age of 12.

O'Connor walked on stage smiling, wearing a formal sky blue suit top and black trousers. She said "thank you" as a wave of loud booing swept the crowd. O'Connor was confused and wondered if the crowd didn't like her top. Then she realised that the booing was a response to her tearing up the photo of the Pope on *Saturday Night Live* two weeks previously.

She stood there for a while in silence, enduring the crowd's anger, her expression impassive. The band struck up the opening chords but could barely be heard over the boos. They tried to start the song again, but O'Connor motioned to them to stop.

Eventually, O'Connor defiantly shouted her a cappella version of Bob Marley's 'War' again, just as she had done on *Saturday Night Live*. It would be the only non-Dylan track to be performed that night. It would not appear on the tribute CD released after the concert; instead, O'Connor's dress rehearsal rendition of 'I Believe In You' would be included.

Kristofferson walked over and wrapped his arms around O'Connor to comfort her. She eventually walked off the stage. All the press reports from the event said she was in tears, but she vehemently denied this to *Hot Press* in an interview a month later.

She explained that the discordant noise of the crowd half-booing and half-cheering "went directly to my stomach. It made me want to puke – I was just trying not to puke. So when they said I was crying – I was not fuckin' crying. In fact, I was puking."[2]

O'Connor said she felt like vomiting for the next two weeks. "That night is what aged me – the venom, the hatred." She said the toxic atmosphere terrified her because it reminded her of suffering at the hands of her mother.

"[The organisers] told me to get her off the stage, and I said, 'I'm not about to do that,'" Kristofferson recalled years later to Miriam O'Callaghan on RTÉ. "I went out and I said, 'Don't let the bastards get you down.' And she said, 'I'm not down,' and she sang. It was very courageous. It just seemed to me wrong, booing that little girl out there, but she's always had courage."[3]

In the *Hot Press* interview, O'Connor described Kristofferson as "an angel from heaven."[4]

The pair became friends because of the incident, despite their 30-year age gap. In 2009, Kristofferson would release an acoustic song he'd written about O'Connor called 'Sister Sinéad', inspired by the event. The lyrics compared her to Picasso and Catholic saints, and spoke highly of her courage.

Despite this supportive song, their friendship didn't end well. In 2019, O'Connor revealed on Twitter that she'd slept with Kristofferson. This was in response to a Twitter user telling the story of the concert and describing Kristofferson's actions as an alternative to toxic masculinity: "I would not agree Kris wasn't toxically masculine. He took full advantage when he got the chance and then immediately turned nasty ... #NoHeroOfMine."[5]

In a follow-up tweet, O'Connor added that the sex was consensual.

She clarified: "In case my use of the words 'took advantage' in an earlier tweet might be misconstrued, I wish to make clear that in no way, shape or form was I in any way sexually assaulted by Kris Kristofferson. And that the one time we did have sex, it was consensual."[6]

Irish music journalist Stuart Bailie spoke about the events of 1990–92, saying, "The *Saturday Night Live* thing happened, and it was like 'Oh wow, OK.' I think the Frank Sinatra national anthem thing happened first, and it was like, 'OK, she's taking on America! She's taking on the entire nation' and it was like, 'OK ...'

"And by that stage, they were parodying her. She had become so big you become public property, which is very tough for any artist, but obviously recognition that you're so huge. Apparently she enjoyed the Claire Grogan parody in *Father Ted* – as the stern, hectoring Niamh Connolly.

"Then I was there at the Dylan gig where it all kicked off, and that was just incredible. Nobody had expected it, I don't think. Here's a major artist who's the most pertinent protest singer of that generation, and then there's this noise [from the crowd]. And then she rode it out and obviously the rest is history. She confronted them and did Bob Marley's 'War', the Haile Selassie speech, and turned it into a whole thing about child abuse again.

"And there were definitely people cheering, but I don't think she was quite as successful again after that."

No, she never had another hit record in America.

"And the album *Am I Not Your Girl*, was that a good idea or not?" Stuart asked. "I don't know. Just to do jazz standards and things ... But yeah, it would have been hard to recover from that.

"But as sort of a fan and someone who's watching it, [she seemed to have been] still riding it out to a degree ... and I think it was only when I watched that film, the recent documentary *Nothing Compares*, that I could see what it was like to be in the centre of that hurricane ... I almost felt embarrassed for myself and for everybody who had written mean things.

"And obviously the stuff about the Magdalene Laundries and child abuse and colonialism, and all the things that she was saying, 90% of it was valid. It was absolutely on the money."

28. Supporting Peter Gabriel (1993)

In 1993, O'Connor sang duets and backing vocals for her lover Peter Gabriel on his *Secret World Tour*. The pair had originally met on 13 October 1990 in Santiago, Chile, at the Amnesty International human rights benefit concert. Gabriel asked her to record backing vocals on two tracks for *Us*, 'Blood of Eden' and 'Come Talk to Me'. O'Connor flew to Real World Studios in Wiltshire to lay down the tracks.

The pair had immediate chemistry. Gabriel had divorced his first wife six years previously. He asked O'Connor to join him on tour, replacing British singer Joy Askew. O'Connor agreed and the two had an on-off fling. However, O'Connor said in *Rememberings* that Gabriel messed her around romantically, asking her to spend weekends with him, then saying he didn't want anything serious. O'Connor finally left the tour of her own volition, and Gabriel hired singer-songwriter Paula Cole instead.

O'Connor said that Gabriel caused her pain, but that he was also extremely tender and that she still thought highly of him.

On 7 September 1993, O'Connor took an overdose of sleeping pills. She insisted after the incident that it wasn't a suicide attempt, but said she'd been depressed and had just wanted to sleep for three days. This was to blot out the fact that Gabriel had left her alone in order to spend time with glamorous models instead. She told a publication that he was still a good friend of hers.

The incident would be the precursor to many suicide attempts.

Of O'Connor's worsening mental health, Neil Perry told me, "As a music journo I lived through the whole Kurt Cobain era and it was horrible, you knew what was coming. You just hoped someone sensible was close by who could spirit [Cobain] away from the madness of fame, but it never happened.

"You need an absolute steel will to negotiate sudden global fame, and many people don't [possess that]. It drives them mad. When Sinéad would crop up in the news in more recent years, I would hope the same thing, that she had people around her who cared for her and could help her."

29. Advert in *Irish Times* (1993)

On 5 June 1993, the Peace Together concert was held at Dublin's Point Theatre (now renamed 3Arena) to advocate for peace in Northern Ireland. O'Connor was booked to perform, alongside bands New Order, Hothouse Flowers, The Stunning and Something Happens.

However, she didn't turn up, and received a barrage of criticism. She reacted by taking out a full-page advert in the *Irish Times* and filling it with a long poem asking for compassion.

O'Connor begged *Irish Times* readers to stop hurting her, stating that she was only 20 when she became famous, and that she'd never recovered from her traumatic childhood. She explained that she hadn't turned up to the concert due to feeling that she didn't want to be the famous Sinéad O'Connor that day.

She ended the poem with her handwritten signature.

Though the advert attracted some cynical responses, it also evoked a lot of heartfelt emotion. Kate Holmquist, who had interviewed O'Connor back in 1986, wrote a touching response in the *Irish Times*, saying the letter had left her in tears, and that she couldn't be the only one.

"You don't have to have been abused as a child to identify with these lines. Like a mischievous pamphleteer, Sinéad sent us an emotional letter-bomb, shattering our equilibrium and demanding that we look honestly at the deep feelings of abandonment, pain and sadness which so many of us keep repressed."[2]

30. *Universal Mother* (1994)

O'Connor's fourth studio album was deeply emotional and beautiful, raw and exposing. Produced by O'Connor with Tim Simenon, John Reynolds and Phil Coulter, it was released on Chrysalis on 13 September 1994. It was recorded after O'Connor started taking lessons in *bel canto*, an Italian style of vocalising designed to allow singers to sing from the heart.

The record starts with a speech by Germaine Greer about the sexes co-operating. This is followed by the impassioned opener 'Fire on Babylon', a track about O'Connor's mother's abuse, which includes a sample from 'Dr. Jekyll' by Miles Davis.

Maggie Poulos of *Diffuser* placed the track at number 5 in a 2013 list of her top ten O'Connor songs, saying, "The vocal is haunting, and coupled with the subject matter, it's chill-inducing."[1]

The song is followed by two sweet and gentle lullabies, 'John I Love You' and 'My Darling Child', the former about her piano teacher and the latter about O'Connor's six-year-old son Jake.

'Am I Human?' is a track by Jake. Next is 'Red Football', ostensibly about O'Connor's mistreatment by the media, which starts softly and ends raucously. Her cover of Nirvana's 'All Apologies' is softer and far more chilled than the original.

Lovely and delicate piano ballad 'A Perfect Indian' is about the actor Daniel Day-Lewis, a friend of O'Connor's who was starring in the film *The Last of the Mohicans* at the time, hence the title. O'Connor said in her memoir that they were great friends until she blew her fuse at him one night, which destroyed their friendship.

'Scorn Not His Simplicity', another deeply touching piano ballad, was written by Irish musician Phil Coulter about his son, who was born with Down's Syndrome and tragically died at the age of four.

'All Babies' is a track about child abuse, about how all babies are born pure and innocent into a world of great pain.

'In This Heart' is a soft a cappella track sung by O'Connor with male voices.

'Tiny Grief Song' is also an a cappella song, but has a darker sound, in a minor key, with sombre lyrics.

'Famine' is a hip-hop track about the tragedy of the Irish potato famine, with O'Connor proving herself a credible rapper. Featuring two lines from the chorus of The Beatles song 'Eleanor Rigby', it features a strong groove and saxophone backing, under O'Connor's assertion that the Irish potato famine was caused by all the other food in Ireland being shipped to England.

Final track 'Thank You for Hearing Me' was written by O'Connor about her past lover Peter Gabriel. Mellow and sweetly repetitive, it features a retro drum machine and synth backing.

The album was awarded four stars by *Rolling Stone*. Writer Stephanie Zacharek said, "On *Universal Mother*, Sinéad O'Connor tells us more about herself than we probably should know. It's record making as therapy

... It wobbles between being an awful record and a remarkable one, and maybe that's why it works: It swings so wildly that it never sinks into that deathly muddy middle ground."[2]

31. Reconciling with U2 (1994)

In 1994, Bono, Gavin Friday and Maurice Seezer were looking for a singer to record a song they'd written, 'You Made Me the Thief of Your Heart', for the film soundtrack of *In the Name of the Father*. They chose O'Connor.

Bono told Gavin Martin in *NME* that the pair had gotten along for a while. "The real problem was falling out with Fachtna, her manager, and she was very loyal to him. But she came down during the Zoo TV tour to talk about that and clear things up. Even through it all, I've always had a good feeling about her. I've always liked her."[1]

Of the song, Bono revealed that it was a murder ballad, a type of Irish song dating back to the 1300s. It was about a woman who murdered her boyfriend so he would always be hers.

32. A Second Child (1995)

O'Connor announced publicly that she would be having a second child and was pregnant by her friend, Irish journalist John Waters. She told Gay Byrne on *The Late Late Show* that Waters, who was 11 years her senior, was a wonderful person, but maintained the pair were not romantically involved.

Waters had worked as a columnist, writing features and op-eds for outlets including *Hot Press*, *Magill*, the *Irish Independent* and *Irish Times*, and had also had a book published, *Jiving at the Crossroads*, about socio-economics and politics in the Republic of Ireland.

On 6 March 1996, the pair's daughter Roisin, officially named Brigidine Roisin Waters, was born in London. However, O'Connor and Waters soon became embroiled in a custody dispute lasting three years, which only ended when O'Connor acquiesced and allowed Roisin to live in Dublin with Waters.

33. Guesting on *Broken China* (1996)

In 1996, O'Connor provided the main vocals for two tracks on Richard Wright's second solo album. Wright played keyboards in Pink Floyd. The songs O'Connor guested on were called 'Breakthrough' and 'Reaching for the Rail'. Pink Floyd's David Gilmour played guitar at the sessions for 'Breakthrough'.

34. Represented by O'Ceallaigh a Second Time (1996)

O'Ceallaigh briefly managed O'Connor again for seven months in 1996–97, just before her EP *Gospel Oak* was released. O'Connor wanted O'Ceallaigh to get her out of her then-deal with EMI. She said she only wanted a short record deal with a new label, so she could try them out.

O'Ceallaigh extricated her from the deal with EMI and set O'Connor up with a new deal for the new EP with Donnie Ienner, Head of Columbia Records in NYC, for a six month period – enough time for her to decide if it was the right home for her music. However, when O'Ceallaigh informed her of this arrangement, she fired him and signed a huge contract with Atlantic all on her own.

35. *Gospel Oak* (1997)

O'Connor wrote this EP, her last original record for Ensign/Chrysalis under the EMI umbrella, during a period while she was visiting a psychotherapist in Gospel Oak, an area of North London just above Kentish Town, NW5. The cover of the record showed the bridge of Gospel Oak overground line station. O'Connor dedicated the EP to "the people of Israel, Rwanda and Northern Ireland."

Morton Schatzman was O'Connor's psychiatrist – she wrote in *Rememberings* about therapy sessions with him and how fond she was of him, despite the fact that his dog would sit at his feet throughout her sessions, licking his balls. She said this made her uncomfortable.

Aged 86, Schatzman spoke to the *Camden New Journal* after O'Connor's death. While he didn't reveal anything she had told him, bound by confidentiality, he said he thought of her as a potent figure in social history and was unsurprised by the press's effusive reaction celebrating her life.

Of his dog, Caius, he said, "I do think she liked [him]. What I will tell you is that one of my sons used to joke that what she was saying there in her book was actually all 'transference' – meaning it was actually her wanting to lick my balls. But, of course, that was just a joke." It was one O'Connor would probably have appreciated.[1]

The first five tracks of the seven were written solely by O'Connor.

The EP's soothing, gentle opener 'This Is to Mother You' has comforting lyrics and tender instrumentation which complement each other perfectly, and is arguably the strongest track on the album.

Second track 'I Am Enough for Myself' has a similarly lullaby-esque vibe and reassuring lyrics.

'Petit Poulet', sung partly in French, is a song about child sexual abuse.

'4 My Love' has a traditionally Irish feel at the start, with military snare drums, and an Arabic-influenced ending.

Only these four tracks appeared on the UK release of the EP, whereas the US release featured six tracks on one CD and a bonus track on another (the Eternal Recurrence Mix of 'Fire on Babylon'). The EP sold 70,000 copies in the US.

The exceptional O'Connor track 'This Is a Rebel Song', track 5 on the US release, is ostensibly about an abusive relationship, but is actually about the historical conflict between England and Ireland, with England in the role of an abuser, and O'Connor in the role of Ireland, appealing for reconciliation.

An arrangement of the traditional song 'He Moved Through the Fair' concludes the first six tracks.

Music industry trade magazine *Music Week* awarded the album four out of five stars, saying, "Motherhood is treating O'Connor well, judging by this angst-free, truly beautiful EP on which the acoustic, traditional instrumentation is the perfect foil for her stunning voice. Another Chrysalis number one?"[2]

Rolling Stone's Greg Kot gave the record three stars and wrote, "Too often, *Gospel Oak* suggests the mystic easy listening of Enya. At the very least, *Gospel Oak* is well-crafted: the melodies are slight but stately; the production unobtrusive, although the occasional use of unnatural reverb and multitracking is a distraction. [O'Connor's] at her best when gimmicks and sweeteners are cleared away."[3]

While promoting the album, O'Connor told the *Tampa Bay Times* that she wasn't keen on being a pop star – she only wanted to sing. "I've made some money and I'm very lucky. I want to ... make records I want to make, and make enough of a living to look after my children. I want to do something that's healing. I want to use my voice for soothing not just myself, but other people."[4]

After O'Connor's death, Sam Sodomsky wrote in *Pitchfork* that *Gospel Oak* was "a brief collection that stands among her finest work – easily her most hopeful. The sense you got was an artist who, having used art as an outlet for rage, sorrow and self-immolation for a decade, had developed a more nourishing perspective that she wanted to share with her audience."[5]

36. *So Far ... the Best Of* (1997)

The first Greatest Hits compilation of O'Connor's most popular tracks was released on 10 November 1997, and would be her last record on Ensign/Chrysalis. The singer Morrissey claimed after O'Connor's death that she was dropped by the label; however, there is little corroborating information on this.

Reaching number 28 in the UK and number 3 in Ireland, the album would be echoed by the *Essential* Greatest Hits release in 2005.

37. Changing Record Label (1998)

In 1998, O'Connor left Ensign/Chrysalis and signed a new deal with Atlantic Records, a subsidiary of Warner Music Group. She started to record a new album, *Faith and Courage*, but the album was delayed by her acrimonious custody battle with daughter Roisin's father John Waters, which led to serious mental health struggles and her first suicide attempt.

O'Connor said that her new album would be about survival, charting her struggles and life events.

38. Her First Suicide Attempt (1999)

On O'Connor's 33rd birthday, Wednesday 8 December 1999, she was in the midst of her custody battle with John Waters over their daughter Roisin, and had to attend court.

"The only evidence against me in that case was 17 years or so of newspaper stories that made me out to be a crazy person," she told Cole Moreton from the *Independent* in 2005. "So basically, the 20 years in which I was 'Sinéad O'Connor' resulted in people trying to take my fucking baby off me."[1] [O'Connor's calculation here was incorrect – it would have been 12 years of newspaper stories at most, as she had only been in the public eye since 1987.]

That Wednesday, she sat through a court session where it was implied that she would only see her daughter once a month for the rest of Roisin's childhood. This triggered recollections of O'Connor being taken away from her mother at the age of eight.

As a result, that evening, at the home of dub producer Adrian Sherwood, O'Connor took a "shitload of tablets."[2] Sherwood got O'Connor to hospital. She told Moreton she didn't recall anything about the incident.

The pressure on O'Connor was so great as social services in the UK had conducted a two-year investigation into whether or not she was an 'unfit mother'. In early 2000, they finally closed it.

39. Being Ordained as a Priest (1999)

The Catholic church still prohibits women from becoming priests. Despite her aversion to the Catholic church, O'Connor was nevertheless ordained a priest of the officially unrecognised Latin Tridentine sect in 1999 by a dissident bishop called Michael Cox. She took the clerical name Mother Bernadette Marie.

The ordination came about after O'Connor made one of several appearances on *The Late Late Show*, informing host Gay Byrne that if she hadn't become a singer she would have loved to have been a priest.

Cox got in touch with O'Connor as a result, and offered to ordain her. In gratitude, O'Connor made a donation of €150,000 so that Cox could set up a healing centre for Irish travellers in County Offaly.

However, Pat Buckley, another breakaway priest, described the act of charity as disturbing, suggesting it might count as simony – buying a sacrament.

O'Connor told Byrne, "It would be a lie to say I bought my priesthood. [Cox] would not have ordained me [if he hadn't known being a priest was what I was meant to do]."[1]

She also said sorry for tearing up a photograph of the Pope on *Saturday Night Live*, telling Byrne down the line from Lourdes: "I'm sorry I did that, it was a disrespectful thing to do. I have never even met the Pope. I am sure he is a lovely man. It was more an expression of frustration."[2]

On a follow-up *Late Late Show* appearance, O'Connor sat in a white dog collar and black robe, her dark brown hair in a short crop, saying, "I became a priest because I believe in the church and I don't want the church to die ... I have a lot of respect for everybody who would be critical, I think it's wise, because a person shouldn't become a priest unless they take it dreadfully seriously."[3]

O'Connor said she now had the authority to baptise babies, say mass and administer the last rites to the dying, despite the Catholic church lagging behind society in officially recognising women priests. She said she would dress as a priest daily from that day forward.

She later told Sean O'Hagan in a 2002 *Observer* interview, "I am someone who has been in a relationship with the Holy Spirit since I was small. It's everything to me in my life. Now, this might sound odd, but there are certain things it asks me to do for the benefit of my relationship with it. And [being ordained as a priest] was one of those things."[4]

Poking fun at the move, Dublin bookmaker Paddy Power opened a book on O'Connor being chosen as the next Pope, giving extremely long odds of 10,000–1.

A year later, O'Connor was ordained as an Archdeacon, in recognition of her work with homeless people in Dublin.

40. Dating Dermott Hayes (1999)

Between 1999 and 2000, O'Connor spent a year dating journalist Dermott Hayes. He had written *So Different*, a meticulously researched and in-depth biography about the early years of O'Connor's career which was originally published in 1991. After her death, he wrote a feature for the *Sunday Times* reminiscing about their year as a couple, explaining how he had taken O'Connor to watch bellringers on Millennium Eve.

"Sinéad was fascinated and spent the next half-hour questioning the assembled bellringers on their art and its resonance," Hayes wrote. "When they began their perennial task of ringing in the new year ... we shared our wishes; I remember hoping the new year would be kinder to her, and she laughed."[1]

41. *Faith and Courage* (2000)

O'Connor's fifth studio album had a memorable cover featuring a picture of her topless, cropped above her breasts, looking downwards with a flame coming out of her head and flames in the background. Released on 13 June 2000 on Atlantic Records, it listed ten producers, including such celebrities as Dave Stewart, Brian Eno and Wyclef Jean. It also featured her first female producer, Anne Preven.

Opener 'The Healing Room' is a gentle up-tempo track with just two chords, about spirituality and therapy.

The second track, 'No Man's Woman', was the first single and is equally up-tempo, with O'Connor singing feminist lyrics about emancipation over a hip-hop beat.

The third track, 'Jealous', is my personal favourite of O'Connor's songs (alongside '8 Good Reasons' from 2014's *I'm Not Bossy, I'm the Boss*). O'Connor's stunning voice full of pain sings about a broken relationship, over a slow dubby groove. The second single from the album, the song didn't chart except for in Belgium, but received plaudits. Davíð Logi Sigurðsson of Icelandic newspaper *Morgunblaðið* considered it to be the best song on the record, while Jon Pareles of the *New York Times* included it in his 10 essential songs by O'Connor.

Pareles described 'Jealous' as "a not-quite-breakup ballad she wrote with Dave Stewart of Eurythmics. The beat is measured. But the singer's partner is keeping her dangling ... she makes her harshest judgments in her most fragile voice."[1]

The next track, 'Dancing Lessons', is a sweet love song produced by Wyclef Jean and Jerry 'Wonder' Duplessis.

'Daddy I'm Fine' is great fun – a punky track about O'Connor quitting school to enter the music business, co-written by O'Connor and Dave Stewart.

The next track, 'Til I Whisper U Something', is another co-write between the two – a more downbeat song about trying to soothe a depressed partner. It has a traditional Irish feel.

Written by Robert Hodgens, aka Bobby Bluebell, the lead singer of The Bluebells, 'Hold Back the Night' has the same kind of feel as 'Jealous' – a tender, impassioned vocal about trying to save a relationship, laid over a steady, rhythmic groove.

'What Doesn't Belong to Me' is one of four songs on the album solely written by O'Connor. With oblique lyrics, the track is down-tempo yet has a pure major key melody, except for the first six bars of the middle eight. It seems to be addressed to O'Connor's mother.

Written by Scott Cutler and Anne Preven, 'The State I'm In' is an upbeat song in a major key with a soaring chorus.

'The Lamb's Book of Life' is an upbeat Irish-influenced spiritual track which O'Connor sings passionately.

'If U Ever' is a mellow Irish-influenced ballad written solely by O'Connor, about missing a lover and imploring him to come home.

'Emma's Song', another self-penned track, is a very gentle ballad.

The final track, the traditional 'Kyrié Eléison', has both Irish and Rasta influences.

The Metacritic score for the album is a respectable 64 out of 100. *Billboard* gave it the maximum score, saying, "*Faith and Courage* is head and shoulders above what came before it. In fact, it is brilliant."[2] Conversely, *Pitchfork* gave it 3.8 out of 10, with a review mocking the record.

Rolling Stone's Barry Walters awarded the record 3.5 out of 5, calling it an album "of approachable pop that's both defiant and diverse and that flaunts rock's swagger, electronica's experimentalism, folk's introspection and hip-hop's social critique. O'Connor doesn't abandon the national identity she quietly asserted on her previous two releases, [layering] playful Irish folk whistles ... while navigating between inner spirituality and the conflicted outside world."[3]

And music industry publication *Music & Media* wrote, "Musically the album glows with a strongly commercial sheen, combining reggae elements, Irish influences, contemporary programmed beats and a strong pop sensibility. 'It's exciting and a little scary to be back,' O'Connor says. 'I wanted to make a record which was strong and positive ... getting my spirit back on its feet.'"[4]

42. Saving Shane MacGowan (2000)

In 2000, O'Connor saw her friend, The Pogues' frontman Shane MacGowan, slumped on the floor of his home after using heroin. She reported him to the police in the hope that he'd stop using, and they charged him with drug possession after finding a small quantity of heroin on him. However, Highbury Corner Magistrates' Court in Islington, London, later decided that the charges against MacGowan should be dropped.

At the time, MacGowan was disgruntled, but in the end he credited O'Connor with saving him from the clutches of heroin addiction, most probably saving his life. O'Connor said, "I love Shane, and it makes me angry to see him destroy himself selfishly in front of those who love him."

MacGowan died on 30th November 2023 at the age of 65, four months after O'Connor.[1]

43. Coming Out ... And Coming Back In (2000)

In a 2000 interview with LGBT publication *Curve*, which back then had a main demographic of lesbians, O'Connor was asked why she thought lesbians had taken to her and her songs. She replied that "they see themselves in me", and was asked if this was because of her personality and non-gender-conforming appearance.

She eventually said, "I would say that I'm a lesbian. Although I haven't been very open about that and throughout most of my life I've gone out with blokes because I haven't necessarily been terribly comfortable about being a big lesbian mule. But I actually am a dyke."[1]

The words 'big', 'mule' and 'dyke' were left out when the interview was reproduced after O'Connor's death.

O'Connor went on to say that in Ireland, it's hard to be gay as it's a homophobic culture, and so she hadn't felt comfortable with her true sexuality, but now she felt more at ease with it. She claimed not to have come out to anyone in her life except for a few very close friends.

However, soon after, she confessed in a piece in the *Irish Independent*, "I believe it was overcompensating of me to declare myself a lesbian. It was not a publicity stunt. I was trying to make someone else feel better. And have subsequently caused pain for myself. I am not in a box of any description."[2]

She said that, of the thirty sexual partners she'd had since the age of 11, only two were women – one when she was 20 and another more recently. The pair weren't together anymore, "but I love her deeply." She explained that this woman was hurt when O'Connor said she was more attracted to men than women, prompting her to come out as a lesbian.[3]

Around the same time, O'Connor told *TIME* magazine that she had, "a huge calling toward celibacy, which will probably ultimately be the way I'll go. Obviously I am a very sexual person, and that's why it's always been a struggle. And I don't feel that being celibate means I have to cut off my sexuality, because that's my life force."[4]

In 2005, in an interview with *Entertainment Weekly*, she declared herself bisexual again. "I'm three-quarters heterosexual, a quarter gay. I lean a bit more towards the hairy blokes."[5]

Nine years later, in 2014, she was interviewed by LGBT publication *Pride Source* and asked about her sexuality. O'Connor replied, "I'm 47 years of age and I hope ... I've matured somewhat. I think that if you fall in love with someone, you fall in love with someone and I don't think it would matter what they were ... green, white and orange ... whatever the opposite of gay or straight is." She said she was anti the idea of labelling people in any way, and if she were to fall for someone, she wouldn't be bothered whether they were male or female.[6]

The same year, O'Connor wrote on her blog: "Having no joy anyway in the dating department. Dating site has thrown up fuck all.

"I'm not exactly a great prospect once they've googled me."

She said she was changing her dating app settings to say she was seeking a female partner, to see if her chances improved.

O'Connor said it hadn't escaped her attention that at gigs and in life, it was generally women who made overtures towards her.

"I've been thinking for a few years anyway it ain't really working out with men," she finished. "So we'll see what happens."[7]

44. Nursing Steve Fargnoli (2001)

O'Connor struck up an unlikely friendship with broadcaster Janet Street-Porter, who was 20 years her senior, when O'Connor's manager Steve Fargnoli was dying of bladder cancer. Fargnoli was a close friend of Street-Porter's, and after O'Connor's death she explained that the pair had nursed him.

"When her manager Steve (my pal) was dying with bladder cancer in 2001, Sinead and I moved into his hotel in Los Angeles for his final days," Street-Porter tweeted.

"Sinéad was utterly unpredictable, enchanting, and special, extraordinary in concert.

"Now Saint Sinéad's gone – if only she'd been cherished."[1]

Fargnoli died in September 2001, at the age of just 52. O'Connor had been aware that he had cancer since he was diagnosed in 1999 in Atlanta. In recent months, the cancer had attacked his liver and other organs, and four weeks before his death doctors had given him three months to live.

O'Connor told *Hot Press* her career had been on the back burner for much of this time as they'd both been hoping Fargnoli would go into remission. She said she was "devastated" by his death, as he had been a father figure as well as a close friend.[2]

She recalled that, when she was being bothered at a party, she'd just say "Princess Anne" and Fargnoli would come over and hurry her away. A month before he died, when he was in hospital, the pair had spoken on the phone and O'Connor had asked how grave the situation was. "Well, I guess it's Princess Anne," Fargnoli had quipped.[3]

O'Connor had taken a flight to LA to see him, instead of Fargnoli having visits from people he didn't want to see.

45. Getting Married Again (2001)

The BBC reported on 25 June 2001 that O'Connor would be marrying her boyfriend Nick Sommerlad, a journalist who was also distantly related to Sweden's Queen Silvia. He met O'Connor after getting a new role in Dublin with the Press Association.

The *Irish Times* reported, "He said [in February that] he did not have any problems with her star status. 'We fell for each other very quickly. Both of us have been out with various people in the past, but we are both very happy now.'"[1]

Sommerlad confirmed to the *Irish Sun* that the pair were getting married. "I am delighted and so is she."[2]

The BBC reported that Sommerlad said: "A journalist friend of mine and hers introduced us. We have been going out since February.

"I asked Sinéad to marry me a couple of weeks ago, but I'd rather not say how because it's a private thing."[3]

Daily Mirror writer Pat Flanagan reported that O'Connor had married Sommerlad after a whirlwind three-month relationship, two months less than the BBC's estimate.

The wedding took place at a secret location, which later turned out to be Anglesey, a Welsh island where Sommerlad's family lived. "One of the very few people there said the 35-year-old mother of two put James Bond star Pierce Brosnan's wedding to shame when it came to secrecy ... [saying] 'Most of Sinéad and Nick's pals still don't know they are married.'"[4]

Working at the *Daily Mirror*, Sommerlad handed in his notice due to the paper covering a libel action taken by John Waters, the father of O'Connor's second child Roisin. Waters had taken legal action against the *Irish Sunday Times* as he felt they had insinuated in an op-ed that he had been a useless dad to Roisin.

"I am much more confident these days," O'Connor told the *Essex Chronicle* after marrying Sommerlad, saying she was living in Ireland and had reconciled with her family.

"I am not caught up with being a rock star – and I am in love. I feel as if I have died and gone to heaven.

"I intend to be a non-politically correct wife, baking and cooking all day and making myself sexually available," she joked.[5]

Unfortunately, the couple separated with mutual agreement after just under a year of marriage, and announced their separation in February 2003, by which point Sommerlad was living in the UK again. They divorced in 2004.

The *Irish Independent* quoted a friend of O'Connor's as saying, "Neither [is] apportioning any blame and both are saddened ... They fell madly in love when they first met ... having married so early in the relationship was a pressure that neither could cope with. This was on top of the usual pressure of a rock star married to a media figure."[6]

The source claimed that, as a result, O'Connor had stated her intention never to remarry.

46. *Sean-Nós Nua* (2002)

O'Connor's sixth studio album was a collection of traditional Irish covers, its title meaning 'the old made new'. Produced by O'Connor, Adrian Sherwood, Dónal Lunny and Alan Branch, it was released on Vanguard Records on 8 October 2002.

Rolling Stone's Milo Miles gave the album three stars out of five, saying that O'Connor was trying "to 'sexy' up [traditional Irish tunes] with bits of Jamaican rhythm and electronic tweaks. But *Sean-Nós Nua* gets plenty sexy just when she wraps her warm-blooded voice around a fine old melody. Fiddles and pipes are the prominent accompaniment ... Her most rapturous work in a decade."[1]

The *Guardian* gave the record three out of five stars, with writer Betty Clarke saying that O'Connor "seeks to make peace with her country. But, just as her relationship with Ireland has been one fraught with deep affection and passionate scorn, her interpretation of these traditional Irish songs – embracing subtle nods to reggae and electronica – is set against conflicting agendas of history and personal belief."[2]

Similarly, *Pitchfork* gave the album 6.3, with reviewer Mark Richardson musing that it was strange "hearing Sinéad singing songs that seem removed from her direct experience. When Shane McGowan sings an Irish ballad about struggle, it's easy to get lost in the theatricality of his presentation ... but Sinéad is always Sinéad; despite her considerable vocal talents, she was born to sing her own words."[3]

47. *She Who Dwells in the Secret Place of the Most High Shall Abide Under the Shadow of the Almighty* (2003)

This two-CD double album comprised a selection of rare tracks and a live concert. The title was taken from Verse 1 of Psalm 91. The rare tracks included covers of Aretha Franklin, ABBA and the B-52s, liturgical hymns sung in Latin, and collabs with Asian Dub Foundation and Massive Attack.

The live performance was a 2002 concert recorded at the Vicar Street Theatre in Dublin. It featured 13 tracks, including six from *Sean-Nós Nua*, three from *Universal Mother*, three from *I Do Not Want What I Haven't Got*, and also 'You Made Me the Thief of Your Heart'.

48. Early Retirement ... But Not for Long (2003)

In 2003, O'Connor posted on her official website that she was retiring from music: "I am a very shy person, believe it or not. So I ask with love, that I be left in peace and privacy by people who love my records too."

At this point, she was pregnant with Shane. She said *She Who Dwells in the Secret Place of the Most High Shall Abide Under the Shadow of the Almighty* would be her final record.[1]

The *NME* hypothesised that her retirement might be due to a pain and fatigue syndrome which had recently caused her to pull out of gigs with Massive Attack. The condition, fibromyalgia, is worsened by stress, emotional upheaval and tiredness.

49. A Third Child (2004)

On 10 March 2004, O'Connor gave birth to a son called Nevi'im Nesta Ali Shane Lunny, known as Shane. She gave him the middle names 'Nesta' after Bob Marley's middle name, and 'Ali' after Muhammad. His father was the traditional Irish folk musician and producer Dónal Lunny, who was 20 years O'Connor's senior.

O'Connor was misdiagnosed with bipolar disorder shortly after Shane's birth, when she was 37. She wouldn't find out she didn't have the condition until she was 46, after being on meds for it for eight years – including strong antipsychotics.

50. Advert in *Irish Examiner* (2004)

In September 2004, O'Connor paid for a full-page 2,000-word advert in the *Irish Examiner*, asking readers for mercy. She said that, since the age of 17, she had been "ridiculed, lashed and called mad" as a "national pastime" and was tired of being called a "crazy bitch".

"I beg ye," she wrote, "I can't live with the pain of being this nation's whipping post any longer. Untie me please and wash me down I ask ye."

She said she'd reached breaking point when a tabloid in Dublin had made fun of her suggestions for a National Delousing Day to beat childhood nits. The paper had compared her unfavourably with her brother Joseph, whose novel *Star of the Sea* had recently become a bestseller, reaching number 1 in the book charts after being praised by Bob Geldof on *Richard & Judy*.[1]

51. *Collaborations* (2005)

O'Connor's compilation album *Collaborations* was released on Capitol Records on 5 June 2005. It featured her guest appearances on 17 tracks – including 'Heroine' with the Edge, the brilliantly dark 'Kingdom of Rain' with The The, the brooding and edgy 'Special Cases' with Massive Attack and '1,000 Mirrors' with Asian Dub Foundation. Only one track, 'Monkey In Winter' with The Colourfield, had never been released on CD before.

During my interview with him, Simon Hattenstone asked if I'd seen the video of O'Connor duetting with Terry Hall on a song called 'All Kinds of Everything' – which also features on *Collaborations*. I hadn't, so he played it for me on YouTube. O'Connor was so playful in the clip, smiling sweetly, and had grown back her hair into a crop. I'd never seen her looking so happy.

It's funny, I said to Hattenstone, because much of her own music wasn't as melodic as that song. Her music was almost resolutely uncommercial, from the subject matter of the lyrics to the often quite discordant sound. Does he think that she set out to be uncommercial, or she was just doing what she wanted, or kind of a mixture?

"I think she did what she wanted. I'm not an expert on music, but she was brilliant in that she could go from the most tender vocal to the loudest, most aggressive vocal. The only other person I can think of who could do that is Stevie Nicks."

52. *Throw Down Your Arms* (2005)

In 2004, O'Connor flew to Kingston, Jamaica, to record a roots reggae album of cover versions with greats Sly and Robbie (Lowell Fillimore 'Sly' Dunbar and Robert 'Robbie' Shakespeare). The production duo had previously worked with artists Grace Jones, Joe Cocker and Chaka Demus & Pliers.

O'Connor felt so passionately about the record, which was named after a *Burning Spear* track, that she funded the production to the tune of

$400,000. Recorded at Tuff Gong Studio, founded by Bob Marley, and Anchor Studios, where Shaggy recorded 'Boombastic' and The Fugees recorded *The Score*, 10% of the album's profits went to support Jamaican Rastafari elders.

Reviews for the album were generally positive, though the *Pitchfork* reviewer said she didn't think the music world required an "album of Sinéad O'Connor reggae covers. Nothing here betters the originals, and nothing takes them out into new, unexplored terrain. The world of reggae is so vast, with so many great records to explore, that unless you're a huge Sinéad O'Connor fan, this isn't much more than an enjoyable curio."[1]

However, the *Observer* gave the record 4/5, calling it "far better than you'd expect". The review said, "The directness of O'Connor's approach has a lot to do with the success of *Throw Down Your Arms*... she has stayed as close to the originals as possible ... the results are clean, lively takes of hallowed sides by Spear, Marley, Abyssinians, Israel Vibration et al."[2]

And *Hot Press* wrote, "*Throw Down Your Arms* sees Sinéad O'Connor impressively navigating another fresh avenue in roots exploration. In the five years since the excellent *Faith and Courage*, she's tackled two of the great musical pillars in her life. Perhaps now she'll get around to writing songs and give us the ultimate thrill."[3]

The album was released on a label called That's Why There's Chocolate and Vanilla Records, named by O'Connor after a saying by Steve Fargnoli. She told *Hot Press* after his death that Fargnoli always had "respect for people whatever their situation. He was a very wise man. He used to say to me: 'There's a lot of different people in the world, Sinéad, that's why there's chocolate and vanilla.'"[4]

The label was a subsidiary of Ministry of Sound reserved for O'Connor releases from 2005–08. *Throw Down Your Arms* is no longer available on streaming services, though it can be heard on YouTube.

53. A Love Rivalry and Fourth Child (2006)

O'Connor gave birth to her fourth and last child on 19 December 2006, naming him Yeshua. She was pictured smoking in March 2006 in the blog *Hollywood Rag*, and the story was picked up by *People* magazine, who posted a link to the site with a letter from a reader, saying: "Sylvia sent us this link to a photo of a pregnant Sinéad O'Connor, asking, 'What the heck is she doing smoking while pregnant?'

"And you thought Britney was bad."[1]

After O'Connor sent both sites 'cease and desist' letters from her lawyer, *People* posted an apology and correction: "We stand corrected.

Sinéad O'Connor was NOT pregnant while photographed smoking. We apologise for jumping to any conclusions."[2]

A follow-up story in *People* said, "Sinéad was *not* pregnant with the baby while photographed smoking in Manhattan earlier this spring with Frank. She told the *Daily Mail*, 'I want people to know the baby is due on Christmas Eve, so they will know I could not have been pregnant when I was smoking.'"[3]

Her relationship with Yeshua's father, Frank Bonadio, lasted from January 2006 to February 2007. The pair split up due to the displeasure of Bonadio's wife, the fêted Irish blues singer Mary Coughlan, to whom Bonadio was still married.

However, Bonadio and Coughlan had been separated for more than 18 months by the time he met O'Connor. Coughlan had left Bonadio soon after marrying him, after eight years and two children together, when it came out that he'd had sex with the couple's au pair.

Despite there being no overlap between the relationships, Coughlan did not take kindly to O'Connor spending time with Bonadio in the marital home.

On 28 March 2006, the *Irish Mail* printed photos of O'Connor kissing Bonadio in New York. This kicked off an abusive text message war between O'Connor and Coughlan, who was ten years O'Connor's senior. Clearly exasperated at being made to feel like a bad person despite Bonadio being single, O'Connor sent her love rival texts such as: "Be very afraid, by the time I'm finished, you will be crying for your Mummy. I eat crazy bitches like you for breakfast," and "I'll break your face, Mary." Of the messages, O'Connor said, "I let her know not to fuck with me and I sincerely mean it."[4]

The *Irish Independent* claimed that Bonadio had been lonely since splitting with Coughlan, and O'Connor had been a shoulder to cry on. He had apparently not dated anyone else since his split with Coughlan, and Coughlan felt possessive towards him.

"This is where the whole business turned toxic and left the realms of marital breakdown, catfight, call it what you will," wrote Anne Harris in the paper. She said O'Connor was "fighting Frank Bonadio's battles (apparently without his knowledge) and [battling] to defend herself ... [in] a war between two women who didn't get where they are today without fiercely developed competitive streaks."[5]

Despite feuding, Coughlan and O'Connor had much in common. Both female Irish singers who loved jazz and were most successful in the 1980s and 1990s, they had also both advocated for Irish women's rights, experienced sexual and physical abuse as children, suffered mental health problems, and spent time in psychiatric hospitals. O'Connor gave birth to four children, Coughlan five.

The *Irish Times* reported that Coughlan had succumbed to alcoholism and cocaine earlier in her career: "She was hospitalised on 32 occasions for alcohol poisoning. She did eventually face down her demons, though the failure of her second marriage tested her hugely. She left her new husband, Frank Bonadio, just weeks after they had tied the knot when it emerged he'd slept with their au pair."[6]

For her part, O'Connor left Bonadio two months after giving birth to Yeshua, telling the *Irish Sunday Independent*, "I wanted to be able to spend two nights a week with the father of my baby, but it's impossible. Frank is still stuck in his marriage, so is Mary.

"The best thing I can do is end the relationship and let Frank and Mary work out their differences."[7]

However, O'Connor and Coughlan eventually forgave each other, with Coughlan telling the *Irish Mirror* in 2020: "[O'Connor] was up for Christmas, the following Christmas [after the text message war]. We've celebrated, I think, four Christmases together at this stage. I've been in her house and they've all been up here to my house with the kids three or four times as well. Yes, we're all the best of [friends]."

Coughlan said she had realised that her own alcoholism had contributed to the breakdown of her marriage with Bonadio.[8]

Speaking to *People* in 2021, O'Connor told the magazine that their son Yeshua was an "incredible musician ... plays piano and everything incredibly and an incredible singing voice." She suggested he "could do anything" career-wise. "He's half-American, so he's interested in going to college in America," she said. "His father is a scientist. So we'll see. But I would not be surprised if he got into music, because he likes money."[9]

54. *Theology* (2007)

O'Connor's eighth full-length studio record was a religious-themed double album, released on Rubyworks (and Koch Records in the States). The first disc was 'Dublin Sessions', acoustic songs, and the second 'London Sessions', songs with a full band.

There are several covers on the record, including the single 'I Don't Know How to Love Him', penned by Andrew Lloyd Webber and Tim Rice and made famous by their musical *Jesus Christ Superstar*. Other covers included Curtis Mayfield's 'We People Who Are Darker Than Blue' and The Melodians' 'Rivers of Babylon', later popularised by Boney M.

The album didn't chart and received mixed reviews. *Hot Press* said, "Fair play to Sinéad for re-invigorating the ancient genre of the hymn in her own inimitable way, bringing it back to a contemporary public. So many of us frequently feel lost in the spiritual wilderness of this violent world; here is a record that can help heal this particular pain."[1]

However, the *Observer* wrote, "Word-heavy, tune-light songs don't help, whether they're soul-searching prayers or the cryptic meditation that is 'If You Had a Vineyard'. Her cover versions also disappoint. Worse, O'Connor's delicate voice can be heard puffing, straining and – horrors – singing flat! Two stars for the music, one for courage."[2]

And *Rolling Stone* only gave the album a single star, asking, "How awesome is it being God? Not only do you get Sinéad to praise you in her reggae hymn 'The Glory of Jah', you get a bonus acoustic version! If you're not Jah, however, you may lack the stomach for Sinéad's megasincere tributes to Curtis Mayfield and *Jesus Christ Superstar*."[3]

55. *Live at the Sugar Club* (2008)

On 8 November 2006, O'Connor performed a live set at Dublin's Sugar Club. The recording was later released as a CD and DVD, only available from her official website, with a limited run of 2,000 pressings. It featured nine tracks, including six O'Connor originals.

56. Represented by O'Ceallaigh Again (2008)

In November 2008, it was announced that Fachtna O'Ceallaigh was managing O'Connor for the third time. She described it as "brilliant" that they were working together once more, and said that his music industry successes hadn't been paid enough attention by Irish journalists.

O'Connor explained that when her romance with Fachtna had failed, the two had let their working relationship slide too. "I think we have always regretted that . . . I don't think I would have got into nearly as much trouble if Fachtna had remained my manager."[1]

However, privately, O'Connor warned O'Ceallaigh that she was "unmanageable".

57. Collaboration with Mary J. Blige (2009)

O'Connor teamed up with R&B singer Mary J. Blige in 2009 to re-record her song 'I Will Mother You'. This was in aid of the Girls Are Not for Sale campaign, which aimed to stop child sex trafficking, and the proceeds from the track went to GEMS (Girls' Educational and Mentoring Services), an American non-profit which supported trafficked girls in the US aged 12–21.

"I am moved by the really important work that GEMS is doing," O'Connor said. "I was delighted to contribute my song to the campaign if it can help and inspire women and children to feel safe."[1]

Blige, who was asked to take part by O'Connor, said, "I really fell in love with the song." She stated that she had previously been unaware of the scale of US child trafficking.[2] The song was recorded in the iconic Windmill Lane Studios in Dublin, which were dubbed 'the U2 studio'. Alexis Petridis wrote in the *Guardian* that, although Blige was considered one of the greatest singers of all time, "O'Connor isn't remotely cowed or overwhelmed by her presence. Instead, they sound perfectly, if improbably matched. O'Connor's accent certainly provides an intriguing counterpoint to the sound made by Blige, steeped in a very different musical tradition, but it's no less authoritative or commanding." He said O'Connor sang in the chorus "a harmony that soars over Blige's voice".[3]

58. Song Used Without Permission on Real IRA Website (2009)

In September 2009, one of O'Connor's songs was used without permission on a YouTube video produced by Real IRA-linked group 32CSM (the 32 County Sovereignty Movement). The Real IRA staged the Omagh bombing, which killed 29 people.

'He Moved Through the Fair' from *Gospel Oak* was used to soundtrack the 32CSM recruitment video, which described what the group hoped to achieve and stated that the reason behind the conflict was the UK's refusal to accept "the integrity of Irish sovereignty".[1]

Fachtna O'Ceallaigh announced, "They are not authorised to use the song. We will be in touch with them to remove it."[2]

The song was taken off the video after O'Ceallaigh appealed to 32CSM chairman Francie Mackey. It was replaced by an up-tempo instrumental.

O'Ceallaigh responded, "I am appreciative of the fact that the material was removed as soon as the issue was raised."[3]

The video featured a man in a mask with an AK-47 assault rifle.

59. A Third Marriage (2010)

On 22 July 2010, O'Connor's website displayed the following message: "We who run this site are very happy to announce the marriage of Steve Cooney and Sinéad O'Connor has taken place this morning. Thanks be to the Great Lord Jah. Rastafari. Dread I. Conquering Lion I. One love."[1]

Cooney was an Australian music producer 12 years O'Connor's senior, who had Irish roots. The guitarist with O'Connor's touring band, he was a former member of Irish band Stockton's Wing, who had been a support act for superstars Michael Jackson and Prince on tour.

Cooney had also previously played on albums by bestselling traditional Irish artists such as Clannad and The Chieftains, as well as releasing his own guitar album on Irish label Claddagh Records. During his marriage to O'Connor, he was studying for a PhD while she recorded her album *How About I Be Me (and You Be You)?* [In the features about the couple's split, the album was due out in June 2011 and was called *Home*; perhaps due to the separation, it wasn't released until March 2012.]

O'Connor and Cooney separated after just eight months, announcing their intention to divorce.

A member of her family told the *Irish Independent*: "The negative tone of the media coverage of her marriage sparked her illness and she became suicidal."

For her part, O'Connor told the paper, "Steve is lovely, so it's not his fault but mine.

"It was an extremely happy marriage. I'm heartbroken about it breaking up."[2]

She said that people on the street commenting on her weight gain had caused a strain on the couple. She had been taking the mood stabilising drug Lithium for bipolar disorder, but discontinued it due to it causing her to go up several dress sizes.

"I didn't mind putting on weight – the problem is strangers telling me I was fat. That was hard on our marriage," she told the paper.[3]

O'Connor then joked that she couldn't wait to be sent freebies from international fashion houses, as Cooney had left and she now had double the wardrobe space in her house in Bray.

"When Nicole Kidman and Tom Cruise split up, she said 'at least now I can wear high heels again'. Well, now I have twice the wardrobe space so I'm just waiting for all those gifts to start coming in. Size 14 please!" she laughed.[4]

60. Vindication (2010)

In 2010, Pope Benedict XVI finally apologised for child sex abuse in the Catholic church in Ireland. CBC News reported that he wrote in a letter he released: "Your trust has been betrayed and your dignity has been violated. I am truly sorry. I know that nothing can undo the wrong you have endured." Pope Benedict revealed he'd experienced "shame and remorse" over what the sufferers had gone through, and lauded their bravery in coming forward with their stories.[1]

He accepted that in the majority of cases, the victims had not been listened to. 18 years on from ripping up the picture of the previous Pope, O'Connor's allegations had been proved right.

She was subsequently interviewed by many outlets, who were keen to discover her response.

Simon Hattenstone, a long-time *Guardian* journalist, interviewed O'Connor twice – once in 2010 and again in mid-2021, spending the best part of a day with her in total. I interviewed him at the *Guardian* offices in Kings Place, North London.

In my experience, I told him, most celebrities are quite guarded and bland in interviews and their PR often sits in. It sounded as though meeting O'Connor was absolutely the opposite, which must have been refreshing.

"Yeah, it was great," he replies. "It was totally un-PR'd. The first interview was at her house in Bray, where the funeral procession went through, and I think she was still a Catholic priest at that point. I remember she wore a big tweed suit and she looked like an early 20th century industrialist! She looked very different from how she had, but you look back now and you think she still looked great."

The prompt for the interview was the Vatican finally apologising to sufferers of sex abuse as children at the hands of the Catholic church in Ireland.

"She had campaigned and screamed for years about abuse in the church," Hattenstone said, "and a lot of the time people had said she was talking out of her arse, she was untrustworthy, she had mental health problems ... She *did* have mental health problems, but it didn't mean she was talking out of her arse. I think it was a real massive moment of vindication for her."

O'Connor could substantiate her claims, too. "I remember thinking she had so many documents and details. It wasn't as if she'd just said, 'I think there's abuse going on in the church' – it was something she'd researched so closely, it was almost like she had a PhD on Vatican Abuse and the Catholic Church."

She'd really done her research and this wasn't just off the top of her head.

"No, it was the opposite," Hattenstone replies. "She kept giving me documents and references and saying 'You know, this is proved here and here.' It was almost like a full-time occupation for her.

"I remember we were in a room and it was full of documents. Obviously she'd had four kids already and she was still singing, but she'd given so much time to [the research]. That's another thing about Sinéad that I don't

Looking soulful and street, 1988.
(*Mike Owen / Wikimedia Commons*)

Leaving Roxbury nightclub in Los Angeles, 1991. (*Bart Sherkow/Shutterstock*)

A picture of a young Sinéad exhibited in the Church of Santa Maria Annunziata.
(*Gualtieri Sicaminò/Wikimedia Commons*)

Singing at the Festivalitaliano, Milan, 1994.
(*Fabio Diena/Dreamstime*)

Gigging at the 1 Maggio Festival in Rome, 1997. (*Fabio Diena/Dreamstime*)

In concert at the Festivalbar in Verona, 2000. (*Fabio Diena/Dreamstime*)

Guesting on the Rai CD Live broadcast in Milan, 2007. (*Fabio Diena/Dreamstime*)

With producer Daniel Lanois, 2007. (*cinetech/Wikimedia Commons*)

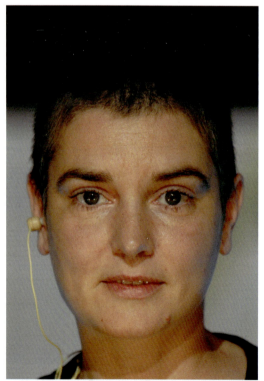

Performing at the Malta Festival in Poznań, Poland, 2007. (*Grzegorz Sulima/Wikimedia Commons*)

Gigging at the City Culture Zone Festival, Warsaw, 2008. (*Dariusz Majgier/Shutterstock*)

Performing in Belgium, 2009.
(*Rob D/Wikimedia Commons*)

Appearing at the amfAR Inspiration Gala, Chateau Marmont, West Hollywood, 2011.
(*S. Bukley/Shutterstock*)

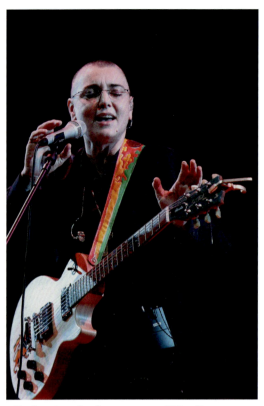

Performing the first concert of The Crazy Baldhead Tour at the Teatro la Fenice, Venice, 2013. (*Matteo Chinellato/Shutterstock*)

Gigging at the WrocLove Fest, Wroclow, Poland, 2013. (*Dziurek/Shutterstock*)

Singing at ParkPop, The Hague, The Netherlands, 2013. (*Steven Lek/Wikimedia Commons*)

Performing at the Ramsbottom Music Festival, 2013. (*Man Alive!/Wikimedia Commons*)

Playing live at the Westport Festival in County Mayo, Ireland, 2014. (*Paul Keeling/Dreamstime*)

Performing at the Festival de Cornouaille, France, 2014. (*Thesupermat/Wikimedia Commons*)

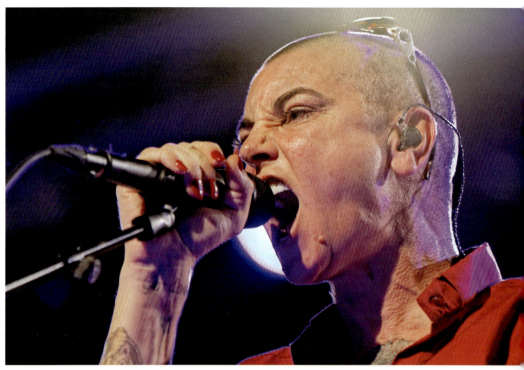

Performing at the Festival de Cornouaille, France, 2014. (*Thesupermat/Wikimedia Commons*)

Gigging at the the 50th Anniversary of the Cambridge Folk Festival, 2014. (*Bryan Ledgard/Wikimedia Commons*)

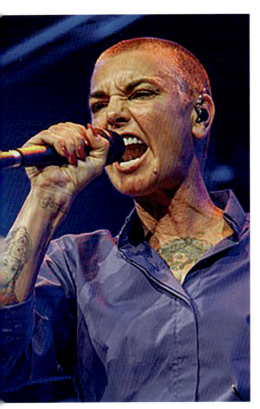

Gigging at the the 50th Anniversary of the Cambridge Folk Festival, 2014.
(*Bryan Ledgard/Wikimedia Commons*)

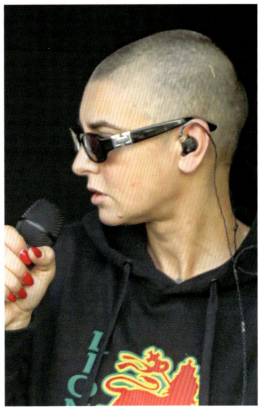

Singing in Lugano, Switzerland, 2014.
(*Grussworte/Wikimedia Commons*)

Fans paying tribute at a memorial in Dublin. (*Liam Murphy/Shutterstock*)

A posthumous mural by Emmalene Blake on South Great George's Street, Dublin. (*Liam Murphy/Shutterstock*)

AI images by a Thai artist of O'Connor created after her death. (*Lanang Banget/Shutterstock*)

think people realise, is just how smart she was. I mean, she was bonkers, but lots of the best people are bonkers. She was incredibly smart, and she saw things differently from lots of people."

Why does he think it is, I ask, that when O'Connor died, there was this outpouring of grief, but during her life, people mocked her? People felt that she was 'TMI', oversharing, mad ... why this sudden shift? Was it a case of 'you don't know what you've got 'til it's gone?'

"I think it's partly that," Hattenstone tells me. "I think a lot of it is to do with that. But also, she was a woman challenging the establishment. She told everyone she had bad mental health problems, which was an easy excuse for people to write her off. She did do incredibly incendiary things, even if she didn't realise it, that made it look as if she was out purely for the attention.

"But when she ripped up the picture of the Pope, I think that came from her heart, from her soul. She was shaking afterwards – it was like, 'Fuck me, what have I done?' – because it came from somewhere inside her.

"We understood a lot less about mental illness back then, and we were prepared to rubbish people.

"So yeah, there were lots of reasons," Hattenstone concludes, "and of course, society was more Christian or Catholic then. Even now, if you attack the Vatican, there's going to be loads of establishment figures having a go at you, and this was a more Christian and religious country.

"So she was attacking the very heart of the establishment. And she wasn't stable, which is not surprising because she'd been through so much shit. She'd been abused by her mum, she'd been abused all her life, she didn't really like fame ... She gave people who would want to [mock her] the perfect excuse to do so.

"When we were interviewing her, about ten years ago, a valid question was, 'Is she in a good enough place to be interviewed, or is it a kind of exploitation?'

"Purely dismissing someone as having a mental illness to rubbish them ... people who wanted to could do that."

Why does he think she shared so much of herself? Does he think that maybe comes from having such a dysfunctional childhood that you're not properly socialised, so you don't have all the usual strictures because things are just so crazy at home? You're not really taught how to behave in polite society ... at least, that was my own experience.

"I don't know," says Hattenstone. "I don't want to present myself as an expert on either Sinéad or what was going on in her head, because I'm not. But I think she was very different from the rest of her family, who she said were also abused but didn't like to talk about it, didn't want to talk about it and hated the fact that she *did* talk about it.

"So it wasn't like she followed the pattern of everyone in her family. I think that was probably just her makeup."

And she said at the end of her memoir that she absolved her parents of responsibility for her mental health problems, because she thinks they didn't stem from her abusive childhood. But I'd be amazed if they had nothing to do with the abuse she experienced when young. That kind of thing leaves scars.

"Yeah, I'm sure it does. Also, the best psychiatrists or doctors couldn't definitively say it was nothing or it was everything to do with it. I'm sure it was massively to do with it but to actually be able to scientifically separate the two, it's just impossible."

Absolutely. I think maybe her saying that was a gesture of kindness on her part towards her parents.

"Yeah," says Hattenstone, "I think it was."

61. Looking for Love on Twitter (2011)

After splitting from Cooney, O'Connor took to her website and Twitter – on which she created and deactivated many different accounts over the years, including @magdadavitt77, @786OmShahid, @vampyahslahah, @howryeh and @OhSineady – and wittily bemoaned the lack of love in her life.

"My shit-uation sexually/affectionately speaking is so dire that inanimate objects are starting to look good, as are inappropriate and/or unavailable men and/or inappropriate and/or unavailable fruits and vegetables," she confessed.[1]

But she said that being famous meant meeting a genuine man was difficult, and that she was depressed being single.

However, O'Connor insisted she had a very specific idea of the perfect boyfriend. She was after a middle-aged, sweet, sex-starved partner over 44 who didn't gel his hair, was based in Ireland and had a great relationship with his mum.

Ed Vulliamy of the *Observer* stated, "The successful applicant, O'Connor stipulated, would be 'preferably sterile' with 'no addictions other than sex, cigarettes or coffee' and 'has to be blind/mad enough to think I'm gorgeous'."[2]

Firemen, rugby players and Robert Downey Jr were of particular interest, O'Connor stated.

She asked for any serious applications to be made through her secretary.

"I must end now," she finished the advert, "as I have a hot date with a banana."[3]

Billboard interviewed O'Connor in 2014 and asked her about this. She stated that the more outraged people were by her openness about her sexuality, the more amused she became.

The magazine reminisced that O'Connor's tweets "left nothing to the imagination", [saying things such as] "'Let me now take time to make VERY clear that yes I "do anal" and in fact I would be deeply unhappy if "doing anal" wasn't on the menu.' Not surprisingly, O'Connor's Twitter feed gained thousands of followers as women and men emailed her."[4]

Around the same time, Irish podcast producer Liam Geraghty (@Liam_Geraghty on Twitter/X) put a slideshow of O'Connor's tweets together on YouTube, backed by a recording of her singing 'Someday my Prince Will Come' from *Snow White and the Seven Dwarves*. The funny tweets, from her @howryeh account, included: "A good nine-incher up the chocolate wiz-way would probably take my mind off it." "Going for a nice relaxing wank and a bath now after that busy week." "Want to clarify. Sex with banana was 12 years ago." And a joke about the doctor telling O'Connor she had to stop masturbating. "I said 'why?' He said 'cuz I'm trying to examine u.'"

O'Connor sent Geraghty an email saying she'd "pissed her Levis" when she saw the video, uploading it to her official website under the heading "Funniest thing ever" with the text "Thanks to Liam Geraghty!"[5]

62. A Cry for Help (2011)

However, just two weeks after publicly looking for a boyfriend on Twitter and being criticised for making rude jokes, O'Connor suggested on her Twitter account that she was going to commit suicide.

"All this shit we're not supposed to say, including suicidal feelings, sex, etc," she tweeted. "U just get treated like a crazy person. I want to go to heaven SO bad. Have for [years] ... Can't manage any more. Badly wish cud die without it ruining my kids' lives."[1]

She then retracted this via two open letters on her website, and said it was merely a cry for help. "People who express suicidal feelings are least likely to act on them," she said. "Anyone who gives u the remotest bit of shit for expressing suicidal feelings is a wanker."[2]

She said that she'd posted the jokey request for a new boyfriend to try and have fun and make herself feel better about her life.

However, sadly some people close to O'Connor didn't see the humour. She hit back at cruel and unrealistic claims. "It was said to me that '14 years from now' my children would be damaged emotionally because I wrote openly and crudely about sex," she said, retorting: "I reject that entirely ... they will know very well I did not actually shag an unpeeled banana."[3]

63. A Fourth Marriage (2011)

One man who responded to O'Connor's requests for a boyfriend was Irish addiction counsellor Barry Herridge. The couple married in Las Vegas's famous Little White Wedding Chapel four months later in a pink Cadillac on 9th December 2011. It was a secret ceremony not attended by either of their families or O'Connor's children.

"I've been married before, but I've never had my dream wedding in Vegas," O'Connor explained. "I wanted to do it there because it's casual, quick, not religious and, most of all, very romantic."[1]

Unfortunately, the couple split up after they had "lived together for 7 days only."[2]

The celebrity blog Gawker published an unusually cruel short piece about the wedding, which began: "In the textbook definition of classy, Irish science experiment Sinéad O'Connor got married to her fourth husband ... in the back of a pink Cadillac at the wedding chapel on the Vegas strip that Britney used when she was married for 48 seconds ..."

They later snarked, "The divorce, oh, sorry, got ahead of myself ..."[3]

Soon after the wedding, O'Connor uploaded the following paragraph to her official website: "Dear friends ... amongst whom I include whomever may be reading this ... Am blogging this cus media people are naturally seeking me. On Sunday I will put up blog. Too glorious for words. For now though, as you will appreciate, it's a bit of a 'Can't. Talk. Cock. In. Mouth'. Situation."[4]

However, just two weeks later, on 26 December, O'Connor posted a letter on her website explaining that the pair had split up: "From the moment [we] got together not long ago, there was intense pressure placed upon him by certain people in his life, not to be involved with me. These were people who had never met me but had formed opinions of me based on what they read about 'Sinéad O'Connor'."[5]

She said that as soon as the wedding had concluded, the union was "kyboshed" by these people. She also confessed that she'd taken the two of them on a hunt for marijuana that night, and she'd been given crack too. This had scared her new husband, who was employed by the Irish government as a counsellor for drug-addicted young people.

The *Mirror* later reported that it was O'Connor who had decided to end the relationship.

90

"We ended up in a cab [on our wedding night] in some place that was quite dangerous. I wasn't scared – but he's a drugs counsellor. What was I thinking?" the tabloid reported that O'Connor confessed to *The Sun*.

"Then I was handed a load of crack. Barry was very frightened – that kind of messed everything up really."[6]

In early January that year, O'Connor suffered depression and voluntarily checked into hospital. The *Guardian* reported: "Sinéad O'Connor has been admitted to hospital for treatment of her depression. The singer expects to spend 'two weeks' in doctors' care, with a view to [being] 'back and smiling' soon. 'Good team,' she said. 'They will put me back together quick.'"[7]

Soon after leaving hospital, O'Connor announced that she and Herridge were back together, tweeting from her new account @vampyahslahah: "Yay. My sweet husband is coming home. Very happy girl. Must get pretty-fied by 8pm. Thank u God. Me love me sweet husband so bad. Yay!! :)" "Sorry if too much info or too personal ... Just ... Me so happy. Wus sad without him. Love him rotten bad. So me all happy now ... Hurray!!!"[8]

She followed this up with: "Guess who had a mad love making affair with her own husband last night?"

"Yay!!! Me husband is a big hairy caveman and came to claim me with his club :) and now I'm in cave-land."

The married pair were trying to return to dating in order to slow their relationship down, she said: "We decided to be boyfriend and girlfriend again an stay married but we did rush so we gonna return to b friend g friend.

"we all in love an f— every other mother— who don't like it ... so me all happy!! me love me hubby ... he love me ... f— who no like it ... God is good!"[9]

The *International Business Times* reported: "The couple, who have decided not to move back in together, nevertheless showed signs of domestic bliss when they were spotted bringing in the bins at her home in Bray."[10]

In July 2012, while O'Connor was, the *Irish Independent* said, "on a sunshine holiday with husband Barry Herridge in Majorca with kids and nannies", they phoned her. The paper's diarist wanted to ask about her purported relationship in the early 1990s with Red Hot Chili Peppers' frontman Anthony Kiedis, who had revealed in his autobiography *Scar Tissue* that the pair had had a fledgling romance.

"We would drive around and listen to music and kiss and whatnot, but she wasn't exactly letting me all the way in the door," wrote Kiedis.

"This went on for weeks and it became the most wonderful, non-sexual relationship I've ever had and I adored her," he finished, saying O'Connor had brusquely split up with him.[11]

O'Connor told the reporter: "This is just pure fantasy. I never even kissed Anthony Kiedis. He did try it on with me once – but it was at the most inappropriate time. It was all purely platonic."[12]

In 2013, O'Connor also told *Uncut* that Kiedis thought he was irresistible, and added "It must have been some other bald bitch, 'cos it certainly wasn't me. I'd have to wash my mouth out A LOT if I did anything like that, for fuck's sake!"[13]

Red Hot Chili Peppers track 'I Could Have Lied' is said to have been written by Kiedis about O'Connor.

O'Connor's marriage to Herridge was one of her longer marriages: in February 2014 she said on her official website that she and Herridge had not divorced and intended to renew their wedding vows. She also tweeted a snap of her wedding ring, and wrote: "Am delighted to say ... since you'll all notice me wearing a very pretty engagement and wedding ring and may wonder ... I haven't married a fifth time ... Robert Downey Jnr just isn't going to happen ... My lovely king of a husband has asked if we would renew our marriage vows."

O'Connor added that he treated her like a "goddess".[14]

However, a fortnight later the two decided not to renew their vows after all.

The *Irish Mirror* reported; "Sinéad claims she has now been told by her doctor that she isn't allowed to have any romantic relationships after suffering post-traumatic stress disorder.

"Instead, she revealed she has been advised she's only allowed to have 'meaningless sex'."

O'Connor told the paper, "We have decided we will not ... renew our vows and ... risk non-recovery."[15]

In March 2013, O'Connor told *Uncut*, "If there's one thing I've learned over the last year, it's to keep my love life to myself."[16]

And in September 2014, she self-deprecatingly confessed to the *Irish Independent*: "I wish I hadn't ever got married. Silly cow. Four times. What a twat. Now I can't ever get married once and properly. Anyway, I look stupid in dresses. And clearly, I'm a crap wife."[17]

64. *How About I Be Me (and You Be You)?* (2012)

On her ninth full-length studio album, O'Connor wrote on every track but one, and wrote two of the tracks solo. The record was produced by

John Reynolds in his house in London. Released on independent label One Little Indian (which was later renamed One Little Independent in response to criticism), the record was reasonably well-received but arguably deserved more than its average 3/5 rating.

The *New York Times* wrote that the record "blends idealism and cynicism, love and loss, in equal measure."[1]

John Reynolds told the US newspaper that O'Connor was "a very emotional person ... But it's why her music connects with people. She says what she feels, sometimes painfully."[2]

"[From O'Connor, who] tore up the pope's photo and tends to get filed under 'batshit crazy', the viscera isn't surprising," wrote *Rolling Stone*. "What may be is the empathy, wit and beauty on this focused LP. On [one] power ballad, O'Connor cops, 'I was always crazy' – true, perhaps. But it's a condition still fuelling fierce art."[3]

Pitchfork wrote, "By so thoroughly humanising the spectacle, [the album] makes it impossible not to sympathise with and even root for O'Connor."[4]

And *Billboard* said, "With Sinéad O'Connor's propensity to generate sensational headlines, we sometimes forget just how exceptional and original of a singer/songwriter she can be. Her ninth studio album, *How About I Be Me (And You Be You)?*, is a slap-upside-the-head reminder, a collection of heartfelt confessionals, evocative insights and provocative position statements."[5]

The first single, a jaunty guitar pop number called 'The Wolf Is Getting Married', reached number 40 in Ireland.

It featured an eerie video, a piece of performance art set in one room, which was directed by Roman Rappak, frontman of the band Breton.

MTV reported that the video "shows a woman sitting in a chair while wrapped head-to-toe in white lace that connects to a spiderweb-esque network of threads stretching from wall to wall. Halfway through the video, threads begin to pull at the lace and lift the fabric away so that the woman's eyes are slowly unmasked."[6]

'4th & Vine' was the opening track and second single, all about a bride about to get married. The upbeat skiffle-bhangra groove fused with traditional Irish fiddle and O'Connor's pure vocal to form a gorgeous pop song.

Kitty Empire wrote in the *Guardian*: "Jaw-dropping revelations about Sinéad O'Connor have come thick and fast ... latest bombshell: a breezy pop album about love. On '4th & Vine', O'Connor, 45, four-times married, most recently last December, anticipates her latest wedding with infectious delight ... this breathy Afro-reggae lope sweetly recalls Althea and Donna's 'Uptown Top Ranking'."[7]

Pitchfork said, "Against a rhythmic acoustic strum that gently mimics a hip-hop beat, '4th and Vine' captures the excitement of new love and the invigoration of devoting yourself to another person."[8]

The joyous video was filmed by Kathryn Ferguson, ten years prior to her documentary about O'Connor, *Nothing Compares*.

The song contrasted with the downbeat piano and guitar track 'Reason With Me', a moving ballad about a guilty drug addict wanting to reform. ("I don't want to waste the life God gave me/And I don't think that it's too late to save me.")

Reviews were mixed for 'Reason With Me': the *Guardian* review described the song as cringeworthy, while the *New York Times* thought it was the strongest track on the album: "At [the record's] best, as on the mesmerising 'Reason With Me', it matches the intensity and drive of her debut album."[9]

The next track, 'Old Lady', is an ode to unrequited love and hope of its realisation in old age.

'Take Off Your Shoes' is a more serious lament about the child abuse scandal in the Catholic church, and how it will see the end of the institution.

Penned solely by O'Connor, 'Back Where You Belong' is a gently heartfelt track about caring for someone.

'Queen of Denmark' is a cover of the John Grant song from his eponymous 2010 record. O'Connor and Grant were friends and performed the track live together, as well as collaborating on other tracks, including 'GMF', 'Glacier' and 'It Doesn't Matter to Him'.

Despite O'Connor not writing the song, several of Grant's lyrics are reminiscent of her sense of humour and honesty.

In 2021, Grant told the *Irish Independent*, "Singing with Sinéad was surreal for me, more than anything, but also just joyous ... I'm singing with Sinéad, so how bad can anything be? I was just ... completely wowed by that incredible voice she possesses. That she counts me as one of her peers now is just incredible."[10]

The beautiful, melodic and wistful track 'Very Far from Home' features self-deprecating lyrics full of longing.

'I Had a Baby' has a similar vibe but a very different theme. O'Connor sings about getting pregnant by Frank Bonadio while he was still technically married, and wonders what she should tell their son Yeshua.

The *Guardian*'s review says the last, virtually a cappella track, 'V.I.P.', is O'Connor having a disguised rant at Bono for meeting the Pope.

Bonus track 'Song to the Siren' is a Tim Buckley cover, though the production and arrangement are in keeping with the sweet and gentle mid-tempo feel of the rest of the album.

Guardian pop writer Caroline Sullivan interviewed O'Connor when the latter was promoting the album. "She was very brisk, almost businesslike, I'd say," said Sullivan. "Not particularly friendly. She wasn't falling apart at that point. She approached the interview as 'OK, let's just do this interview and get it over with so I can get on and do something I'd rather do!' It wasn't as though she was constantly fragile.

"We did it in the green room of *The Graham Norton Show*, and what really came across to me was that she seemed together. Really bossing it. Maybe she was just feeling 'large and in charge' or something like that, but I didn't go away thinking 'this is a girl who really needs help', or anything like that."

So she did have periods when she was much healthier?

"Yes, and I think I met her during one," Sullivan replied.

I think in order to record upbeat and happy songs, I said, and to write songs that are optimistic – because she was always very true to herself and always wrote from the heart – to write optimistic lyrics, I would imagine that you would have to be feeling good about your life.

"Yes," agreed Sullivan. "And also when she married Barry Herridge she was clearly on top of the world at that point, she was very happy with him. Though I remember his family tried to split them up almost immediately, and that was difficult. And also she wanted to [score drugs] on their wedding night. But she actually talked about that, she said 'He was really upset about that and I don't blame him.' I don't know when they got divorced – maybe they were even still married when she died?"

[The pair were definitely still married in 2014, and O'Connor said in a *Billboard* interview that year that they were best friends.]

When it comes to being on top of the world and then falling apart, I explained, the thing about having BPD is that you have these amazing highs and really crashing lows, and virtually nothing in between.

"So that's the exuberance followed by the horrendous depression," Sullivan said perceptively.

Yes – and the other thing with BPD is that it makes it very difficult to maintain relationships. So Sinéad had these four very short marriages, and also three short relationships with her three older children's dads ... speaking from experience, it's not her fault at all, because you feel as though you're so much in the grip of this disorder. It's a very difficult thing to beat.

I asked Sullivan why female artists who have had poor mental health, such as O'Connor, Britney Spears and Amy Winehouse, get a hard time from the tabloids. Is it just that women are more open about their mental health struggles?

"I think women have been socialised from a very young age to share," she explained. "When we don't feel so well, when we're unhappy, it's easy to talk about it with other people – as an extreme example, Sinéad talking about it on social media. So I don't think female artists are hunted down … I think it's generally that women are more used to expressing ourselves."

65. Splitting with O'Ceallaigh for the Third Time (2012)

In May 2012, O'Connor ended her agreement for Fachtna O'Ceallaigh to manage her, much to his dismay and anger. The split happened while she was on tour in Germany.

"Fachtna received a very colourful email from Sinead," a source told the *Irish Sunday Independent*. "And things deteriorated after that.

"He was very upset about the whole thing. But he's an impressive manager with huge talent, he is incredibly well respected within the industry. He'll be OK."[1]

When the *Sunday Independent* asked O'Ceallaigh if he still represented O'Connor, he answered: "I don't represent anyone that you are talking about."[2]

On and off, the pair had worked together for over 25 years.

O'Connor would go on to be managed by Simon Napier-Bell and then Carl and Kenneth Papenfus of 67 Management.

66. A Very Candid Interview on Mental Health (2012)

Italian psychology website *State of Mind* have generously allowed me to reproduce the following interview with O'Connor, 'The Psychiatrist and the Rock Star', conducted by psychiatrist Gaspare Palmieri in 2012.

"Sinéad kindly took some time out from her schedule as a busy mother of four to speak to me," wrote Palmieri at the start of the piece. "Despite the impersonality of online conversation, I felt as though on the other side of the screen I was talking to someone authentic, who isn't ashamed to share their own fragilities and is extremely precise when describing her own journey towards healing."

Palmieri started the interview by saying to O'Connor, "Well Sinéad, first of all I want to thank you for your kindness and willingness in giving this interview. I must confess, I was really surprised that you accepted. I don't know how much you want to talk about yourself specifically, but

I would like that our talk be of some help for people who struggle every day against depression."

"I am interested in the issue obviously," O'Connor replied. "Well, the only reason I am qualified to speak is because I have direct experience."

"So ... you have been diagnosed with bipolar depression, haven't you?" asked Palmieri.

"Yes," O'Connor answered, "I was diagnosed eight and a half years ago, but it took twelve years to get the right diagnosis."

"Did your disorder start with a manic state or with a depressive state?" Palmieri wanted to know.

"I don't get the highs and the manic particularly, I get the lows," confessed O'Connor. "When I was younger though, I had a very bad temper, that's my being a bit of a manic; not in a happy way, but I was like ... fuck that!

"I have always had a good functioning in my artistic life, but I had problems mostly in my private life. I got very angry with my boyfriends and stuff ... I would probably have good reasons to be angry but the volume would be too high, just getting to some level of wounding that perhaps was not appropriate to the actual offence committed."

Palmieri asked, "So you never had a proper manic episode?"

"I did have once where I was addicted to shopping," disclosed O'Connor. "That's unheard of for me because I fucking hate shopping, but I did actually about two years ago. That was as manic as I ever got. I bought a lot of clothes."

"Do you think that your experience of depression has been of some inspiration for your creative process at some point?" Palmieri wanted to know.

"I think the other way round," replied O'Connor. "I don't agree with this romantic fantasy that people who suffer from depression are more likely to be artists. I find that I am more creative when I am happy actually.

"I think that music has been a great help to me and this has been confirmed by every psychiatrist I have seen. I would probably be dead if not for music. They think that the reason that I have this depression is for what I went through growing up. I have also Post Traumatic Stress Disorder, and I wouldn't have survived that if not for music. So I think for me, music was a soothing thing and it was also a place where you could say all the stuff that you couldn't say anywhere else.

"When I grew up in Ireland in the seventies there was no such thing as therapy ... I mean, we didn't even have cappuccinos until 1998! So for me, music was therapy. It was also the place where you could speak about yourself, where you were allowed to speak about your traumatic experiences. I grew up in a situation of extreme abuse, but there was no chance to talk about it, so music became the escape if you like."

"In what way has music helped you?" Palmieri questioned. "More in the creative process of songwriting or more in the cathartic process of performing?"

"I think all of it," replied O'Connor. "I think, in the first place, hearing the music inside of you is very soothing, very comforting. For me, there always been, if you like, a spiritual connection between myself and music. What I like about being a musician is that I find the thing soothing, but I also give the soothing to other people; I guess for some people particularly, I think people who come from abuse and/or people who have mental illnesses, have terrible self-esteem problems. And for me I have always found being a musician a place where I find a lot of self-esteem. I feel that I'm a useful contributor to society, and that I couldn't be a contributor to society in any other way.

"I think when you have a mental illness you can feel very bad about yourself because you are always fucking up in life. Making music perhaps makes you feel you are not such a dreadful person and there is something you can do that is not fucked up ... because there is a terrible lack of self-esteem that comes with mental illness, especially if you live, like I do, in a society such as Ireland, where having mental illness has a dreadful stigma.

"And also I suppose it's very cathartic to do a show to the masses and you get to make magic in a manner that you can't do in regular life, but I suppose that self-esteem effect is one of the most powerful."

"I think that the problem of stigma in mental health is as important as the illnesses themselves," Palmieri ventured. "Can you tell me something more about the stigma situation in Ireland?"

"Well I suppose in some ways, all over the world 'crazy' is a term of abuse and I think that is something that should be stopped," replied O'Connor. "In Ireland, 'crazy' is a term of abuse and people are terrified of anything that they conceive to be crazy.

"And the people believed to be crazy won't be treated compassionately, they will treat you horribly and use it as a reason to dismiss anything you would think, do, say or feel, so you're rocking into a self-esteem trap.

"I had a letter from a man back in January, an old man aged 73, he lives in Goolen (Ireland), I was thinking about him this morning, he has been taking antidepressants for 30 years and he has not told his wife and his adult children because of the stigma. That is Ireland, you know. We are very ignorant about the nature of mental illness. People assume all over the world, for example, that schizophrenia means you have a lot of personalities, like multiple personality disorder, but it is not. It is completely different.

"When you have mental illness, you don't have a plaster or a cast or a crutch that lets everyone know that you have the illness, so people expect the same of you as from anyone else. And when you are different, they give you a hard time and they think you're being difficult, or they think you're being a pain in the ass and they're horrible to you.

"You spend your life in Ireland trying to hide that you have a mental illness. I'm always checking with my friends: 'Do I seem crazy?', 'Am I being crazy?', and I shouldn't have to keep checking – if I'm being crazy I should be left in fucking crazy peace!

"You have to hide what you are and it's really stressful and very bad for your self-esteem. Because it's not obvious to people that you are ill, they treat you as if you're a pain in the ass, then you beat yourself up and you are already beating yourself up as a part of mental illness, you know.

"I mean, I understand that we are actually complicated people but we are also dreadfully simple, but you know it's a hard world where there is this gap between the supposedly sane and the supposedly insane, the sane are not familiar with the insane, which in itself is insane. We are all stuffed behind these kind of, you know, the actual bars that don't exist anymore, the metaphorical bars do exist."

"I know that you have always had a difficult relationship with the Catholic Church," said Palmieri. "What do you think about the attitude toward mental illness of the Catholic Church today? Is there acceptance and compassion for the mentally ill?"

O'Connor laughed: "If there was acceptance of the mentally ill in the Catholic Church, the entire Curia would resign! You need the best psychiatrist in Italy to take a little time in there! The very top guys are insane. They are more insane than the lot of us put together. If they investigate mental illness they have to start out by checking themselves into hospital.

"Anybody who can claim that paedophilia and the ordinance of women are equal has a mental problem. When one criticises the Church, what we usually mean, especially in Ireland, are the top guys. We all know that 99.9% of priests and nuns are incredible people, that do a lot to help people of all kinds.

"But the regular priests down the road haven't got the training to go around the country breaking statements, all the poor priests can do is mop up the mess, which is usually suicide, 'cause stigma leads to suicide. Because of the stigma, people don't stay in treatment and they don't get the help they need, because they know they are gonna be treated like shit.

"For example: I checked into hospital about two years ago, because I wanted to make doubly sure that the diagnosis was right. While I was in the hospital (I was there for two weeks), there was a woman about my age who had been there for six months. She wasn't that unwell, and I was talking to her one day about why she was there and she showed me her arms, they were all cut.

"Her mother had died of cancer and she'd nursed her. Nothing had happened to this woman before, but the night her mother died, she probably lost her mind and she sliced up her arms. But the reason she stayed in the hospital so long was that in the village that she came from, they wouldn't have her back, she couldn't have her job back, none of her friends wanted to talk to her. She was a pariah in the village because she had done this to her arms, everybody thought she was mad. So she couldn't go back to her town and she was based in the hospital."

"How many times have you been admitted to hospital?" asked Palmieri.

"I took myself to the hospital twice," replied O'Connor. "The first to get a clear diagnosis. The second was last year when I was taken off medication very stupidly and I got very sick, I couldn't eat or sleep."

"Why did you stop the medication," Palmieri questioned. "Was it [because of] the side effects?"

"I was getting a lot of pressure from people in show business about my being overweight because of medication," O'Connor replied. "I was on 200mg of amitriptiline. When I said this to my doctor, for some reason she took me completely off medication and she didn't really supervise me properly. The mental health system here is really terrible.

"After I was taken off the medication, I got sick, but I didn't realise I was sick. Then I got carried away with losing weight so I wanted to pretend I was not sick. It was not my choice to be off medication, but the psychiatrist took me off, so I thought it was ok. Unfortunately in my case, because of what I do for living, here in Ireland it's very hard for me to find a doctor who can just deal with me as a person, that can get beyond Sinéad O'Connor. I had to go to England to find a psychiatrist for my case."

"How long were you without medication?" Palmieri wanted to know.

"I was off medication from August last year until April," said O'Connor. "I was told to come off by the doctor, so it took me a long time to know I was sick because when you stop those meds it takes a long time to get sick, so I didn't know what the fuck was going on."

"Nine months without medication is really a long time," said Palmieri. "Weren't you warned by the psychiatrist about the possible risks of relapse?"

"Because of what I do for living, in Ireland all that the psychiatrist did was to complain about the stuff that was in the newspapers instead of talking about my sickness," O'Connor told him. "The same psychiatrist was very involved in the Church's public struggle in Ireland ... on the opposite side to me. At the same time as coming off meds, when I was going to her, she complained to me that she didn't like what I was saying about the Church in the newspapers, so we fell out and I was left stranded.

"Then in Ireland the mental health system is so shit that you can't get an appointment with the doctor for treatment for months, so I would wait for another doctor to tell me the same shit. One doctor sent me home with anti-histamines and told me to take 100mg every night. So I said, 'OK!'

"In Ireland, people think doctors are God, they don't question them. But this meant I was sick for three more fucking months! And the funny thing is that it was a private doctor, and the only alternative is to go to the fucking hospital. Nobody wants to go to the hospital, the worst thing that can happen if you are sick is to leave your family and your children, that's the only thing that makes you feel safe."

"It sounds strange," said Palmieri. "In Italy, you can choose a private doctor and pay more, but you can see the doctor more often."

"Here you have six weeks in agony," replied O'Connor, "but unless you want to check into hospital, you are fucked. Moreover, here people don't have money. I have, but the guy next door can't pay for a private psychiatrist and can wait up to six months for a consultation.

"I'll give you an idea about how bad our system is: a friend of mine works in a child drug counselling service, run by the National Health Service for children aged between 12 and 18, and there is a fridge in the toilet! That is the picture of the health system in Ireland."

"I can imagine you really had terrible times," empathised Palmieri. "Was it in the last months when you couldn't finish the tour?"

"Yes, I almost died," revealed O'Connor. "It was in June this year that I was very sick, like never before. I was put on carbamazepine in April and I had a very unusual reaction that made the symptoms worse. Now I feel better taking 200mg of lamotrigine and 100mg of quetiapine. I also take a very high dose of vitamin B12, prescribed by the psychiatrist. They have just discovered that it helps with the depressive phase of bipolar disorder."

"Have you ever tried psychotherapy?" asked Palmieri.

"Yes, fucking never stops, I still do," O'Connor disclosed. "At the moment I have counselling every week. From July to August this year I also worked for 12 weeks with a therapist at a Suicide Prevention Centre in Dublin. They are fantastic. One of the main symptoms when I was very sick was the constant suicidal thinking and I found that many therapists are not specifically trained in the area of suicidal thinking, so you can go on for years and it is not fixed.

"Because I was not on medication, the suicidal thinking got worse and worse and I actually made an attempt in January, and then there were three more attempts. The therapists in the Suicide Prevention Centre just work on suicidal thinking. They don't just talk about killing yourself, they help to rebuild your life, they help you to focus on the life you want. I saw them once a week for individual sessions. While you do that you don't do any other therapy."

"What do you mean by rebuilding your life?" asked Palmieri.

"They helped me identify a number of issues," explained O'Connor. "The 'off-switch' was one, learning how to fucking do nothing, just sit the fuck down and put energy out. Then you sit down and realize how tired you were, when you have depressed or suicidal thinking you don't know how tired you are.

"Then they focused on the thing with me that I am too inclined to take on board other people's negative opinions of me. If ten people stood in a room and nine said you are fucking great and one said you're an asshole, that would be what I'd worry about and believe in, that person, getting depressed if someone says I'm an asshole.

"They were able to teach me, which I hadn't learned before, how to really not give a fuck about them. And then another important thing is fun, I mean 'What are you doing just for fun?', 'Are you doing anything just for fun?'

"They made me put together a bucket list, so first of all you deserve better, to hang out all the people that make you feel like shit, then you need to rest your body, to take time for yourself and they made me put together a list of the things I would like to do in my life, and that was great!

"They very quickly put you out of the misery part and start to build a fun life. It's quite witchy how therapy works, it's a kind of subconscious, you don't know how the fuck they've done it but suddenly you start living differently and thinking differently. I've been able to build the life I want, do you know what I mean? When you have a mental illness I think it is important to work with prevention services when one of your symptoms is suicidal thinking."

"Did you struggle with interpersonal problems that drove you to think about suicide?" Palmieri wanted to know.

"In that period, I was not on medication, and at the same time a lot of awful stressful things were happening. If I had been on medication perhaps I would have responded differently. In my case it was purely the sickness that made me think of suicide but it was a compulsion. I got to the point where the physical symptoms of bipolar disorder made me feel as if I was walking underwater."

"Walking underwater really gives the idea of how you could have felt," empathised Palmieri. "Well, Sinéad, I think you were really brave in telling your difficult story, and I want to thank you on behalf of *State of Mind* and of all the people who have to face mental illness every day."

67. An Argument with Miley Cyrus (2013)

In an interview with *Rolling Stone* in 2013, the young singer Miley Cyrus said her video for the track 'Wrecking Ball', in which she appeared naked and licking a sledgehammer, had been inspired by O'Connor's video for 'Nothing Compares 2 U'. Though O'Connor was fully clothed in her video, both featured the singers crying tears while gazing at the camera. Cyrus told the magazine:

"It's like the Sinéad O'Connor video, but, like, the most modern version. I wanted it to be tough but really pretty – that's what Sinéad did with her hair and everything. Getting the camera up above you ... like you're looking up at someone and crying. I think it will be ... iconic."[1]

Worried that the then 20-year-old was being exploited by her record company, O'Connor responded to this by publishing an open letter to Cyrus. She said that she was flattered to be considered a role model by Cyrus, but also highlighted her fears for the young singer.

"I am extremely concerned for you ... you will obscure your talent by allowing yourself to be pimped, whether it's the music business or yourself doing the pimping. Nothing but harm will come from allowing yourself to be exploited, and it is NOT an empowerment of yourself or other young women."[2]

O'Connor stated that she herself had never sexualised herself and that she was glad, as it had meant she hadn't ended up on the scrap heap in middle age.

In response to this letter and clearly smarting from it, Miley Cyrus posted screenshots of old tweets of O'Connor's from 2012, in which O'Connor pleaded for help. Cyrus captioned her tweet, "Before Amanda Bynes ... [a US actor who suffered from bipolar disorder] There was ..." and also posted a picture of O'Connor tearing up the photograph of the Pope.[3]

The screenshots from O'Connor read: "Does anyone know a psychiatrist in Dublin or Wicklow who could urgently see me today please? I'm really unwell ... and in danger ... I desperately need to get back on meds today."

Replying with another open letter, O'Connor pulled no punches: "Miley . . . Really? Who the fuck is advising you? Because taking me on is even more fuckin' stupid than behaving like a prostitute and calling it feminism. You have posted [old] tweets of mine posted when I was unwell and seeking help . . . in doing so you mock myself and Amanda Bynes."[4]

O'Connor asked Cyrus to take the tweet down and threatened legal action.

After this, Cyrus appeared on *The Today Show*, telling host Matt Lauer: "I don't know how someone can start a fight with somebody who said, 'I really respect you. And I really love what you what you did.' 'You know what? You suck! I don't like you!' That was kind of crazy. But I'm a big fan of hers . . . it's all good."[5]

This prompted a fourth open letter to Cyrus from O'Connor: "You've said on Matt Lauer's show (where you again refer to me as 'crazy') that you don't understand why I have been upset with you. Until you exposed me (and Amanda Bynes) to abuse I had no problem with you whatsoever. I would very much like you please to apologise."[6]

Cyrus replied on Twitter: "Sinéad. I don't have time to write you an open letter cause I'm hosting & performing on *SNL* this week.[7]

"So if you'd like to meet up and talk lemme know in your next letter. :)"[8]

After O'Connor's first open letter, she also received a long open letter response from feminist rock singer Amanda Palmer, who stated that O'Connor had been a huge formative influence on her. In the kindly, balanced letter, Palmer wrote: "Miley is, from what I can gather, in charge . . . She's writing the plot and signing the checks, and although I think it's tempting to imagine her in the board room of label assholes and management, I don't think any of them masterminded her current plan to be a naked sexpot."[9]

She said there needed to be room in the industry for both women who wanted to wear nothing and women who wanted to cover up, and ended by exhorting people to listen to O'Connor's music.

After she died, O'Connor's first letter to Miley Cyrus went viral again, along with Cyrus's response mocking O'Connor's mental health, for which Cyrus received criticism.

Cyrus recently confessed to *Vogue* magazine that she "carried some guilt and shame around myself for years because of how much controversy and upset I really caused" due to the 'Wrecking Ball' video and her twerking at the MTV Video Music Awards.[10]

After O'Connor died, Cyrus released a new special, *Endless Summer Vacation: Continued (Backyard Sessions)*, in which she spoke about the spat with O'Connor. She said she'd expected a strong reaction from the

'Wrecking Ball' video, but didn't imagine that "other women [would] put me down or turn on me.

"I had no idea about the fragile mental state that [O'Connor] was in, and I was also only 20, so I could only wrap my head around mental illness so much ... God bless Sinéad O'Connor, for real, in all seriousness."[11]

In addition, Cyrus said her live performance of her track 'Wonder Woman' was for O'Connor.

Opinion was divided on O'Coneor's original letter. Feminist Melissa Bradshaw wrote in the *Guardian* that the letter wasn't wholly "helpful to women ... the implication is naked or other sexual images of women inevitably entail the woman being a victim. Why should this be the case? How boring a world without any images of nudity would be. There would be no celebration of the immense power of sexuality, no eroticism."[12]

I asked *Guardian* pop writer Caroline Sullivan what she made of the feud.

"[Pop stars] like Britney and Christina started dressing incredibly scantily about 10 years before that, and Paris Hilton," she recalled, "all of those girls that hung out together. They weren't wearing panties and they wore tiny miniskirts. So by the time Miley was virtually naked on a wrecking ball, we'd had about a decade of women saying they felt empowered by being naked.

"And there's Sinéad, who's coming at it from a motherly perspective, because she would have been old enough to be Miley's mother, but also the perspective of being a veteran in the music business. And Miley, despite the fact that her father was a pop star in his own right – I think Miley, being so much younger than Sinéad, was thinking, 'How dare this old woman judge me? She's not even related to me, she doesn't even know me! How dare she make a comment? She's trying to rob me of agency.'

"But I actually sympathise what Sinéad was saying, because I was just watching all this kind of female nudity where they were telling themselves and had come to believe that they were being massive feminists by being naked and being overtly sexual. Talking about 'fucking', using that word.

"And I thought that Sinéad offered a very good and timely corrective. But I don't think she expected Miley's reaction. I think she thought she was doing a very nice thing, that she was being motherly and kindly. I don't think she was expecting this kind of furious reaction from Miley, and I think she was probably shocked by it, and probably felt very put down as well, very kind of diminished.

"And if you notice, she never reached out to any other young woman star again after that.

"[The journalist] Liz Jones had a similar run-in with Rihanna about ten years ago. Rihanna had this gun tattooed on the side of her body and Liz Jones had a go at her, saying 'Why is Rihanna doing this, she's a role model?!' [She wrote a *Daily Mail* column titled 'Pop's poisonous princess: Glorying in drugs, guns and sleaze, Rihanna's toxic role model for her army of young fans.']" [13]

"Rihanna's reaction was vicious. She was like, 'Who's talking to me, this sad sloppy menopausal mess?!' It was far worse than anything Miley said. So younger female musicians now are as quick to anger as men when pushed beyond endurance, and unlikely to just let things ride, they just won't do it. I suppose it's a kind of legacy of third-wave feminism. Young women of about 30 now, they learned from the Spice Girls, who were enormously influential, that you should do what you want ...

"With Miley, I thought it was mean, but ... you know ... and I do feel for what Sinéad must have felt at that point."

I mentioned to Sullivan that it's an interesting and age-old debate in terms of feminism – it's the sex-positive feminists versus more old-school feminists. Is it OK to flaunt your sexuality or is that just playing into the patriarchy and what men want?

When Sinéad was first out there, I said to Sullivan, the record company told her to sexualise herself and wear miniskirts, and instead she wore combat trousers and Doc Martens and shaved her head. I guess maybe Sinéad was thinking, 'If I could cover myself up and make it, surely Miley could do the same thing?' But maybe the pop landscape has changed.

"Lily Allen is one of the few major pop stars to completely dress the way she's wanted to dress," Sullivan commented. "Do you remember when she came out with the first album, and 'Smile'? She wore these massive prom dresses and these big trainers. And so it was almost like she was taking the piss out of a look. She never did anything to be sexy. I don't know what Sinéad thought of Lily, but I'm sure she would have approved in a way."

68. Getting Face Tattoos (2013)

In September 2013, O'Connor gigged at Bestival and revealed two new facial tattoos: a letter B on her right cheek and a letter Q on her left, both in red ink.

She posted a blog titled 'Face Tattoo' on her website, writing "Brendan Quinlan ... 'It's what it is' ... Un ange passe ;). There's a bottle of Agent Provocateur in someone's room that Belongs to me." [1]

The French phrase means 'uncomfortable silence'. Quinlan was most probably a love interest. O'Connor soon had the tattoos lasered off.

69. Recognition of Misdiagnosis of Bipolar (2013)

In October 2013, O'Connor told the *Irish Mirror* that she had been assessed at three hospitals in Ireland, and that all had confirmed without a doubt that she didn't fit the criteria for bipolar disorder.

She explained that she had originally been misdiagnosed after a traumatic incident when Shane was five months old.

She was relieved to be able to get off the meds, telling the paper, "They are extremely debilitating drugs."

She had found that the meds "fuck up your liver, your kidneys, your eyes, your appetite, your entire way of thinking and generally your entire life. They can cause suicidal or self-harm type thinking. I can shortly begin the very, very slow indeed, process of getting them out of my system."[1]

In 2021, while promoting *Rememberings* in the *Guardian*, O'Connor told Simon Hattenstone that she had voluntarily checked into St Patrick's Hospital in Dublin in 2016, which she affectionately dubbed "the nuthouse". She had been resident there for so long, the book was dedicated to the hospital, as well as to her father and musical influences.

She said St Patrick's had rediagnosed her mental health conditions: "10% bipolar apparently, 40% complex traumatic stress and the rest [50%] is borderline personality disorder."[2]

Borderline personality disorder (BPD) seems more of a fit for O'Connor than bipolar, with many people living with the severe condition having been abused as children. An article about BPD in the research journal *Frontiers in Psychiatry* states that "in 30% up to 90% of cases BPD is associated with abuse and neglect in childhood." These numbers far outweigh those associated with other disorders.

The article continues, "BPD is characterised by severe functional impairment, intense use of health services, medications, and a suicide rate of 10–50 times higher than the rate in the general population."[3]

The NHS website states that BPD is characterised by "emotional instability", "impulsive behaviour" and "intense, unstable relationships".

It also says sufferers can experience "severe mood swings over a short space of time.

"It's common for people with BPD to feel suicidal with despair, and then feel reasonably positive a few hours later."[4]

A study in *BMC Psychiatry* states that BPD is associated with "adverse and traumatic experiences during childhood. BPD is a disorder primarily characterised by emotion[al] dysregulation and indeed, patients with BPD show heightened emotional sensitivity, inability to regulate intense emotional responses, and a slow return to emotional baseline."

It added that "Symptom overlap has been reported between BPD diagnosis and ... Post-Traumatic Stress Disorder (PTSD)."[5]

70. *I'm Not Bossy, I'm the Boss* (2014)

O'Connor's tenth and final studio album was originally titled *The Vishnu Room* after the eponymous track on the record, but O'Connor then became aware of Facebook CEO Sheryl Sandberg's campaign 'Ban Bossy'.

The idea behind it was that girls and women who display leadership qualities are often lambasted as 'bossy' where boys and men aren't, discouraging girls and women from being assertive.

Sandberg, along with her website LeanIn.org and the Girl Scouts, advocated banning the word, and many female celebrities agreed as well as O'Connor, including Beyoncé, Condoleezza Rice, Victoria Beckham and Jennifer Garner.

In the campaign video, Beyoncé said, "Girls are less interested in leadership than boys" [because they're concerned about being considered bossy], with Garner suggesting, "Let's just encourage girls to lead."[1]

Not every celebrity saw it as a positive campaign: Joan Rivers called it "so stupid. I find it outrageous and I find it petty ... and I find we're so damn uptight in this country that this whole country is being divided."[2]

O'Connor wrote on her blog that, "a few months back, when I saw the phrase 'I'm not bossy, I'm the boss' and Sheryl Sandberg's Ban Bossy campaign, I wished I could rename the album ... It can be tricky being a female boss, and I think Sheryl's campaign is a terribly important one."[3]

The striking cover image shows O'Connor wearing a shiny black wig in a straight bob style, dressed in a skintight black latex dress with long sleeves, while clutching an electric guitar. The background is an empty industrial-style studio.

O'Connor claimed that none of the tracks except for the first one, 'How About I Be Me', were autobiographical, saying she was writing about characters. However, this may have been a defence mechanism, as tracks such as '8 Good Reasons', which make allusions to being a pop star, feel extremely autobiographical. O'Connor also admitted in an interview that the eight reasons were her children's eyes.

Reaching number 1 in Ireland and 22 in the UK, the album was seen as a return to form. Released on 11 August 2014 on the record label Nettwork Group, it was produced by John Reynolds. It received a Metacritic score of 66 and a Best Album nomination for the Choice Music Prize.

The opener 'How About I Be Me' is a glorious pop song with a mid-tempo groove and optimistic lyrics. It was the album's third and final single.

Second track 'Dense Water Deeper Down' is a 1960s-esque mid-tempo three-chord rock track with vocal harmonies and lyrics about falling in love with a bad boy.

'Kisses Like Mine' has a similarly retro feel, with vocal harmonies and crunchy guitar.

'Your Green Jacket' still has harmonies forward in the mix, but more modern production. The song is about still loving someone even though you know it's not going to work out between the two of you.

'The Vishnu Room' is the laid-back yet wistful song which originally gave its name to the album. Half-love song, half-prayer, O'Connor sings sadly.

'The Voice of My Doctor' is a guitar-filled, angry track reminiscent of U2's more rocky songs.

'Harbour' starts off as a gentle, stripped-back ballad, then gives way to thrashy hard rock, as O'Connor howls lyrics about combat, oppression, sadness and a longing for death.

The bop 'James Brown', as its name would suggest, features a funk groove. Seun Kuti plays jazz saxophone as O'Connor sings heavily sexual and breathy lyrics.

'8 Good Reasons' is possibly my favourite O'Connor song – emotionally heartwrenching and haunting.

The music video, too, is moving, featuring O'Connor singing on a local bus, dressed as the priest she was at the time, as strangers interact in a kindly way with each other and O'Connor, including one playing her younger self.

The album's first single, 'Take Me to Church', didn't chart in the rest of the world but reached number 55 in Ireland. An Irish-influenced indie pop song, it features a beguiling chorus with bittersweet lyrics.

'Where Have You Been', while musically jaunty, is the story of a terrifying sexual experience.

The poignant stand-out track 'Streetcars' features O'Connor singing virtually a cappella with only a scant synth piano-bell accompaniment.

On the self-deprecating 'How Nice a Woman Can Be', O'Connor suggests that she is useless.

'Make a Fool of Me All Night' is a sweet, chilled track addressed to a lover.

Bonus track 'Little Story' is another 60s-esque track with an Americana feel, featuring slide guitar and finger-picking.

The *Pitchfork* review of the album said, "O'Connor is pushing herself on every song here – maybe not always in the right or most obvious or safest directions, but always with some purpose. A quarter-century into [an unpredictable] career, she continues to lay claim to every musical possibility and refuses to define herself with only one particular style."

In 2014, O'Connor would also appear on the celebrity Band Aid 30 single organised by Bob Geldof, the fourth official version of 'Do They Know It's Christmas?', which reached Number 1. It also featured Bono, Ed Sheeran, Ellie Goulding, Chris Martin, One Direction and Rita Ora. Proceeds from the single went towards combatting the Ebola crisis.

71. A Second Neil McCormick Interview (2014)

After interviewing O'Connor in an amusingly disastrous interview in 1990, *Telegraph* rock critic Neil McCormick didn't want to interview her again, he said. But he changed his mind 24 years later when *I'm Not Bossy, I'm the Boss* came out.

"Regine Moylett was her PR and would occasionally ask me if I'd like to interview Sinéad, and I would say, 'Not really,'" he told me. "But then I thought about it, and she'd sent me her new record, and I thought the record was really good.

"I was in my 40s by then, and I had a different perspective. I thought, 'You know what? This could be interesting. We were both very young, she's still making great music and this is ridiculous, that was one encounter.'

"So I went out to Bray to her house. It's always nice to go to a pop star's house and get to see the furnishings. It was a big old house. She welcomed me in very warmly, and I wasn't sure where we stood. Obviously I knew who she was, and I didn't know if she knew who I was, 'cause I'm more on the periphery of that Irish music scene. But I said to her, 'We did this before,' and she was like, 'Yeah, I know.' And then we started to talk about it and she just said, 'I'm *so* sorry.'

"And then she was talking about it and said she was very traumatised at the time and that she was singing to stay sane. That they would just be putting her in rooms with men asking her questions, and she didn't really understand why anybody was interested in her music. She felt very vulnerable, and of course that can be when you get hostile.

"And we know the dynamics of the music industry then, and I have an appreciation of mental health issues now. And there's a lot of things that she put into the conversation in music that have been incredibly valuable in the long run, although were very destructive to her own career, when she obviously prioritised just getting her feelings off her chest and speaking her own truth over her career.

"So we had a lovely encounter, but it kind of went on. It's one of those where the day went on, and I've got my interview, I've got more than

I need, and she's not letting me out of her sight. We've sort of retreated to her studio in the back garden, and we're drinking tea and talking about the Pope and the Catholic Church, and she's slightly starting to go off on one.

"She's bringing out of files of things, clippings and stuff. I can't even remember what the issue was, but it was clear she wanted help with something. I mean, I knew what it was at the time: something to do with parenting, or the Catholic Church and kids.

"And so, after that, she would call me up and text me, and that went on for a couple of months, where you get these random phone calls. And you're trying to be supportive, but you're really in somebody's mania. She had some kind of obsession and she's looking for people that would help her. And I'm a journalist, and I've listened sympathetically, because that's your job when you're interviewing somebody.

"And maybe when I was younger I had a more challenging approach to interviewing, but now I'm just going there and you just want somebody to talk, and asking questions. You're listening but you can't help them because it would be a full time job.

"So that kind of drifted off and she stopped calling me, but I've spoken to a few other people – Olaf Tyaransen – he worked for *Hot Press*. He had been writing her autobiography for years."

And it never came out, I said.

"No, she kept changing her mind. I was talking to him about this time, and he said, 'Yeah, the four in the morning phone calls' – she'd call up anytime and just expect you to pick up. And I've had some experience of that before with other people, where they are on a cycle, if it is manic depression or bipolar or whatever they call it, if they're in a very up part of it, they can want to talk and it can be a little bit disjointed and hard to follow. And then other times, they don't want to do anything.

"She talked to me a lot about her medication and whether it was helping or whether it was a correct diagnosis. And then she'd go off the medication ... and also that she's in the public eye, and she always puts on weight with the medication.

"And that was a funny thing. Being known in the public eye, being famous, is so tough on people. Obviously some people are born for it, but it's a very hard place to be. And then for women, probably even more so for all kinds of reasons.

"But one of the things is that you're constantly confronted with the youngest, best version of yourself, in a way that we in the ordinary world aren't. You know, nobody's comparing me with a picture of me when I was 21, because those pictures aren't in the public domain. They're not hanging on walls. People aren't meeting me and going, 'God, he's got old.'

"But that's definitely a real thing [for celebrities]. I was thinking about that when I saw this photograph which I dug out of the two of us together. She had great vivaciousness. One of the things about that encounter in her house was that I really saw her warm side, her soft side, her humour, which I knew was there and people had talked about it, but I hadn't experienced that before. And that was lovely, the twinkle and spark, which even if you were disagreeing on something or arguing about something, it could come back very quickly.

"She was a really attractive woman, but in photographs she didn't look like this elfin girl anymore. And I saw this picture of us out of context, and I thought, 'Well, there's this grey-haired guy wearing a suit rather badly, and Sinéad looking fantastic, this shaven-headed and tattooed middle-aged woman.' If you saw it and you didn't know who she was, you'd go, 'Who's that fantastic-looking woman?'

"But instead, people were looking at it and they would go, 'Oh, she's put on weight.' And you know, that's a tough thing."

Yeah, that's really difficult.

"So after that, I was perceived as an ally. She came on my show, *Needle Time*, and did an interview, and it was very warm. It was a lovely encounter and she spoke incredibly frankly, I thought. That was a really strong interview, and we went out for tea in Soho after that. She'd send me the occasional text message, and I might have seen her in Dublin at some dinner or some party, but our paths weren't crossing.

"Then I reviewed her book, and I wrote the review largely as an apology. To read that book is to see that this is a person who's been through a hell of a life, who has fought a lot of battles and has been mistreated and maltreated by her family and by society and then by the music industry and by the popular culture industry. And I'm part of that, and I felt like we owed her an apology. That it was a very strong book that she eventually had written herself, it really gives a lot of insights.

"So I wrote my review kind of as an apology, but in it I said she was treated as the madwoman in pop's attic. Then somebody said to her on the radio, 'Neil McCormick called you the madwoman in pop's attic,' and she went off on a little rant about me. I remember seeing that, 'cause it was in the *Daily Mail* or somebody picked up on it, and I just thought, 'Don't worry about that because she clearly hasn't read the piece, and that's just the way it is.'

"And actually, she did send me a message via DMs on Twitter, and said, 'I said a few things about you on the radio. I've read your piece now.

I'm so sorry.' So she was apologising to me again and she said, 'You know how it is,' and I said, 'I know how it is.'"

She momentarily retired from music didn't she, after that? And then very quickly reversed and said she wasn't retiring from music.

"Those reversals were just a big part of her way of being in the world, which was to say whatever was on her mind at one point with 100% commitment."

72. Interest in Sinn Féin (2014)

In late 2014, O'Connor declared that she was planning to become a member of the party Sinn Féin, historically seen as the political wing of the IRA. However, she insisted that the elders of the party stand down "in the same way the last Pope did."[1]

This is because, at the time, Gerry Adams and other party leaders were accused of mishandling child sexual abuse cases. One involved Adams' own brother Liam, who was convicted of having sexually assaulted his own daughter. The other involved Irish politician Mairia Cahill, who said she was raped by her uncle – a Provisional IRA member – between the ages of 16 and 17.

"There'd be a zillion per cent increase in membership of Sinn Féin if the leadership were handed over to those born from 1983–85 onward and no one associated in people's minds with frightful things," said O'Connor. "Frightful things belong where they are now, in the past."[2]

A couple of months later in January 2015, having spoken to two Sinn Féin officials, O'Connor withdrew her membership application, accusing the party of not wanting to end partition.

73. Blasting *Rolling Stone* and Reality Shows (2015)

The July 2015 issue of *Rolling Stone* featured reality personality Kim Kardashian on the cover, wearing a very low-cut sailor's vest and cap and a red push-up bra.

O'Connor was horrified, taking to Facebook and asking: "What is this cunt doing on the cover of *Rolling Stone?* Music has officially died. Who knew it would be *Rolling Stone* that murdered it? Simon Cowell and Louis Walsh can no longer be expected to take all the blame. Bob Dylan must be fucking horrified. #Boycott*RollingStone*".[1]

Back in 2013, she had also lambasted Cowell and Walsh, purveyors of manufactured pop acts, saying on *The Late Late Show*, "I feel sorry for the murder of rock 'n' roll [which is the music industry's responsibility]. Because of Simon Cowell, Louis Walsh and the lot of them [judges on reality talent shows] have murdered music. They're murderers of music!

I stand and say it on behalf of every musician in the world and they will all agree with it."[2]

Taking to Twitter, Cowell replied: "I think Sinéad O'Connor would be a real fun guest judge on X Factor. She loves the show and everything I do. Let me know Sinéad."[3]

74. Becoming a Grandmother (2015)

In March 2015, O'Connor told her fans on Facebook that she was about to become a grandmother at the age of 48, thanks to her first son Jake. Her fans had wrongly assumed it was O'Connor's daughter Roisin who was pregnant.

"It's not my 18-year-old daughter who's having a baby! It's my 27-year-old son Jake and his beautiful girlfriend, Lia!" she posted.

"Am so delighted!!! Always wanted to be a granny. In fact that's the only reason I had kids (joking). Baby will be arriving in July."[1]

A few days before the birth, she tweeted, "OMG! Am literally hours away from the greatest dream of my life coming true! #Granny!"

The baby arrived on 18 July, and a joyful O'Connor posted an 'It's A Boy' cartoon on Facebook, accompanying it with the words, "Don't mess with abuelita."

'Abuelita' is Spanish for 'granny'.[2]

75. Being Shafted by Her Agent (2015)

In August 2015, O'Connor alleged on Facebook that she had been the victim of mismanagement by her booking agent and management team. She said that she had performed three shows in Germany, which had brought in an impressive €48,000, but she had been paid a tiny €500 for all three.

The remainder of the money had gone to her agents, band and crew, with a massive €11,700 paid out to her booking agent Rita Zappador and company Modus in Rebus. This was over 23 times the sum O'Connor received, she said.

"MASSIVE negligence cases to be brought by me against every member of my now ex-management team," O'Connor wrote, posting a photo of the costs breakdown, "for several even more appalling and reckless negligences, which have cost me hundreds of thousands of Euros which I was illegally told was my obligation to pay, and it was NOT my legal obligation."[1]

76. A Radical Hysterectomy (2015)

On 26 August 2015, O'Connor underwent a hysterectomy, which artificially kickstarted her menopause. She chose to go under the knife for the procedure rather than having it carried out by laser. It made her suicidal and mentally unstable afterwards and caused her to fall out with her family.

Unaware of what was to come, she posted with customary humour on Facebook prior to the operation.

"Hysterectomy Wednesday, ovaries and uterus," she explained, also posting a picture of the female reproductive system. "Looking at this photo I can't see how my vagina isn't going to fall out."[1]

In 2017, she told Dr. Phil McGraw in an episode of his show which she found traumatic, that she was asked to leave hospital just a couple of days after the operation with only paracetamol, no HRT and no advice or information as to what could occur. She entered surgical menopause immediately and became suicidal.[2]

In 2021, O'Connor spoke to *People* magazine again about her operation. "When I had the surgery, I was terribly triggered," she disclosed, saying that it had led her to post cries for help on social media due to her mental illness.

"The last man that touched my body took out my reproductive system. I've not let a man touch my body in any way since," she told the magazine, joking that "if [US actor] Taye Diggs is available, I'd consider it."[3]

77. Suicide Attempt (2015)

At the end of November 2015, a clearly very distressed O'Connor wrote a heartbreaking post on Facebook, saying that she had overdosed on pills due to her family's "appalling cruelty" and "horrific betrayals". She said she had been driven to suicide as "There is no other way to get respect. I am not at home. I'm at a hotel, somewhere in Ireland, under another name."

She said she'd been "Howling crying for weeks. And been told by them all to go fuck myself. I'm invisible. I don't matter a shred to anyone."[1]

She was discovered to be safe at a Dublin location.

78. Letters to Her Family (2016)

In May 2016, O'Connor took to Facebook and called out John Reynolds and son Jake, though didn't specify what she felt they'd done wrong.

"I will see you all in court," she posted. "I want damages. I have been unable to work. I have lost last year's income and this year's. I have had enormous medical expenses, and enormous trauma because of your torturing of me. Unlike my poor mother, I will not let this drop."[1]

A few days earlier, O'Connor had gone missing after a bike ride in Illinois, *TMZ* said. "According to an alert sent out by cops ... O'Connor is being classified as 'missing suicidal.' She was last seen on a Raleigh motorized bicycle with a pink basket. She's not exactly in typical cycling gear – black parka, black leather pants and a sweatshirt with 'Ireland' on the back."[2]

She was discovered safe and well: "A day after she was reported missing by authorities in Wilmette, Ill., the 'Nothing Compares 2 U' singer is no longer considered missing or endangered," Page Six reported. O'Connor was taken to a local hospital.[3]

Around the same time, O'Connor wrote an open letter on Facebook addressed to her middle son Shane, *Billboard* reported: "Baby, I've been trying to get you out of care but Tusla are being monsters. I have to back off because they are hurting me so badly I get unwell again if I go near them." She told Shane to find a lawyer to advocate for him. "I'm waiting for you and will wait as long as I have to."[4] Tusla is Ireland's Child and Family Agency.

79. Surgery and Complications (2016)

On 13 October 2016, O'Connor said she was planning to have an unspecified "surgery by robot".

Twelve days later, she posted on Facebook after discovering her liver had mistakenly been cut during the surgery.

"Fuck. Gotta go to emergency. Liver all fucked and killing me. Can't breathe properly it so sore."

And she seemed to be feeling very desolate and sad, with a total lack of support: "Am posting as am lonely. Story of life. Wish was not so alone in world. Gotta be worth something to someone after all these years and after all I given.'"[1]

Staying in a hospital in San Rafael, America, she disclosed that she'd lost a lot of blood during her surgery.

O'Connor also said that she'd beaten her 30-year addiction to weed and would be living in a rehabilitation facility for at least the next year. She noted that, given what she'd been through, it was a wonder that she hadn't become addicted to every drug in existence.

The comments on the *Daily Mail* article about the incident were depressingly harsh and unsympathetic, even by the standards of the publication.[2]

80. Dispute with Arsenio Hall (2017)

Prince died of an accidental drug overdose in April 2016. He was found with 67.8 micrograms per litre of fentanyl in his stomach, an opioid fifty times stronger than heroin. The United States Drug Enforcement

Administration (DEA) were investigating whether the drug was prescribed by doctors or whether it came from an illegal source.

In 2017, a year after Prince's death, O'Connor claimed on Facebook that Arsenio Hall was involved in providing Prince with drugs: "[Here's] where Prince got his drugs ... Arsenio Hall. Anyone imagining Prince was not a long time hard drug user is living in cloud cuckoo land. Arsenio I've reported you to the Carver County Sheriff's office. Expect their call. They are aware you spiked me years ago at Eddie Murphy's house."[1]

Soon after, she said on Facebook that Hall had invited her to a post-Grammys party after she'd refused to attend the awards ceremony, and that her non-attendance at the Grammys made him hate her.

"In his unfathomable narcissism, he has deduced that my not attending is specifically an act against him, and all that he holds dear," she posted. "This is, like, the second time we've hung out."[2]

In its report of the accounts, *Rolling Stone* deduced that the ceremony O'Connor referred to must have been held in 1991, as she wrote that her winning an award made Hall angrier. Her account finished with her claiming that Hall had given her spiked cannabis and "actually did stick his tongue in my mouth too".[3]

As a result of this, Hall lodged a $5 million lawsuit claiming defamation in Los Angeles and asking for compensatory damages, decrying O'Connor's "malicious statements" and "heinous accusations" as "despicable, fabricated lies". The entertainer also called O'Connor a "desperate attention seeker ... now known perhaps as much for her bizarre, unhinged internet rants as she is for her music".[4]

O'Connor initially answered this with a Facebook post, saying "I'm more amused than I've ever dreamed a person could be and look forward very much to how hilarious it will be watching him trying to prove me wrong." She poked fun at what she called "Arse-inio's laughable threats".[5]

"I do not like drugs killing musicians," she added. "And I do not like Arsenio Hall. He can suck my dick."[6]

However, soon after, Hall received an apology from O'Connor: "I apologise for my Facebook posts about Arsenio Hall [as people may have assumed O'Connor] was accusing him of acting as Prince's drug dealer and supplying him with illegal hard drugs, or insinuating that Arsenio had something to do with Prince's death. I sincerely apologise because those statements would be false. I retract them unequivocally."[7]

Hall then dropped the libel lawsuit. His publicist stated, "Arsenio's lawyers have confirmed that now that Arsenio's reputation has been restored by Sinéad's unequivocal retraction and apology, the lawsuit will be dismissed."[8]

81. Sued by O'Ceallaigh (2017)

In May 2017, Fachtna O'Ceallaigh launched a case against O'Connor, alleging that in 2012 she'd terminated their agreement for him and his management company TAL Management Limited to manage her without his permission.

He requested damages for breach of contract. He also stated "he was defamed by the singer in an open letter published on her website and on a fans website in 2012," reported the *Irish Times*.[1]

"His client was not a wealthy man with many clients and was aged in his 70s," said the lawyer for O'Ceallaigh, according to the newspaper.[2]

"The singer denies that she ever had any agreement with TAL or Mr O'Ceallaigh."[3] O'Connor also disputed that she had ever defamed him.

The pair settled the dispute in 2019, with no details forthcoming. The *Irish Times* reported, "As part of the settlement, Jim O'Callaghan for Ms O'Connor read an agreed statement.

'The parties are pleased to confirm that they have amicably resolved the differences between them in these proceedings.

'They thank each other for their work together and wish each other well for the future,' the statement added."[4]

82. Charity and Trans Rights (2017)

In May 2017, the *Irish Examiner* ran a story about O'Connor posting on her Facebook page, generously offering three decades of her clothes and unused cosmetics to trans women in Ireland.

She explained that she'd gone up a dress size, growing "from ten to somewhere between twelve and thirteen".

As a result, she wanted to give away her "ordinary clothes and unused makeup" to an Irish organisation "for those youth (over 16) born 'legally' male who wish to enjoy being female".[1]

O'Connor said she didn't know of any organisation like this in Ireland, and asked for contact details. A member of the Transgender Equality Network in Ireland got in touch.

83. Breakdown in Motel (2017)

At the start of August 2017, a distraught O'Connor had a breakdown in a motel bedroom in New Jersey, which she captured in a heartrending video and posted on her Facebook page.

"I'm all by myself and there's absolutely nobody in my life except my doctor," she said, crying. "My entire life is revolving around just not dying ... I love the people who are doing this to me. I'm not staying alive for me, if it were for me I'd be gone – straight away, back to my mum."[1]

She said she'd been alone for two years, with no one looking after her, merely because she was angry and suicidal. She begged her family to come and get her and bring her home.

Her video was widely reported in the press, with fans trying to ensure O'Connor was safe and being cared for.

84. Dr. Phil Interview (2017)

As a result of O'Connor's video, television presenter and former clinical psychologist 'Dr. Phil' McGraw tracked O'Connor down and promised to help her. He checked her out of the New Jersey motel and into a treatment facility, and did an hour-long therapy session with her on his show, which was watched around the world by millions.

The interview would have been insightful and helpful as a private therapy session. McGraw perceptively made the connection between O'Connor's mother attempting to destroy her reproductive parts when she was a child, and her radical hysterectomy, saying it was no surprise this had caused her mental health to decline.

However, the session felt exploitative and unethical because it was televised, sensationalising O'Connor's trauma and pain for ratings. O'Connor talked at length about the child abuse she'd experienced, and when focusing on recent years, confessed that she'd tried eight times to commit suicide in just one year. She said she'd taken an overdose three weeks previously, and produced a guitar on which she'd written a suicide note reading: *Forgive me, I could go no further. #oneofmillions*[1]

"You're not a horrible, evil person," McGraw told O'Connor.

"I actually became a singer because I thought I was so evil that I was going to go to hell, and I wanted to sing so that I might have a chance of going to heaven," O'Connor replied.[2]

She then gave McGraw a picture she'd drawn of herself, explaining that she'd been asked to draw what her perfect life would look like. When McGraw asked her to sign it, O'Connor signed it as 'Magda Davitt'.

McGraw told her that he'd elicited a promise from famed music producer David Foster to work with her. O'Connor was thrilled.

There is no record of her going on to work with Foster.

O'Connor spent at least five weeks in the treatment facility, according to the show – but things there didn't work out for her.

"Dr Phil is on the phone and you sort of feel like Cinderella – to begin with," she told the *Irish Independent* in 2019. "After the interview, I never saw him again and I am bringing proceedings against the facility he sent

me to, from the trauma I went through there ... He said 'I never fail'."
O'Connor assured McGraw he would.[3]

85. Change of Name (2017)

In September 2017, O'Connor changed her name to Magda Davitt. She posted on Facebook on 31 August: "This is to let you all know that I am legally changing my name. In two weeks' time I will let you know what name I have chosen.

"I no longer want the patriarchal name.

"The name I have chosen is beautiful and suits me much better."[1]

She added later: "September 12th you will know my true name."[2]

When people left critical messages saying she shouldn't change both her names, she messaged her fans, saying:

"For those who are hurt by people slagging me off ... fuck 'em all.

"Those who love me will call me Magda. Those who continue to call me Sinéad are uneducated fools. Of the kind who would refer to transgender folks as being the gender they were before they changed."[3]

86. Conversion to Islam (2018)

O'Connor spent a period intrigued by Judaism, and took Kabbalah lessons.

However, she eventually decided to convert to Islam instead. She had long been interested in Islam, and had an 'Allah' tattoo on her arm well before converting.

"I've studied Islam a little, not very much," she previously told David Burke of *R2* magazine in 2009. "Certainly not enough to really understand their scriptures. But I've had on-the-ground experience of Muslim people, just general ordinary workaday Muslim people. From what I can feel when I'm around those people, Islam is a very peaceful religion."[1]

However, she only converted to Islam in 2018, taking the Islamic name Shuhada', translated in Arabic as 'one who bears witness'. She tweeted about her conversion (or 'reversion', as it is known in Islam), posting a picture of herself wearing hijab from her now-deactivated account @magdadavitt77.

Her tweet dated 19 October 2018 read: "This is to announce that I am proud to have become a Muslim. This is the natural conclusion of any intelligent theologian's journey. All scripture study leads to Islam. Which makes all other scriptures redundant. I will be given (another) new name. It will be Shuhada'."[2]

O'Connor then decided to change her surname to Sadaqat, meaning 'truth' in Arabic.

Next, she uploaded a recording of herself singing the Islamic call to prayer, known as the Adhan.

"Here is my attempt at singing the [Adhan]," she tweeted. "I got some pronunciation wrong because emotions took me from my page ... but there'll be hundreds of others onstage to come."

A follow-up tweet said: "Sorry re all the mistakes in my [Adhan] ... first attempt. When I've practised it 30 times I'm gonna make the world stop turning."[3]

She explained a day later that a Dublin friend had helped her dress in hijab for the first time.

"My best friend Elaine just gave me my first hijab and she got chills all over her body when I put it on. Not gonna post a photo because [it] is intensely personal. And I'm an ugly old hag. But I'm a very, very, very happy old hag."[4]

Muslims on Twitter were extremely welcoming, encouraging and supportive in response to O'Connor's conversion.

"Thank you so much to all my Muslim brothers and sisters who have been so kind as to welcome me to Ummah today on this page," she responded. "You can't begin to imagine how much your tenderness means to me."[5]

However, O'Connor was also sent some Islamophobic tweets, and posted in reply:

"I'm terribly sorry. I'm about to say is something so racist I never thought my soul could ever feel it. But truly I never wanna spend time with white people again (if that's what non-Muslims are called). Not for one moment, for any reason. They are disgusting."[6]

She received a huge backlash for this, including from Muslims, with many users alleging she had incited racial hatred. One fellow Muslim, who said she was also white, tweeted back:

"There is never any excuse for racism, there are good and bad Muslims and non-Muslims everywhere. Instead of concentrating on someone's colour or religion, focus on those that are good and kind and spend time with them, never judge someone on colour or faith."[7]

A second Muslim wrote: "No one's ethnicity makes them disgusting, no matter which individuals you've encountered. Likewise, we shouldn't condemn/generalise all non-Muslims as disgusting, especially by citing ethnicity. The Quran says they're not all the same."[8]

O'Connor deactivated her account, but not before tweeting: "Amazing how many people ask me or suggest to me I've 'flipped' or am 'mentally ill' for becoming Muslim.

"I feel like whoever doesn't become a Muslim is actually the mentally ill one.

"Final word. If it's 'crazy' to care. Then by all means, spank my ass and call me fruity loops."[9]

She later retracted these statements, attributing them to the Islamophobic comments she'd received.

O'Connor confessed that she "loves annoying white supremacists", and stated: "I don't really hate white people, it's just the way I see it is Twitter would close my account if I said I did [like they did when I said] I don't like nuns murdering babies in Ireland. I was rather hoping they would close my page if I said I hated white people. But they didn't."[10]

Of her conversion, she told host Ryan Tubridy on *The Late Late Show*, "I read just Chapter Two of the Quran alone and I realised, 'Oh my God, I'm home.'

"I've been a Muslim all my life and didn't realise."[11]

In 2019, O'Connor apologised for her tweet describing white people as 'disgusting'. *People* magazine reported,

"O'Connor explained that she made the remarks 'while angry and unwell.'

"'They were not true at the time and they are not true now,' she wrote. 'I was triggered as a result of Islamophobia dumped on me. I apologise for hurt caused. That was one of many crazy tweets Lord knows.'"[12]

I asked Simon Hattenstone why, as O'Connor had such a hard and painful life, he thought she had retained her faith in God and spirituality?

"I think it's really interesting," Hattenstone replied. "Because I think she hated institutions, but she was a real purist about faith. She was always looking for the better faith, the faith that took her to a more immediate relationship with whatever God was.

"I think in the end she said she liked Islam as it was a more direct relationship with God, because there was less stuff in the way and less of a hierarchy. I don't know enough about religions to know the truth of that, but that was her take on it."

And, I said, she was most attracted to the two religions that I suppose people would see as the most hardcore: Catholicism and Islam.

"I think part of it was that Sinéad was naturally kind of sympathetic or empathetic to what she regarded as the underdog," Hattenstone explained. "And I think it was a time when Muslims and Islam were being attacked. She was like, 'If they're being attacked, I'm with them!'"

As a pushback to the racism they were receiving?

"That's just me guessing," Hattenstone said, "but there were so many issues or organisations that she supported that were attacked by the mainstream. So, with Islam, that might have been an element of it. She was very religious, but in her own way. She was still drinking."

Neil Perry said he wasn't religious, but that O'Connor's faith "was obviously important to her, despite her views and experiences regarding the darker side of Irish Catholicism. I've known lapsed Catholics who say it never really leaves you, if you've been brought up with it.

"What was more mystifying was her conversion to Islam, that being a religion not known for its enlightened attitude towards women. After all her raging against the patriarchy, I think that was a decision that was hard to understand. But she was a believer, God was always going to be in her life in some shape or form."

87. *One More Yard* (2018)

Despite her new name and conversion to Islam, O'Connor decided to continue recording under her birth name.

Her next involvement with a record was an appearance with a new supergroup titled Evamore, on an EP titled *One More Yard*, which she recorded with the Rolling Stones' guitarist Ronnie Wood, Pink Floyd's drummer Nick Mason, Irish film actor Cillian Murphy and singer Imelda May.

A tribute to an Irish teenager, Michael Thomas Wall, who only lived to 19 and perished while fighting for the Royal Irish Regiment in the First World War, the EP takes its lyrics from ninety letters Wall wrote home to his mother in Dublin during the fighting.

One More Yard was released on 2 November 2018 to mark 100 years since Armistice Day. All proceeds went to the newly set-up Cancer Awareness Trust.

88. Performing Live Again (2019)

O'Connor sang live in a rare performance in September 2019. She hadn't gigged for four years. Backed by the Irish Chamber Orchestra, she performed 'Nothing Compares 2 U' on *The Late Late Show*.

Three months later, she performed her first UK gig since 2015, dressed all in black, singing in hijab at the Shepherd's Bush Empire to rapturous applause.

"When she's on form, as tonight, she's radiant. The more broken the song, the more strength she siphons from it," wrote pop writer Caroline Sullivan in her four-star *Guardian* review, saying, "Performance is a serious business for this outstanding singer. She speaks infrequently – perhaps because she gives so much of herself in her lyrics – and focuses on finding solace in the music."[1]

89. Studying Healthcare (2020)

In May 2020, O'Connor announced her intentions to qualify as a healthcare assistant, saying the Covid pandemic had given her the incentive she'd needed. "I've been accepted onto the course to start in Bray Institute of Further Education in September," she told *The Late Late Show*. "So it's the FETAC Level 5 healthcare support course."

She had chosen the specialisms of "hospice work" and "palliative care", "companioning people who for one reason or another don't have family 'round or are on their own," she added.

It is unclear whether or not O'Connor started or finished the course.[1]

90. 'Trouble of the World' (2020)

On 2 October 2020, O'Connor put out her version of the Mahalia Jackson song 'Trouble of the World', which she had recorded with producer David Holmes. Jackson was a black gospel singer from New Orleans. O'Connor donated 100% of the proceeds from the single to Black Lives Matter charities.

In a statement, she said the song, which has lyrics referencing returning to God and dying, wasn't about those things for her: "For me the song isn't about death or dying. More akin, a message of certainty that the human race is on a journey toward making this world paradise and that we will get there."[1]

NME reported, "The accompanying video – which was directed by Don Letts – features footage from Black Lives Matter protests, including O'Connor herself protesting in a BLM jumper and holding a sign with Jackson's picture on."[2]

She told *Rolling Stone* that the single had originally been meant for her next album, slated for release in a year, provisionally titled *No Veteran Dies Alone*. "I'm writing more about personal matters, being a mother," she announced. "I don't know what the tone of the whole record will be, but that's what it is so far."

Of the single, she said, "The soundtrack for the Black Lives Matter movement was written and recorded in the Fifties by artists like Mahalia Jackson."[3]

O'Connor did a 2020 interview with *MOJO* to promote the song, explaining why she hadn't released a new studio album since 2014: "I had a hysterectomy in 2015... [and needed] five years to recover," she explains. "I [couldn't] work; I was in hospital for eight months, and when I came out I had 8000 quid in the bank and got a 2000 quid gas bill. That was my catalyst for getting the fuck back to work."[4]

91. *Rememberings* (2021)

In early 2021, it was clear O'Connor was desperate to get back to public life. "I'm fed up not working but apart from that I'm grand," she replied, when the *Sunday World* asked after her well-being in February 2021.

"I've a new album coming out, which will most likely be released early next year, if we are lucky it will be late this year," she continued. [Unfortunately the album was postponed, most likely due to Shane's death, and hadn't been released by the time this book went to press.]

"I have also got my book coming out in June, my autobiography."[1]

On 1 June 2021, O'Connor released her memoir, *Rememberings*. A tender, moving and often hilarious collection of vignettes, it wasn't your average chronological memoir, in part as there were large swathes of time which O'Connor couldn't remember – she says because she was self-medicating with weed.

She revealed a lot in the book – including that she dated Peter Gabriel for a while. She also wrote in detail about her experiences of child abuse at the hands of her mother, and wrote a little about her father's melancholy nature. And, as promised, she finally told the full story of her altercation with Prince.

Writing in the *Telegraph*, Neil McCormick said, "The structure is scattershot, and a lot of the stories familiar to anyone who has followed her career closely, but the accumulation of subtly awful details renders this first-person account quietly devastating."

He added that she "calls out pervasive bullying, sexism and racism wherever she sees it … I hope this brave book helps rehabilitate [her]."[2]

To promote the book, O'Connor did a series of press interviews, many of which focused on her mental health and the fact that people had insinuated she was crazy in the past.

"The media was making me out to be crazy because I wasn't acting like a pop star was supposed to act," she told the *New York Times*. "It seems to me that being a pop star is almost like being in a type of prison. You have to be a good girl."[3]

O'Connor was a great writer, I remarked to Simon Hattenstone, saying I thought *Rememberings* was really well-written, incredibly entertaining and very funny.

"She was really poetic," Hattenstone replied. "One of the things about that book is that it's so elliptical. A normal memoir tells you everything, but this was like kind of vignettes, wasn't it, and little short stories. I felt particularly the first half … the second half was written more when she was in 'the nuthouse' [as she called it], in Saint Patrick's. But [the first] part of it was really beautifully written."

92. A Retirement Announcement and Retraction (2021)

On 5 June 2021, O'Connor posted on Twitter that she was retiring "from touring and from working in the record business." Her tweet continued, "I've gotten older and I'm tired. So it's time for me to hang up my nipple tassels, having truly given my all."[1]

However, two days later, she issued a retraction, saying that she'd simply had enough of the press response to *Rememberings*. She was specifically upset about an interview on Radio 4's *Woman's Hour*, in which host Emma Barnett asked her how she felt about journalist Neil McCormick describing her as "the crazy woman in pop's attic" in his otherwise sympathetic *Telegraph* review of the book.

In response to Barnett's question, O'Connor replied, "I think it's a bit extreme to make the Jane Eyre comparison, I don't think I've ever been perceived as 'the crazy lady in pop's attic' as represented [in the Charlotte Brontë novel] ...

"It's not like I'm trying to attack people with knives or trying to strangle people while I'm walking around in my nightdress."[2]

O'Connor wrote later: "I was already so badly triggered by the time the BBC fucked me up the ass, with no warning, lube or permission, I lost my shit after *Woman's Hour*: I felt like I did thirty years ago ... That I'd be better off (safer) if I ran away and gave up."[3]

Clearly enraged by the *Woman's Hour* interview, she also lambasted Barnett for asking about her having four kids with four different fathers.

O'Connor tweeted: "Actually found the interview with @Emmabarnett extremely offensive and even misogynistic. One abusive and invalidating question or statement after another: 'madwoman in the attic.' At that point I should have ended it. I will absolutely never do *Woman's Hour* again."[4]

The BBC put out a statement, replying: "During an interview about her new book, Sinéad O'Connor was talking about her mental health and was asked what she made of a comment by a music critic reviewing her book in recent days."[5]

O'Connor revealed that she had requested the press to be sensitive and refrain from quizzing her about child abuse or "dig deep into painful shit about mental health which would be traumatising for me to have to think about" while she promoted the memoir.[6]

However, she stated that only the American press had adhered to this, and asked that the UK and Canadian media "might have a look at themselves and learn from this so that no other survivor of violent trauma will be as triggered as I was."[7]

She wrote, "I'm a 5′ 4″ soft-hearted female who is actually very fragile. When people ridicule or invalidate or disrespect or abuse or misuse me on the grounds I suffer from severe long-term effects of the barbaric physical and sexual abuse I grew up with … it triggers me."[8]

After announcing her retirement, O'Connor tweeted that she would definitely be touring as planned in 2022. "Also, I lied when I said I'm past my peak," she wrote. "Ain't no such fuckin' thing :) I'm just past listening to any more shite about how crazy people are invalid."[9]

93. Putting Her Own Stamp on the World (2021)

In July 2021, O'Connor was honoured by the Republic of Ireland postal service An Post, which dedicated a postage stamp to her. It featured a photo of her singing, her t-shirt tinted orange and purple, against a background of a blue-green planet with rings and stars around it. The image of O'Connor was taken by Martin Goodcare for Getty Images. Sold in a €5.40 booklet of four called Irish Singer Songwriters at Glastonbury, the official An Post site announced, "On 15 July, we launched a set of very special stamps that celebrate Ireland's world-renowned songwriting and performing traditions. The stamps feature iconic photographs of four leading Irish artists who have graced the Pyramid and Acoustic Stages at the famous Glastonbury Music and Arts Festival."

From every purchase 2% went to the Irish Music Industry Covid relief fund, up to €50,000. A total of 300,000 booklets were printed.[1]

94. Shane (2022)

O'Connor's 17-year-old son Shane tragically died by suicide after going missing on 6 January 2022. He had broken out of an Irish psychiatric hospital in Newbridge, County Kildare, after being put on suicide watch.

The Gardai, Ireland's national police force, had appealed for information to locate him. "Shane was last seen this morning in the Tallaght, Dublin 24 area," their tweet had said.[1]

O'Connor had posted many tweets begging Shane to give himself up to the Gardai.

"Shane, your life is precious. God didn't chisel that beautiful smile on your beautiful face for nothing," she wrote.[2]

"My world would collapse without you. You are my heart. Please don't stop it from beating. Please don't harm yourself. Go to the Gardai and let's get you to hospital."[3]

"This is a message for my son, Shane. Shane, it's not funny anymore all this going missing. You are scaring the crap out of me. Could you please do the right thing and present yourself at a Gardai station. If you are with Shane please call the Gardai for his safety."[4]

She also asked how he was able to go missing from the hospital:

"Like, how has a 17 year old traumatised young person WHO WAS ON SUICIDE WATCH in Tallaght Hospital's Lynn Ward been able to go missing??? Hospital of course so far refusing to take any responsibility. Anything happens to my son on their watch? Lawsuits."[5]

The Gardai sadly found Shane's body the next day.

"Following the recovery of a body in the Bray area of Wicklow on Friday 7 January 2022, a missing person appeal in respect of Shane O'Connor, 17 years, has been stood down," a Gardai spokesperson said to the *Irish Mirror*. "An Garda Síochána would like to thank the media and public for their assistance in this matter. No further action is required and no further information is available at this time."[6]

O'Connor tweeted: "My beautiful son, Nevi'im Nesta Ali Shane O'Connor, the very light of my life, decided to end his earthly struggle today and is now with God. May he rest in peace and may no one follow his example. My baby. I love you so much. Please be at peace."[7]

O'Connor then dedicated the Bob Marley track 'Ride Natty Ride' to Shane, saying "This is for my Shaney. The light of my life. The lamp of my soul. My blue-eyed baby. You will always be my light. We will always be together. No boundary can separate us."[8]

She also posted: "Just to say, suggestions there'll be any performances this year or next year or ever again are erroneous.

"There will never be anything to sing about again."[9]

O'Connor lambasted Ireland's Child and Family Agency Tusla for how they had dealt with Shane's case, and for their lack of communication with her after he died.

"Now Tusla want to discuss with me 'a media release' no doubt wishing to have me join in their efforts to make this death of my child seem like it wasn't at the hands of the Irish State. I have now formally identified the remains of my son, Shane. May God forgive the Irish State for I never will."[10]

She added: "I'm going to take private time now to grieve my son. When I am ready I will be telling exactly how the Irish State in the ignorant, evil, self-serving, lying forms of Tusla and the HSE enabled and facilitated his death. Magdalene Ireland never went away. Ask the youth."[11]

She later retracted her statements about Tusla, saying the organisation had done their best: "OK, I'm gonna do the right thing here and apologise for my lashing out. Tusla are working with very limited resources. They loved Shane. They are broken-hearted. They are human. I am sorry I have upset them. We are a third world country. It's not their fault."[12]

O'Connor received many condolences on Twitter. Pogues singer Shane MacGowan tweeted, "Sinéad you have always been there for me and for so many people, in this world you have been a comfort and you have been a soul who is not afraid to feel the pain of the suffering and you have always tried to heal and to help." He prayed that O'Connor and Shane would find peace.[13]

Cáit O'Riordan, a formerly bass guitarist with the Pogues, said: "I'm so sorry Sinéad."[14]

O'Connor posted a message for Dónal Lunny, Shane's father: "You did your best too, Dónal. And Shane adored you. I will always remember how sweet you have been to him. You have been a lovely father. I am sorry for your loss." To Shane, she added the heartbreaking words, "Shaney, babba, stick with me ... My baby ... I don't know how I'm going to live without you."[15]

Six days after Shane's death, O'Connor posted on Twitter: "I've decided to follow my son. There is no point living without him. Everything I touch, I ruin. I only stayed for him. And now he's gone."

In a follow-up tweet, she posted, "I'm sorry. I shouldn't have said that. I am with cops now on way to hospital. I'm sorry I upset everyone."[16] Another tweet said: "I am lost without my kid and I hate myself. Hospital will help a while. But I'm going to find Shane. This is just a delay."[17]

O'Connor held a Hindu funeral for Shane.

"We just said goodbye to our beautiful angel, Shaney," she tweeted.

"Very lovely Hindu ceremony. Shane will have loved it. He was always chanting 'Om. Shanti.'"

"I put a few packs of fags in the coffin for him in case there's none in heaven. He'll have loved that too. Om. Shanti."[18]

95. *Nothing Compares* (2022)

In 2022, a documentary about O'Connor was released with her permission, featuring interviews with her about the events between 1987 and 1993. *Nothing Compares* was made by Irish film-maker Kathryn Ferguson, the long-time O'Connor fan who directed the video for '4th and Vine', and was narrated by O'Connor herself.

"The film was a love letter to Sinéad," Ferguson told *Hot Press*. "Having her voice in it was critical. When we were granted the interview, it became crystal clear that her voice *was* the film. She didn't regret a thing ... I wanted the film to encapsulate the absolute essence of that."[1]

96. Choice Music Prize (2023)

In March 2023, at the RTÉ Choice Music Awards, O'Connor was given the first ever award for Classic Irish Album, for *I Do Not Want What I Haven't Got.* She said the award was for "each and every member of Ireland's refugee community. And not just the Ukrainian one", telling them, "You're very welcome in Ireland. Mashallah. I love you very much and I wish you happiness. Thank you." She received a standing ovation from the audience. Photos from the event show her smiling and waving.[1]

97. Struggling with Grief (2023)

O'Connor was clearly desperate to feel better after Shane's death and enjoy life again. Her final post on Instagram was the subject of a *Sun* news story after her death: "Shared on 7 June 2016, O'Connor's last Instagram post was a black-and-white picture of herself smiling.

"In the snap, the singer is dressed simply in a black t-shirt against a plain background.

"The post's caption read: 'Love the life you have and be grateful for what you are.'"[1]

BirminghamLive also reported: "In a Twitter post on 6 June, Sinéad quoted a Hawaiian prayer.

It ran: 'This is dedicated to the many upon whom I have in my life so far brought suffering and is also, with love, for anyone who has in their lives so far brought suffering upon me.'"[2]

While trying to come to terms with his death, O'Connor was still grieving Shane deeply. On 17 July 2023 she posted on Twitter: "#lostmy17yr OldSonToSuicidein2022. Been living as undead night creature since. He was the love of my life, the lamp of my soul. We were one soul in two halves. He was the only person who ever loved me unconditionally. I am lost in the bardo without him."[3]

In Tibetan Buddhism, 'bardo' means a kind of limbo between death and reincarnation.

By this point, she had left St. Patrick's hospital, and was spending her time between Co. Roscommon and South London.

98. Death (2023)

Sinéad O'Connor died alone and was discovered unresponsive at her flat in Herne Hill on 26 July 2023, aged just 56. Police said they were not treating her death as suspicious. On 9 January 2024, it was disclosed by Southwark Coroner's Court that O'Connor had died of natural causes.

Her family released a statement on the day of her death, saying, "It is with great sadness that we announce the passing of our beloved Sinéad.

Her family and friends are devastated and have requested privacy at this very difficult time."

Her fans began to leave bunches of flowers and tributes in front of her house in Strand Road, Montebello, where she had spent 15 years living.

At The Mansion House in Dublin, a new book of condolences was started, and fans and the public were invited to write messages to O'Connor. They came in droves to write in the book, which was placed on a table next to a photograph of O'Connor, with a lit candle beside them.

Fans massed in Barnardo Square in Dublin to sing 'Nothing Compares 2 U' together, many holding black and white posters of O'Connor featuring the slogan 'Fight the real enemy'. The gathering was organised by Rosa, a socialist feminist group.

Activist for the group Ruth Coppinger said at the event, "An exceptional and unique voice that could be both a whisper or a scream in one line, she captivated audiences.

"She wasn't fearless — she felt the fear but did it anyway. That's the real definition of bravery."

Before the All-Ireland football final between Dublin and Kerry, a tribute appeared to O'Connor. The audience cheered as an image of her face appeared on the screens inside Croke Park pre-match, contrasted with a dark background, while 'Nothing Compares 2 U' played. Fittingly, Dublin went on to win the match.

99. Tributes (2023)

There was an outpouring of grief from the world. The Irish President Michael D. Higgins wrote a long and considered tribute to O'Connor, part of which read: "My first reaction on hearing the news of Sinéad's loss was to remember her extraordinarily beautiful, unique voice. What was striking in all of the recordings she made and in all of her appearances was the authenticity of the performance, while her commitment to the delivery of the song and its meaning was total."[1]

Taoiseach Leo Varadkar wrote on Twitter: "Really sorry to hear of the passing of Sinéad O'Connor. Her music was loved around the world and her talent was unmatched and beyond compare. Condolences to her family, her friends and all who loved her music."[2]

Irish boxer Conor McGregor posted photos of him with O'Connor. He tweeted: "The world has lost an artist with the voice of an angel.

"Ireland has lost an iconic voice and one of our absolute finest, by a long shot. And I have lost a friend. Sinéad's music will live on and continue to inspire!"[3]

Northern Ireland's First Minister Michelle O'Neill wrote that she was "saddened at the news. Ireland has lost one of our most powerful and successful singers, songwriters and female artists. A big loss not least to her family and friends, but all her many followers across the world."[4]

Dublin City Councillor James Geoghegan tweeted: "Awful news. Thoughts with her family. May she rest in peace."[5]

Tanaiste of Ireland Micheál Martin wrote: "Devastated to hear of the passing of Sinéad O'Connor. One of our greatest musical icons, and someone deeply loved by the people of Ireland, and beyond.

"Our hearts go out to her children, her family, friends and all who knew and loved her."[6]

Dr Umar Al-Qadri, an Irish Muslim leader, posted a video of himself together with O'Connor. His tribute read: "Renowned Irish singer formerly known as Sinéad O'Connor and now as Shuhada', @MagdaDavitt77, proclaimed the Shahadah.

"We pray that Allah grants her Peace in all aspects of this life and hereafter, Ameen. She has a truthful soul."[7]

Stephen Donnelly, the Irish Minister for Health, wrote on Twitter: "Devastating to hear that Sinéad O'Connor has died. An extraordinary, passionate, fearless woman, an immensely talented artist. Deepest sympathies to Sinéad's family and friends. Ar dheis Dé go raibh a hanam."[8]

RTE presenter Ryan Tubridy, a long-time friend of O'Connor, wrote on Instagram Stories:

"Like everyone, I'm devastated by the awful news about Sinéad.

"We spoke days ago, and she was as kind, powerful, passionate, determined and decent as ever.

"Rest in peace Sinéad, you were ahead of your time and deserve whatever peace comes your way."[9]

Irish comedian Al Foran said: "The worldwide tributes to Sinéad O'Connor really do encapsulate the fact that she was probably one of Ireland's greatest exports, she was the definition of pure raw talent."[10]

Music journalist David Stubbs wrote: "Sinéad O'Connor RIP. One of the most remarkable ever women in pop, who doubtless never got the support, respect and understanding she deserved, for all her fame. What must it have been like to put herself out there, the way she did? What courage, what loneliness?"[11]

Bono wrote: "I first heard Sinéad sing 'Take My Hand' when she was aged 15. The U2ers are heartbroken for Sinéad, for her family. She loved God by so many names ... she will now reach what has so conspicuously eluded her ... the peace that passes all understanding."[12]

U2 quoted the lyrics to 'Heroine', the track O'Connor had recorded with the Edge adding, "Rest In Peace Sinéad."

O'Connor's former lover and friend Peter Gabriel tweeted: "Sinéad was an extraordinary talent. She could move us with a candour and a passion with which so many people connected. The path she chose was always difficult and uncompromising but at every turn she would show her spirit and her courage."[13]

Kate Bush said: "It's like a light has gone out, hasn't it? A beacon on a high mountain. Sinéad didn't just move us with her incredibly emotive voice, she stood up with it. I salute her. We were lucky to have such a magical presence move among us."[14]

Amanda Palmer wrote a long tribute on Facebook, part of which referenced O'Connor's appearance at the Bob Dylan 30th Anniversary Concert: "Now that she is dead, she'll be lauded. But back then? How do you imagine she felt that night, crawling into bed, having been abused by a crowd of thousands? Would you care if the world turned around, forty years later, and said: 'Sorry about that, you were actually very brave?'"[15]

Charity HIV Ireland thanked O'Connor for her support for people living with HIV and AIDS, writing: "We are incredibly sad to hear of the passing of Irish music legend, activist, and proud ally of people living with HIV and impacted by AIDS, Sinéad O'Connor. A profoundly talented artist and a trailblazer in every sense. We remember her talent, her courage, and her honesty. RIP."[16]

Shane and Victoria McGowan said: "We don't really have words for this but we want to thank you Sinéad for your love and your friendship and your compassion and your humour and your incredible music. We pray that you are at peace now with your beautiful boy."[17]

Irish Fiction Laureate Colm Tóibín told Radio 4 that he had great admiration for O'Connor.

"Her voice is personal. You can hear the sort of courage, the bravery, the ferocity, and the sense of mission, I think, also.

"She began at a time when those things she did were so necessary in Ireland, for somebody to emerge like that, who would speak in that way."[18]

Journalist and broadcaster Caitlin Moran tweeted: "Sinéad: and she was the first to talk about abuse in the Catholic church – tearing up the picture of the Pope on TV – but 99% of the music industry hung her out to dry. She was decades before her time, and fearless. Rest in power, queen."[19]

Fachtna O'Ceallaigh said: "It wasn't just that she was unique looking – her willingness to speak what she believed to be the truth forged a new path for women in the music industry to be as close to their true selves as they could possibly be."[20]

Three days after O'Connor's death, Bob Geldof and the Boomtown Rats headlined the Cavan Calling Festival in County Cavan, Ireland. Geldof divulged that he'd known O'Connor and her brother Joseph when the three were children, as the O'Connor family had lived 75 yards from the Geldofs and travelled to school from the same bus stop.

Geldof told the audience that she was the Maud Gonne of their era – an Irish revolutionary. He said that he'd been close to O'Connor, and the last time they'd spoken had been a few weeks previously. In some of her messages to him, she'd sounded depressed, and in some she'd seemed elated.

Before performing the song 'Mary of the 4th Form' and dedicating it to O'Connor, Geldof recalled that O'Connor would bring the album the song was on to school, which would send the nuns crazy. He also revealed that she had affixed a picture of him to the school noticeboard.

Geldof said he thought O'Connor had torn up the photograph of Pope John Paul II on *Saturday Night Live* because he himself had previously appeared on *Top of the Pops* and ripped up a picture of John Travolta.

"It was a little more extreme than tearing up fucking disco," he joked.

"Tearing up the Vatican is a whole other thing, but more correct actually, I should have done it.

"We love her very much ... [some of the band] watched her this afternoon and we were just speechless at how beautiful, how brilliant she was."[21]

Hot Press produced a whole tribute issue, 'Thank You for Hearing Me', devoted to O'Connor. Editor Niall Stokes introduced it by saying "O'Connor was one of the most important Irish artists of the past 50 years." He praised her talent "of transcendent ability. Her voice was an awe-inspiring instrument, capable of moving from a whisper to a banshee wail and back in nano-seconds ... she traversed the full spectrum of where the human spirit can take us."[22]

100. Pushback to Tributes (2023)

Singer Morrissey wrote a scathing yet eloquent open letter on his website, saying O'Connor had been treated badly by the media and record industry while alive, and lambasting tributes from them now as fake.

"She had a proud vulnerability ... and there is a certain music industry hatred for singers who don't 'fit in' (this I know only too well), and they are never praised until death – when, finally, they can't answer back. The cruel playpen of fame gushes with praise for Sinéad today."[1]

What progressive O'Connor would have made of the right-wing Morrissey's support for her can only be imagined.

Many on Twitter suggested that Morrissey was angry because he envisaged only being truly appreciated after his own death.

Singer Lily Allen – herself the target of negative tabloid attention for years – also posted a series of angry tweets:

"It's hard not to feel incensed when there are so many people posting about Sinéad and how fearless she was, people who would never in a million years align themselves with anybody who stood for something or had anything remotely controversial to say. It's so spineless."[2]

101. Pushback to Obituary (2023)

Paradoxically, while Morrissey and Lily Allen were furious at the effusive eulogies, others were angry at a less effusive obituary which ran in the *Guardian*. Pop writer Caroline Sullivan, who has worked for the paper for more than three decades, wrote a measured account of O'Connor's life, similar in tone to the *Telegraph* obituary for her. While recognising some of O'Connor's positive qualities, Sullivan also spoke about the singer's complexities, flaws and the trials she'd endured.

The piece described O'Connor as "a passionate and highly engaged musician ... one of her generation's significant talents" and added that she was "startlingly beautiful" with an "unswerving commitment to activism".[1]

However, Sullivan received pushback for saying O'Connor "lacked the obsessive drive needed to keep a top-flight pop career aloft" – even though O'Connor had professed many times that she had never intended to be a pop star – and that O'Connor had "an inability to edit her pronouncements", "regularly revealed troubling personal details" and was "oblivious to the usual dividing line between pop stars [and fans]".

Feeling this was unduly negative, O'Connor fans took to Twitter to complain, some directly to Sullivan. Tracey Thorn, singer for Everything But the Girl and one of the few vocalists of the same generation whose voice rivalled O'Connor's, had posted the following tribute: "Oh Sinéad O'Connor, no, that's a terrible loss. What a singer and what a brave brave woman. Heartbreaking news."[2]

"As always, when someone like that dies, you hope they knew how much they were loved."[3]

"And now I've read an obituary that has made me furious, fucking hell."[4]

"I think what's so hateful about that *Guardian* Sinéad obit is the way it frames her whole life in negatives – 'she lacked the obsessive drive needed

... never had another hit ... inability to edit her pronouncements ... constitutionally unable to compromise ...' Talk about removing agency."[5]

"Compared to the outpouring of love and good feeling I have seen on here, it is extraordinarily tone deaf, and really upsetting."[6]

She added a follow-up tweet: "Here, I've fixed it for you – 'She was free of the obsessive desire to have hits at any cost ... she saw no need to edit herself for public consumption ... she stuck to her guns when powerful forces tried to make her compromise ...'."[7]

Feminist writer Julie Bindel also wrote: "This is such a mean-spirited obit, I don't know where to start ..."[8]

To my surprise, given the response to her obituary, Sullivan granted me an interview for this book. She was warm, generous and funny, and at one point came close to tears while talking about O'Connor's death.

I asked her if, given that she'd said so many nice things about O'Connor over the years – describing her voice as 'an object of wonder', doing a positive write-up of an interview with her and reviewing her albums and live gigs favourably – she felt the response to the obituary was unfair?

"I think I was generally positive about her," Sullivan said, "and the negative stuff, I thought and still kind of think was in the interests of a balanced view. An obituary can't just say 'she was wonderful and saintly' – it's not a eulogy or an appreciation piece – [it has to acknowledge that] there were bad things in her life as well.

"I used the phrase 'she lacked the obsessive drive to keep a top-flight pop career aloft', and a lot of people were very angry at that particular statement. She never wanted to be a pop star, and I knew that. But I didn't express well enough that she basically couldn't care less that 'Nothing Compares to You' was a fluke in her catalogue – it was her only big hit.

"I thought I was being journalistic by using that phrase, but all these people thought I was judging her for not having the wherewithal to be a massive pop star, and so they were furious about that. It was really hard to explain to them what I'd meant.

"There were a couple of other things I would have written in a slightly different way ... At the very beginning, I started off by saying her childhood had been difficult. A lot of people were angry that I started on what seemed like a negative note. Also, I might have said 'she never got the enjoyment out of her career that she should have', rather than 'it was the apex of a career that tormented rather than fulfilled her'.

"I think the piece stands up journalistically, because it gives you both sides of her. But I now realise from this incident that people who really love the artist you're writing about will be reading this, and there's no point in upsetting them needlessly if you can think twice about it. I don't just want to go running roughshod over people's finer feelings."

I asked Sullivan how it had felt to be on the receiving end of so much criticism.

"I found it very, very hard to get over the monstering from Twitter. It really affected me – I know it sounds melodramatic, but it knocked me for six."

Before the internet, I pointed out, the obituary would have come out and there wouldn't have been any pushback, save for the odd letter.

"Exactly," Sullivan replied, saying that she'd been upset by Tracey Thorn's tweets, but that she could also have made Thorn's suggested edits. "Tracey Thorn said I 'removed agency' from Sinéad, asking why I hadn't said 'she chose to do this' instead of 'she failed to do this'. So instead of saying she had 'an inability to edit her pronouncements', she suggested I should have said 'she chose not to edit her pronouncements'."

I took a different view: as I suffer from the same disorder as O'Connor had, borderline personality disorder, I know how hard it is for BPD sufferers to regulate our emotions, filter our speech and not overshare. So 'inability' felt more accurate to me than suggesting it were a choice, even if it may have seemed harsh in an obituary.

Does Sullivan think that, because people were so angry and grief-stricken at the way they thought O'Connor had died, and O'Connor was treated so badly by the media in general, Sullivan bore the brunt of this grief for being a journalist?

"I do. She never got an easy time from the media. Even now, with what we now know about people's mental health, she didn't get an easy time, up to probably the last couple of years. The cause of death hasn't been released yet, but I think the assumption was that she'd [committed suicide]. We don't know, and somebody pointed out that it could have been a heart attack or some kind of physical thing. But her fans were assuming that she'd ended it as she couldn't stand it anymore. They rounded on journalists because we were supposedly part of her misery."

Did the outpouring of grief after O'Connor's death surprise her? She seemed more revered after death than in life. Was it that people realised what they'd lost, in that she was this unique artist, there was nobody like her and there probably won't be again?

"I think that the media response – not the *Guardian*'s response, because it had some real fans on the staff like Simon Hattenstone, so it would always have gone in really big on her passing – but I think the response of the tabloids, who all had her on the cover, was guided by the public response. They realised that people were genuinely grief-stricken and they thought, 'we'd better get onto this'. I don't think it would have occurred to them to commemorate her otherwise.

"I think there was a lot of surprise at how revered she was. To be honest, I was surprised, I guess because she hadn't [released any records for nearly a decade]. I know she was working on a new album, but unless you're a really big Sinéad fan, you wouldn't have been following her career to that degree. I think a lot of people's grief about her was almost retrospective. They remembered what she had meant to them a long time ago, and it all came flooding into people's psyches. They remembered what a hard time she'd had, and how she'd been a truth-teller.

"She knew about child abuse in the Catholic church years and years before anybody else did, and she was right about it. And suddenly all these people who probably hadn't thought about her in a long time were like, 'Oh my God, Sinéad, she's gone – she'll never be there telling the truth again.' And once you see that other people have that same reaction, it kind of becomes a massive wave of grief . . . I think people are now realising that there is nobody else like her, and we won't see her like again."

I think that's a real shame, I told Sullivan, because she was very, very open, and very honest. And what also sets her apart from the average pop star is that she was incredibly intelligent, and extremely funny. Pop star interviews are often very guarded, bland and PR'd. And Sinéad said exactly what she wanted to say at all times.

"Exactly. She wasn't media trained at all. You can imagine her laughing if someone had suggested doing media training! But also, I think she had far more of a sense of humour than her fans give her credit for. Somebody who knew her suggested to me at the height of the furore over the obit that she probably would have just laughed, she wouldn't have found it offensive at all."

102. Funeral and Further Tributes (2023)

O'Connor's body was laid to rest on 8 August 2023 in Bray, Co Wicklow, where she was buried in a private service for family and close friends. The procession and cortège journeyed past the seafront, travelling from the Harbour Bar down to the end of the Strand Road.

Fans and mourners lined the road where O'Connor's house Montebello was located, and where she'd previously spent 15 years living. They laid down bouquets of flowers and carefully-written tributes.

Two days before the funeral took place, a Bray hillside saw a huge tribute created on it, reading "ÉIRE SINÉAD", a heart emoji separating the two words. It was a joint initiative between Dublin creative agency The Tenth Man and signwriters Mack Signs.

"We just wanted to take the opportunity to mark the moment with a bold statement that symbolises what she meant to this little country of ours," said Richard Seabrooke, director of The Tenth Man.[1]

The *Guardian* story about the tribute also added, "Last week, the Samuel Beckett bridge over the Liffey was lit up with lyrics from O'Connor's seminal 1990 hit, 'Nothing Compares 2 U'."[2]

After O'Connor's death, the *Sun* reported that the Irish LGBTQ+ organisation BelongTo had revealed how O'Connor gave them more unused makeup to pass onto trans youths supported by the organisation.

BelongTo said, "Sincerest condolences to the family and friends of Sinéad O'Connor/Shuhada' Sadaqat.

"In 2021, we were lucky enough to get a call from Sinéad herself who wanted to donate her unused makeup to trans young people in our service."[3]

In another of many stories of O'Connor's kindness to the disenfranchised, abused and depressed, her friend Kala Jackson Craft told the *Irish Mail on Sunday* how O'Connor had rescued her from a devastating situation. "I was raped by a well-known businessman and then attacked by his son and when Sinéad read about it in the newspaper she tracked me down ... [she] believed me when no one else would. If she had not tracked me down I probably would have died or walked into the sea."

Jackson Craft revealed that O'Connor had taken her for lunch, given her a place to stay in her own home and a job as her housekeeper. She said she would forever be grateful to O'Connor for her compassion.[4]

103. Family Statement (2023)

Three weeks after O'Connor's death, her family released another statement to the *Irish Times*: "The children of Sinéad together with Sinéad's extended family wish to thank the countless kind people who sympathised and offered condolences on Sinéad's recent passing. Their helpful support for the family is much appreciated."[1]

104. Legacy (2023)

I was interested to know what the people I'd interviewed for this book thought O'Connor's legacy would be. These interviews took place four to five months before it was revealed that she had died of natural causes.

I asked Stuart Bailie what his immediate reaction had been when he'd heard the news in July that she had passed. Had he always feared this would happen?

"Well, not really," he replied. "I don't know ... I sort of thought she'd become a survivor. I spoke to her about her song 'Trouble of the World', saying that sounds like a farewell song. She's going, 'No, no it's not, everything's changing for the better.'

"I know David Holmes a little bit, and he said she drove up early in the morning from Bray with Shane. And was sitting in the car at five in the morning, ready to work. He said, 'We give her a bacon bap and then she records two or three good songs and gets back in the car again.' He had found a brilliant way to work with her and was giving her all the respect she deserved.

"Obviously I'd seen some of the videos she'd put out, where she was distraught. And when her son died, that was awful. That whole thing with that first record 'Troy', and I said it was almost like 'Wuthering Heights', you know, it was like Cathy tapping at the window ... that generational thing that the kids get caught up in and they almost relive past parts of that story all over again.

"I think Sinéad's life, you know, the mother and the daughter and the son have all been touched by mental health issues, and that's just unbearably cruel.

"Obviously the mother died in a car crash. I'm not sure what happened to Sinéad, did she take her own life? I don't know."

We don't know yet.

"Her son took his own life. So it just feels like, my there's three generations that have been touched. I don't know if that's an inherited trait or whatever but it's just horrific beyond words."

Yeah, it's really tragic.

"There's a song on the new record, I haven't heard all of the new record, but there's a song called 'Horse on a Highway', which is her singing to her son, who was at that stage still alive, saying just calm down, son.

"And then you hear the story about the son, and you hear the story about her, and you're going oh no ... those conversations. Like 'Troy', it's sort of there. They're still out there, like phantom songs, you know?"

You said on Twitter that there's a version of an Irish song on her upcoming album and it's amazing, I told Bailie. So you've heard some of the album?

"I've heard bits," he replied. "I don't know if it's completely finished yet. 'Mo Ghile Mear' is a song about Bonnie Prince Charlie. He was beaten by the English and the Irish were waiting for him to deliver them from the English. It's one of those elemental songs. It was sort of forgotten, and now it's becoming huge again. I think 'Trouble of the World' is on it, and at one stage she was going to record 'At 17' by Janis Ian, so I'm not quite sure if that's part of it or not."

So is it mostly not songs she's written herself?

"I think it's a mixture. At one stage when David worked with her, Sinéad had moments of creative energy and then they would stop … And then I think in the interview I did with her she said maybe it'll just be an EP, and then the record companies are kind of going, 'Well, you can't sell an EP.'

"So I think that was the energy and ambition near the end, to get an album out."

It had a working title of *No Veteran Dies Alone*, didn't it?

"Yeah. She wanted to work with American soldiers who'd come back from Iraq or Afghanistan … at one stage, she was talking about getting training to be a counsellor, that was the tenor, and there was a song possibly called that, about that desire to heal them."

Which of her past albums would you say her last album is closest to in terms of its sound? Is it quite mellow or more raucous?

"David Holmes obviously has that whole Phil Spector, Andrew Weatherall sound … he's a hugely accomplished musical visionary, so he's used a very light touch but given her voice a lot of presence. Some of her stuff before was perhaps a bit twee or obvious, so they're just little sonic strokes that make it sound cool, for want of another word."

Sounds great. Do you know when it's likely to be released?

"No, I've no idea. I'd imagine there's a million lawyers talking to each other about it. The single was out on Heavenly, but I think the ongoing project reverted to Chrysalis Records, and they owned Ensign, so it's kind of gone back to her original home."

Do you think Sinéad's legacy will mostly be for her music or her activism?

"I was slightly surprised at the strength of feeling in Ireland. I kind of half-thought people had half-forgotten about her or got bored with her or moved on. And there was just a massive outpouring of grief because I think she represented a generation of women and young people of saying, 'Fuck the Catholic church and fuck the State.'"

"She really kicked in – in the time before that, people were thinking it, but nobody was necessarily saying it. And she said it in a huge way. Bob Geldof had a song called 'Banana Republic' where he was castigating the Irish state and the tradition of gunrunning, and glorifying violence, and police, and priests, and all the things that he had in that song.

"And there was an annoyance that he had dared to say that. But even then, it wasn't obvious what he was saying. Whereas Sinéad was kind of letting it all hang out! There were no fucks given.

"I think that's a huge part of her legacy. Again, I'm talking in Irish terms, but you hear bands like Pillow Queens and that's pure Sinéad in a lot of ways, though it's obviously going to be a different level or different era. Sinéad and The Cranberries and Clannad and Enya are all touched by the liturgy of the church, and the rhythms and the music and singing unaccompanied in a church . . . there's a whole tradition of Irish music that Sinéad was at the centre of, she channelled a lot of that.

"As well as working with MC Lyte and various hip-hop artists. I get the feeling that the hip-hop community was grieving for her when she died. I could be wrong. So I don't know if the English ever totally got her! At the *NME* I sometimes felt like a semi-lonely voice – 'God, this is one of the greatest artists in the world,' and the response was, 'Well, whatever, y'know!'

"So I was just deeply, deeply touched at how Ireland has responded. And possibly people are exaggerating, at funerals grief can be very performative.

"But I think there is actually a great love and respect and a recognition that she moved the state on. Songs like 'This Is a Rebel Song', the fact that she tried to sing about English colonial legacies. And also on 'Famine', where she said there was no famine, it was starvation perpetrated by the English state. I would be very fond of a lot of those songs as well – they're just incredibly thoughtful and incredibly well presented.

"And then the fact that she could have a commonality with people like Christy Moore. She could sing songs like 'Irish Ways and Irish Laws' and absolutely plug into that rebel tradition. 'The Foggy Dew', another song about the Irish Republic called Óró, sé do Bheatha Abhaile.

"And she tussled with Sinn Féin around the centenary of the 1916 Easter Rising and said, 'We all know that the ideals of the Irish Republic are completely lost, it became a church-dominated patriarchal society, and how do we get away from that?' And she's having these huge conversations on Twitter and you kind of go, 'Wow, OK!'

"I think she put a lot of consideration into Sinn Féin as a solution and then she went, 'No, no, you're not the people to deliver this.' So I really value a lot of that as well. I thought that was amazing."

I asked Neil McCormick what his first reaction was to the news of O'Connor's passing.

"It was devastating," he told me. "You know, it's become a big part of my job, the 'death watch', the 'death beat'. Rock and roll's got very old and the first generation have all shuffled off now, and the people from the '60s and the '70s are on their way out. It's become a big part of what I do, and there were a couple of times when Sinéad had seemed close to the edge, and I thought, 'Oh my God I hope she doesn't, I don't know how to write that piece, I don't want to write that piece.'

"And so I didn't prepare anything, whereas if I'd been more professional about it I would have done. I just didn't want it to happen. And then obviously after her son died, it felt like, well, that's a very hard one to get over. But on the grapevine, you heard that she was doing OK."

She'd been in mental hospital for years, hadn't she, at St. Patrick's. I guess she was healing and then that must have knocked her for six.

"It must have. So it was awful, it was just awful. There's only two or three times that the death of a pop star slash public figure has winded me, and that was one, but I just sat down and wrote about it. Because that's what you do, and it's a privilege to be able to do that.

"She's a complicated, complicated figure. She never lived up to, I don't think, her full potential musically, because in a way she would constantly be shooting herself in the foot.

"She was a very good songwriter, but she didn't write that many songs, she didn't make that many albums. But then she played a lot of gigs. Some people are at their best on stage and singing, and she was always great – a powerful presence on stage.

"She had put into the conversation a lot of really important points. From her point of view, obviously the behaviour of the Catholic Church in the world, but in Ireland in particular, is huge. But see, I just took that for granted. I grew up in Ireland.

"Everybody was turning round saying, 'I didn't know the priests did that, we were walking around with blinkers on' and I didn't feel that we were. That our generation, the punk generation ... I'd heard people say these things and so I just assumed the priests and the nuns were the enemy. They weren't part of my world.

"She went about it in a way that was difficult for other people to accept. She was not a diplomat, and so it caused a lot of furore, but that wasn't really the significant point from my point of view. Her theological beliefs were haphazard and wayward and ridiculous really, and you know, one minute she was a Muslim and then she was a Catholic priest even though she hated the Catholics. There was so much God, and I'm an atheist and I wasn't that interested in all of that. It seemed to be enacting her internal dramas.

"But what I do think is interesting is that she was suffering mental health crises that came from an abusive Catholic church background, and came from being a woman in our times, and *those* are the really strong conversations that she was having.

"And she was almost alone out there as a major public figure, because she had achieved, briefly, global superstardom which she burned down. But she was out there having that conversation, putting those things in, and they sounded mad at the time, and with each passing year they sounded less and less mad.

"So that now you listen to the points and you just think, 'Well, we've accepted them now.' I think we kidded ourselves that sexual equality had come in the '60s. I think we were more feminist in that punk generation than people are now. And we just kidded ourselves that equality had arrived, and clearly it hadn't – and neurodiversity, mental health issues, all of these issues which have become very foregrounded in pop culture, that would make Sinéad not even an unusual figure if she was coming out today.

"[But back then] she was alone out there fighting her fight, her mental health battle for her self-esteem and mental health, in a very public forum, and getting a lot of abuse for it. And being treated as the madwoman in the attic, as a stupid woman who was burning down her career, as her own worst enemy. Treated in a hostile way by popular culture and in a very hard way. She becomes a very brave figure."

Do you think that will be her legacy then, her activism rather than her music?

"They'll go together. For most people, Sinéad O'Connor is just one song, and she didn't even write that song. Obviously she's talked about what that song meant to her. And you know, when people sing because it's a matter of life and death, there's something in our ears that hears that.

"And so these figures like Kurt Cobain or Sinéad you know, or Billie Holiday, their struggle is in their voice and you hear it and it's a very powerful thing, and you can have really great singers that just don't have that intensity of expression.

"But because she did so much damage to her commercial prospects, most people don't know much more than that about Sinéad and she wasn't playing arenas – she was playing theatres."

She always said that she didn't want to be a pop star and had no interest in fame or money, I pointed out, and that it was just about being a protest singer. So I guess that's why she was happy to burn it down – she didn't care.

"Was she happy?"

Maybe 'happy' is the wrong word ...

"She burned it down because she couldn't help herself. Other things were more important to her. But she sowed a lot of damage, she wreaked a lot of havoc. Into the mix of the fact that she was a brave person speaking her truth, and she was able to perform in a way that put that self and that truth front and centre, as she was a fantastic singer who sang songs that she believed in, some she wrote and some she just connected to. And that really came through.

"But into that she also had major mental health issues, which meant that she was very very difficult for other people to deal with, and for her own family to deal with. She was not helpful to herself and her own, because the damage that was in her meant she wasn't able to deal with the world in a reasonable way for the world to deal with her.

"And you can always say, 'Well we have to be careful of people's mental health,' and I do think that's the legacy. The legacy is raising awareness of mental health and people's vulnerability and speaking your own truth and truth to power in our times.

"That will be the legacy more than music. It will be attached to the song that she's so famous for.

"But along the way she made her life very very difficult, and the lives of people around her."

While she was at Saint Patrick's she was diagnosed with borderline personality disorder, I said, which makes it very difficult to regulate your emotions, to not overshare – you don't have any kind of filter. BPD is what people who were abused as children get and I think it explains why she just couldn't seem to help herself [from expressing BPD traits]. I think it explains a lot.

"It does explain a lot, and the abuse and the trauma that she experienced you know to the shame of the church, to the shame of Irish society, to the shame of our misogynistic and paternalistic society is common. She's not the only person that I've encountered like that along the way, but she was in a very high profile space and she didn't retreat. She lived her truth."

I asked Caroline Sullivan whether she thought O'Connor's legacy would be to do with her music or her activism, and what her influence on other artists had been.

Sullivan replied, "Her music is inextricably linked to her activism. You feel as if she made music with the express intention of getting people to pay attention to what she had to say.

"She clearly influenced people like Alanis Morissette and P.J. Harvey – outsiders who I think found the courage to be who they are after witnessing Sinéad's example. Roisin Murphy comes to mind, too, and Shirley Manson. She was a beacon, attracting artists who felt different and unruly."

Neil Perry said, "It saddens me that she's reduced to one song ('Nothing Compares 2 U') which wasn't even her bloody song. She wrote better songs than that. And some of the last few albums you can't even buy, they are out of print or very hard to find.

"But then she wasn't prolific with recording, and as the 21st century sped up and digital culture arrived it was very easy to fall out of the public eye. Which she sort of did, musically, which I think is a huge shame. In the last few years she became associated with drama, name changes, religion changes, all that, and talking crap on Twitter – she was definitely someone who should not have had access to social media.

"Our generation who'd grown up with her, we'd just think, 'Oh Sinéad, what are you doing . . . you're still out there, being Sinéad I guess.' It was strangely comforting in one way, I suppose. But for younger generations, I'm sure they were thinking, if they were thinking of her at all, 'Who is this loonball?' Not, 'Oh, that's Sinéad O'Connor, the amazing singer.' Which I find sad . . . not that Sinéad gave a shit, I'm sure.

"The activism was important, especially in the 1990s when artists rarely made a stand for a principle, but nowadays I don't think young people would be especially surprised. Maybe that's her legacy, maybe she normalised speaking your mind in public, having your say, not shutting up and going quietly and putting up with crap, maybe some girls and young women took notice and grew up to be just as mouthy, unafraid to stand up for themselves. It's a nice thought."

I asked Robert Dean if he was shocked when O'Connor died.

"I was very sad, but I wasn't shocked," he replied. "With everything that had gone on in her life in the preceding years, I wasn't shocked at all. I could sort of see it coming. It was sort of getting better for her mentally, I think, until her son killed himself. She couldn't get a break, could she?"

No, it's really tragic. Do you think her legacy will be more to do with her music or with her activism, or both?

"Well, I think they go hand in hand, really. I don't think people will be able to think about Sinéad without the activism side of things. But ultimately I do think she'll be thought of in a far more positive way than in the past. And what came out in the aftermath of her death was so much positivity in the media, which was fantastic. I mean, too late, but it was so very positive that I think she'll be remembered as one of the greats of the 1980s and 1990s."

I suggested to Simon Hattenstone that O'Connor will probably be remembered more for her courage and convictions and beliefs than for her music, excepting her one huge hit. Did he think she'd be happy with that legacy?

"Yeah," he replied. "I think if it was the fact that she was proved right on the church and on abuse, I think that meant more to her than her music. I mean, her music's still there for loads of people who are into it.

And what was interesting is that, in a way, her music wasn't divorced from herself and her issues.

"Her Irishness was a massive part of her, so she recorded Irish folk songs. She did reggae stuff and Rasta stuff because she was really into that. She did loads of covers because she was really into the history of music and kind of traditional Irish songs like 'Danny Boy' as well. So she continued doing different stuff.

"Maybe the album she was working on [at the time of her death] will come out.

"But loads of people looked back at her and said, particularly around the time of her funeral, that she taught me how to speak up for myself. She taught me it was OK to acknowledge mental illness, to talk about it, which is massive. She taught me it was OK to be potty mouthed and swear loads, which is massive. She taught me that I could take on the church and the establishment, which is massive.

"And then, you know, her private life … I wrote a piece after she died and pointed out that the four dads of her children were all different men. And someone said, 'How disgusting, typical man writing that!'

"But she was really proud of it, because again, it was breaking away from the convention that she thought was really hidebound. And she thought you could be really religious, and a really good person, and a person of faith, while pissing on every element of the tradition. So I think [that's a great legacy]. I think she's so important, particularly to women, and women of a certain generation, and women growing up in a suppressive and repressed environment.

"But I don't think she really had any idea. It would be interesting if she could read about herself now."

Author's Note

So far, I've tried to remain relatively impartial about Sinéad's tragic and fascinating life, and not bring my own experiences into this biography. It is about her, not me. But I'm aware that people might wonder why I thought I would be the right person to write about her. It may seem audacious, as I never met her, and was only seven years old when *The Lion and the Cobra* was released. And, while I am from a minority ethnic group, I'm not Irish, much less steeped in Irish musical traditions.

The truth is that sadly I can relate to a lot of Sinéad's personal story, almost all of which I learned from obituaries after her death. We both suffered a brutal childhood at the hands of a violent, volatile and emotionally abusive parent; we both found great solace in music during our childhoods.

We were both diagnosed with borderline personality disorder, made suicide attempts and suffered poor mental health throughout our lives – and were both very slight, petite women who were put on drugs for our mental health conditions later in life, which caused us to gain a lot of weight.

We both fell pregnant at a relatively early age; I had an abortion, Sinéad had two with following pregnancies, and we both suffered the emotional pain of these. We felt an overwhelmingly deep love for our kids, and were single mums to them. We shared custody with their dads, who were quite a bit older than us. We both had dozens of relationships, and, coincidentally, a Las Vegas wedding at the same chapel, yet neither of us managed to hold down a marriage or relationship for any significant length of time.

I understand Sinéad's over-sharing and passion for activism: when you're abused as a child and no one steps in and does anything – when your pain and the horror you went through isn't even acknowledged by anyone, let alone stopped or apologised for, and your families don't want you to speak about it – then you want to make as much noise as possible about the issue, in order that no one can suffer that kind of childhood again.

You're horrified and traumatised by the lack of acknowledgement and action on your behalf. You also crave attention and success to compensate for the lack of attention and sense of failure at being told by your abusive parent that you are worthless. That small child who wasn't listened to is now going to be listened to by the whole world.

I can also empathise hugely with Sinéad's breakdown after offending the Catholic church on *Saturday Night Live*. In 2008, I created an atheist advertising campaign which went global, with the slogan 'There's probably no God. Now stop worrying and enjoy your life' running on buses across the western world. After the hate mail I received from Christians, I became suicidal and didn't write publicly for three-and-a-half years. Feeling like the enemy of the whole world, even if in reality it's just a vocal minority, completely destroys your mental health, so it's unsurprising that Sinéad suffered hugely.

She was about as far from being an atheist as you can get, but this makes sense: traumatic experiences either push you towards faith or turn you off it completely. She was understandably always searching for answers and solace.

So when I was given the chance to pitch a book about a public figure from the past to this publisher, and was told I could suggest anyone from history, Sinéad was the person whose life I felt most connected to and with whom I could empathise most deeply. Telling her story has been extremely moving and a huge honour.

As I hadn't met Sinéad, I carried out several interviews with people who knew her, to talk about her life, music and legacy and give you a better sense of who she was. I'm very grateful to Caroline Sullivan, Simon Hattenstone, Stuart Bailie, Neil McCormick, Neil Perry and Robert Dean for their time and insights, and also to David Stubbs, Liam Geraghty and *State of Mind Italia* for their help.

Thank you too to Peter Weilgony, Peter Archibald, Kevin S. Brodie, Kevin McGeary, Klaas Jan Runia, Justin Lewis, Matthew Sylvester, Phil Adcock, Iain Goldfinch, Trevor Prinn, Steve Bowen, Dave Cross, Rebekah Bennetch, Mark White, Shane Jarvis, Mary and Tim Fowler, Keith Bell and all the other people who allow me to keep writing.

A special thank you to Lily Cariad and John Fleming.

Thank you to my supportive author friends Kia Abdullah and Gary Panton.

Lastly, I wish I had been able to meet Sinéad when she was alive and tell her what an inspiration she was to me, and to the millions of abused children around the globe for whom she stood up. I hope I have done her justice.

Sinéad Marie Bernadette O'Connor,
8 December 1966 – 26 July 2023.
Rest in peace.

Bibliography

1. Childhood (1966–1979)

1. O'Connor, Sinéad, *Rememberings* (Penguin, 2021), p. 283.
2. O'Connor, Sinéad, *Rememberings* (Penguin, 2021), p. 8.
3. 2020, 'On this day in 1987: Sinéad O'Connor releases her debut album *The Lion and the Cobra*' [online], *Hot Press*, available at https://www.hotpress.com/music/on-this-day-in-1987-Sinéad-oconnor-releases-her-debut-album-the-lion-and-the-cobra-22832057# [Accessed: 14 September 2023].
4. Hattenstone, Simon, 2021, 'Sinéad O'Connor: "I'll always be a bit crazy, but that's OK"' [online], *Guardian*, available at https://www.theguardian.com/music/2021/may/29/Sinéad-oconnor-ill-always-be-a-bit-crazy-but-thats-ok- [Accessed: 14 September 2023].
5. O'Connor, Brendan, 2007, 'Sinéad's love of her "devil" mum' [online], *Irish Independent*, available at https://www.independent.ie/irish-news/Sinéads-love-of-her-devil-mum/26297965.html# [Accessed: 14 September 2023].
6. Hayes, Dermott, *So Different* (Omnibus, 1991), p. 17.
7. Hattenstone, Simon, 2021, 'Sinéad O'Connor: "I'll always be a bit crazy, but that's OK"' [online], *Guardian*, available at https://www.theguardian.com/music/2021/may/29/Sinéad-oconnor-ill-always-be-a-bit-crazy-but-thats-ok- [Accessed: 14 September 2023].
8. Guccione Jr, Bob, 2015, 'Sinéad O'Connor: *SPIN*'s 1991 cover story, "Special Child"' [online], *SPIN*, available at https://www.spin.com/2015/09/Sinéad-oconnor-interview-spin-30-cover-story/ [Accessed: 14 September 2023].
9. 2022, '"You, as a priest, must hear this" – singer Sinead O'Connor discusses child abuse on After Dark | 1995' [online], *Open Media* on YouTube, available at https://www.youtube.com/watch?v=hWxz_1TPwEk&list=PLWJRhzV_VIVarWNp4CNT27wYiRb2LEj0b&index=2 [Accessed: 23 October 2023].
10. McNeil, Legs, 1990, 'Sinéad O'Connor: a captivating contradiction' [online], originally published in *SPIN*, available at https://pleasekillme.com/sinead-oconnor/ [Accessed: 22 October 2023].

2. Adolescence (1979–1985)

1. Pattison, Brynmor, 2016, 'Sinéad O'Connor's brother Joseph can't listen to her music because it's too "painful"' [online], *DublinLive*, available at https://www.dublinlive.ie/news/celebs/sinead-oconnors-brother-joseph-cant-11249937 [Accessed: 14 September 2023].
2. Joshi, Tara, 2023, '"She spoke truth to power, always": Sinéad O'Connor's affinity with Black music – and liberation' [online], *Guardian*, available at https://www.theguardian.com/music/2023/aug/14/she-spoke-truth-to-power-

always-sinead-oconnors-affinity-with-black-music-and-liberation [Accessed: 21 September 2023].

3. Guccione Jr, Bob, 2015, 'Sinéad O'Connor: *SPIN*'s 1991 cover story, "Special Child"' [online], *SPIN*, available at https://www.spin.com/2015/09/Sinéad-oconnor-interview-spin-30-cover-story/ [Accessed: 14 September 2023].

4. *Nothing Compares*, 2022, Director: Kathryn Ferguson, UK and Ireland, Paramount International.

5. Ibid.

6. Simons, Roxy, Sheets, Megan, 2021, '"My favourite was the naughty nun!" Sinéad O'Connor reveals she was a kissogram from the age of 16 but admits she was "terrible" at it because she was "shy"' [online], *Daily Mail*, available at https://www.dailymail.co.uk/tvshowbiz/article-9639733/Sinead-OConnor-reveals-kissogram-aged-16.html [Accessed: 3 October 2023].

7. Stokes, Niall, 2023, 'Sinéad O'Connor 1966–2023', *Hot Press*, Sinéad O'Connor tribute issue 'Thank You for Hearing Me', p. 19.

8. Hayes, Dermott, *So Different* (Omnibus, 1991), pp. 34–37.

9. Ibid.

10. Ibid.

3. Starting Out (1985–1986)

1. Capretto, Lisa, 2014, 'Sinéad O'Connor explains why she shaved her head: "It was dangerous to be a female"' [online], *Huffington Post*, available at https://www.huffpost.com/entry/sinead-oconnor-shaved-head_n_4726103 [Accessed: 13 October 2023].

2. Ibid.

3. 1986, Prophyltex advert, BBC, available at https://www.youtube.com/watch?v=oP0mYN9umPE [Accessed: 16 September 2023].

4. Masterson, Eugene, 2021, 'Sinéad O'Connor lashes out at authorities for not legalising condoms until the 1980s' [online], *Sunday World*, available at https://www.sundayworld.com/showbiz/irish-showbiz/sinead-oconnor-lashes-out-at-authorities-for-not-legalising-condoms-until-the-1980s/40115620.html [Accessed: 16 September 2023].

5. Holmquist, Kate, 1986, 'Sinéad O'Connor's first *Irish Times* interview, from 1986: "I don't need to drink or take drugs. All I need to do is sing"' [online], *Irish Times*, available at https://www.irishtimes.com/culture/music/2023/07/26/sinead-oconnors-first-irish-times-interview-i-dont-need-to-drink-or-take-drugs-all-i-need-to-do-is-sing/ [Accessed: 16 September 2023].

6. McAnailly Burke, Molly, 2023, 'Sinéad O'Connor: Revisiting one of her earliest *Hot Press* interviews' [online], *Hot Press*, available at https://www.hotpress.com/music/sinead-oconnor-revisiting-one-of-her-earliest-hot-press-interviews-22981807 [Accessed: 20 September 2023].

5. Affinity with Rastafari and Black Music (1986)

1. Bunce, Kim and Diski, Chloe, 2000, 'It was 20 years ago today' [online], *Guardian*, available at https://www.theguardian.com/theobserver/2000/dec/03/features.review7 [Accessed: 21 September 2023].

2. Joshi, Tara, 2023, '"She spoke truth to power, always": Sinéad O'Connor's affinity with Black music – and liberation' [online], *Guardian*, available at

152

https://www.theguardian.com/music/2023/aug/14/she-spoke-truth-to-power-always-sinead-oconnors-affinity-with-black-music-and-liberation [Accessed: 21 September 2023].

3. Bull, Sarah, 2013, 'Sinéad O'Connor debuts another giant tattoo at Glastonbury ... a reference to her Rastafarian beliefs on her right hand' [online], *Daily Mail*, available at https://www.dailymail.co.uk/tvshowbiz/article-2351472/Glastonbury-2013-Sinead-OConnor-debuts-GIANT-tattoo–reference-Rastafarian-beliefs.html [Accessed: 21 September 2023].

4. 2005, 'Sinéad O'Connor goes Rasta, mon' [online], Associated Press, available at https://www.today.com/popculture/sinead-oconnor-goes-rasta-mon-wbna8894420 [Accessed: 21 September 2023].

5. Elliott, Debbie, 2005, 'Sinéad O'Connor finds new roots – in Jamaica' [online], *NPR*, available at https://www.npr.org/transcripts/4961027 [Accessed: 21 September 2023].

6. Lightbody, Gary, 2023, "I'm a fan of the voice and just as equally a fan of the human being", *Hot Press*, Sinéad O'Connor tribute issue 'Thank You for Hearing Me', p. 5.

6. 'Heroine', and a Fight with U2 (1986)

1. Merkin, Daphne, 2023, 'Sinéad O'Connor remained true to herself at all costs' [online], *The New Republic*, available at https://newrepublic.com/article/174876/sinead-oconnor-remained-true-costs [Accessed: 17 October 2023].

7. First Child and First Marriage (1986–1987)

1. Reynolds, John, 2023, 'Comrades In Arms', *Hot Press*, Sinéad O'Connor tribute issue 'Thank You for Hearing Me', p. 7.

2. Ibid.

3. Bailie, Stuart, 1987, 'Sinéad O'Connor: Skinéad' [online], *Record Mirror*, available at https://www.rocksbackpages.com/Library/Article/sinad-oconnor-skinad [Accessed: 13 October 2023].

8. *The Lion and the Cobra* (1987)

1. Horton, Ross, 1987, 'One for keeps: Sinéad O'Connor, The Lion and the Cobra' [online], *musicOMH*, available at https://www.musicomh.com/features/one-for-keeps/sinead-oconnor-the-lion-and-the-cobra [Accessed: 23 October 2023].

2. Zaleski, Annie, 2023, '"Nothing Compares 2 U is perfect": Sinéad O'Connor's 10 greatest songs' [online], *Guardian*, available at https://www.theguardian.com/music/2023/jul/27/sinead-o-connor-10-best-songs-nothing-compares-2-u [Accessed: 23 October 2023].

3. DeCurtis, Anthony, 1988, '*The Lion and the Cobra*' [online], *Rolling Stone*, available at https://www.rollingstone.com/music/music-album-reviews/the-lion-and-the-cobra-252050/ [Accessed: 23 October 2023].

4. 1988, 'About' [online], *Genius*, available at https://genius.com/Sinead-oconnor-mandinka-lyrics#about [Accessed: 23 October 2023].

5. DeCurtis, Anthony, 1988, '*The Lion and the Cobra*' [online], *Rolling Stone*, available at https://www.rollingstone.com/music/music-album-reviews/the-lion-and-the-cobra-252050/ [Accessed: 23 October 2023].

6. Sodomsky, Sam, 1987, '*The Lion and the Cobra*' [online], *Pitchfork*, available at https://pitchfork.com/reviews/albums/sinead-oconnor-the-lion-and-the-cobra/ [Accessed: 23 October 2023].

7. Nelson, Terry, 2022, 'Sinéad O'Connor's debut album *The Lion and the Cobra* turns 35' [online], *Albumism*, available at https://albumism.com/features/sinad-oconnor-debut-album-the-lion-and-the-cobra-album-anniversary [Accessed: 23 October 2023].
8. Peschek, David, 2007, 'Review: Sinéad O'Connor' [online], *Guardian*, available at https://www.theguardian.com/music/2007/nov/14/popandrock1 [Accessed: 23 October 2023].
9. 1987, 'Troy' [online], *Genius*, available at https://genius.com/Sinead-oconnor-troy-lyrics [Accessed: 23 October 2023].
10. Zaleski, Annie, 2023, '"Nothing Compares 2 U' is perfect": Sinéad O'Connor's 10 greatest songs' [online], *Guardian*, available at https://www.theguardian.com/music/2023/jul/27/sinead-o-connor-10-best-songs-nothing-compares-2-u [Accessed: 23 October 2023].
11. FT, 2023, 'Incomparable' [online], *New York Review of Books*, available at https://www.nybooks.com/online/2023/08/05/incomparable-sinead-oconnor/ [Accessed: 23 October 2023].
12. Erlewine, Stephen Thomas, 2023, '10 essential Sinéad O'Connor songs' [online], *Los Angeles Times*, available at https://www.latimes.com/entertainment-arts/music/story/2023-07-26/10-best-essential-sinead-oconnor-songs [Accessed: 23 October 2023].
13. Amorosi, A.D., 2023, 'Sinéad O'Connor's best: 12 of her finest musical moments' [online], *Variety*, available at https://variety.com/2023/music/news/sinead-oconnor-best-songs-finest-moments-tracks-1235680937/ [Accessed: 23 October 2023].
14. 2023, 'Sinéad O'Connor: 10 essential songs' [online], *Rolling Stone*, available at https://www.rollingstone.com/music/music-lists/sinead-oconnor-best-songs-1234795591/ [Accessed: 23 October 2023].
15. De Sylvia, Dave, 1987, 'Sinéad O'Connor: *The Lion and the Cobra*' [online], *Sputnik Music*, available at https://www.sputnikmusic.com/review/9823/Sinead-OConnor-The-Lion-And-The-Cobra/ [Accessed: 23 October 2023].
16. Hart, Ron, 2017, 'Sinéad O'Connor's "*The Lion and the Cobra*" introduced us to her fearless voice 30 years ago' [online], *Billboard*, available at https://www.billboard.com/music/rock/sinead-oconnor-the-lion-and-the-cobra-debut-album-8031076/ [Accessed: 23 October 2023].
17. Beaumont, Mark, 2023, 'Sinéad O'Connor, 1966–2023: an artist of integrity, intensity and honesty' [online], *NME*, https://www.nme.com/features/music-features/sinead-oconnor-obituary-3473864 [Accessed: 23 October 2023].

10. Support for the IRA (1989)

1. 2005, 'Sinéad O'Connor takes back pro-IRA comments' [online], *Irish Examiner*, https://www.irishexaminer.com/lifestyle/arid-30223283.html [Accessed: 17 October 2023].

11. *Hush-a-Bye-Baby* (1989)

1. 'Sinéad O'Connor: Our Lady, Colleen' [online], *iMDB*, available at https://www.imdb.com/title/tt0118804/characters/nm0640521 [Accessed: 29 October 2023].
2. Beaumont-Thomas, Ben, Cain, Sian and Snapes, Laura, 2023, '"She trembled with the truths she had to tell": Sinéad O'Connor by friends, fans and collaborators'

[online], *Guardian*, available at https://www.theguardian.com/music/2023/jul/27/sinead-oconnor-tribute-by-friends-fans-and-collaborators [Accessed: 29 October 2023].

12. 'Nothing Compares 2 U' (1990)

1. 2023, 'Sinéad O'Connor, troubled Irish pop star who sabotaged her career spectacularly after her hit "Nothing Compares 2 U" – obituary' [online], *Telegraph*, available at https://www.telegraph.co.uk/obituaries/2023/07/26/sinad-oconnor-irish-pop-superstar-nothing-compares-2-u/ [Accessed: 23 October 2023].
2. Sweeney, Ken, 2008, 'Nothing compares to you, Fachtna' [online], *Sunday Tribune* article reproduced on sinead-oconnor.com, available at https://www.sinead-oconnor.com/home/index.php/articles/273-nothing-compares-to-you-fachtna [Accessed: 22 October 2023].
3. Hunt, Dennis, 1990, 'MTV: the naughty envelope, please' [online], *Los Angeles Times*, available at https://www.latimes.com/archives/la-xpm-1990-09-08-ca-599-story.html [Accessed: 23 October 2023].
4. 2023, 'Sinéad O'Connor, Billboard Music Awards 1990' [online], *YouTube*, available at https://www.youtube.com/watch?v=63Z_l9-XBw4 [Accessed: 23 October 2023].
5. Harvilla, Rob, 2023, '60 songs that explain the 90s: How Sinéad O'Connor turned a Prince song into her classic' [online], *The Ringer*, available at https://www.theringer.com/2021/6/2/22464082/sinead-oconnor-nothing-compares-2-u-prince [Accessed: 23 October 2023].
6. Merkin, Daphne, 2023, 'Sinéad O'Connor remained true to herself at all costs' [online], *The New Republic*, available at https://newrepublic.com/article/174876/sinead-oconnor-remained-true-costs [Accessed: 23 October 2023].
7. 2023, 'Sinéad O'Connor, troubled Irish pop star who sabotaged her career spectacularly after her hit "Nothing Compares 2 U" – obituary' [online], *Telegraph*, available at https://www.telegraph.co.uk/obituaries/2023/07/26/sinad-oconnor-irish-pop-superstar-nothing-compares-2-u/ [Accessed: 23 October 2023].

13. Finding a New Manager (1990)

1. Robinson, Stephen, 2001, 'Sinéad remembers Steve' [online], *Hot Press*, available at https://www.hotpress.com/music/sineacutead-remembers-steve-1525753 [Accessed: 22 October 2023].

14. *I Do Not Want What I Haven't Got* (1990)

1. Christgau, Robert, 1990, '*I Do Not Want What I Haven't Got*' [online], robertchristgau.com, available at https://www.robertchristgau.com/get_album.php?id=3163 [Accessed: 23 October 2023].
2. Stafford, James, '25 years ago: Sinéad O'Connor releases *I Do Not Want What I Haven't Got*' [online], *Diffuser*, available at https://diffuser.fm/sinead-oconnors-i-do-not-want-what-i-havent-got-25-years-later/ [Accessed: 23 October 2023].
3. Hocter, Matthew, 2020, 'Sinéad O'Connor's *I Do Not Want What I Haven't Got* turns 30' [online], *Albumism*, available at https://albumism.com/features/sinead-oconnor-i-do-not-want-what-i-havent-got-turns-30-anniversary-retrospective [Accessed: 23 October 2023].

4. Cinquemani, Sal, 2003, 'Review: Sinéad O'Connor, *I Do Not Want What I Haven't Got*' [online], *Slant*, available at https://www.slantmagazine.com/music/sinead-oconnor-i-do-not-want-what-i-havent-got/ [Accessed: 23 October 2023].

16. A Run-In with Madonna (1990)

1. Lynch, Donal, 2019, 'Regrets, yes, she's definitely had a few but still nothing compares to Sinéad O'Connor' [online], *Belfast Telegraph*, https://www.belfasttelegraph.co.uk/entertainment/music/regrets-yes-shes-definitely-had-a-few-but-still-nothing-compares-to-sinead-oconnor/38297432.html [Accessed: 15 September 2023].

17. Affair with Hugh Harris (1990)

1. Rogers, Sheila, 1990, 'Face to face with fame' [online], sinead-oconnor.com, originally printed in *Rolling Stone*, available at https://www.sinead-oconnor.com/home/index.php/articles/161-face-to-face-with-fame-rolling-stone-1990 [Accessed: 22 October 2022].
2. Ibid.

18. Refusing the US National Anthem (1990)

1. Greene, Andy, 2021, 'Flashback: Sinead O'Connor gets booed offstage at Bob Dylan anniversary concert' [online], *Rolling Stone*, available at https://www.rollingstone.com/music/music-news/sinead-o-connor-booed-pope-bob-dylan-concert-1176338/ [Accessed: 12 October 2023].
2. 1990, 'Listeners angered by Sinead O'Connor' [online], *Washington Post*, available at https://www.washingtonpost.com/archive/lifestyle/1990/08/28/listeners-angered-by-sinead-oconnor/b0b89b89-3ec1-4ad8-8978-4dd80513f342/ [Accessed: 12 October 2023].
3. Ibid.
4. Wilkinson, Tracy, 1990, 'Clerk at Upscale Grocery Strikes Sour Note With Singer: Anthem: He's fired from Mrs. Gooch's of Beverly Hills when Sinéad O'Connor objects to his rendition of "The Star-Spangled Banner" while she is shopping' [online], *Los Angeles Times*, available at https://www.latimes.com/archives/la-xpm-1990-10-06-mn-1612-story.html [Accessed: 12 October 2023].
5. Ibid.
6. 2023, 'Sinéad O'Connor: 1966 – July 26, 2023' [online], *Sydney Morning Herald*, available at https://www.smh.com.au/national/troubled-singer-sabotaged-her-career-after-hit-nothing-compares-2-u-20230727-p5drlh.html [Accessed: 23 October 2023].
7. Hilburn, Robert, 1990, 'Nothing Compares 2 Her Year' [online], *Los Angeles Times*, available at https://www.latimes.com/archives/la-xpm-1990-12-16-ca-9231-story.html [Accessed: 22 October 2022].

19. On Abortion (1990)

1. Guccione Jr, Bob, 2015, 'Sinéad O'Connor: SPIN's 1991 cover story, "Special Child"' [online], *SPIN*, available at https://www.spin.com/2015/09/Sinéad-oconnor-interview-spin-30-cover-story/ [Accessed: 14 September 2023].
2. 1992, Marian Finucane In Conversation with Sinéad O'Connor, RTÉ, available at https://www.youtube.com/watch?v=mdalYgfQm38 [Accessed: 16 September 2023].

156

3. Jonze, Tim, 2014, 'Sinéad O'Connor interview: "I deserve to be a priest. Music is a priesthood"' [online], *Guardian*, available at https://www.theguardian.com/music/2014/jul/27/sinead-o-connor-interview-i-deserve-to-be-a-priest [Accessed: 16 September 2023].

20. Breaking the Mic (1991)

1. Didcock, Barry, 2023, 'Jah Wobble on punk, PiL and "unstoppable" Sinéad O'Connor' [online], *The Herald*, available at https://www.heraldscotland.com/business_hq/23729203.jah-wobble-punk-pil-unstoppable-sinead-oconnor/ [Accessed: 22 October 2023].
2. Ibid.

22. A Fist Fight with Prince (1991)

1. Lewis, John, 2013, 'An audience with ... Sinéad O'Connor' [online], *Uncut*, available at https://www.uncut.co.uk/features/an-audience-with-sinead-o-connor-17114/ [Accessed: 21 September 2023].
2. 2018, 'Sinéad O'Connor audio claimed Prince beat women while on drugs' [online], *TMZ*, available at https://www.tmz.com/2018/04/19/sinead-oconnor-prince-death-police-investigation-violent-rages/ [Accessed: 21 September 2023].
3. 2019, 'Sinéad O'Connor claims Prince tried to beat her up' [online], *Good Morning Britain*, available at https://www.youtube.com/watch?v=Q73DVGhsMiE&t=252s [Accessed: 21 September 2023].
4. Mitchell, Gail, 2013, 'Read Prince's in-depth *Billboard* cover story from 2013' [online], *Billboard*, available at https://www.billboard.com/music/music-news/prince-billboard-cover-story-2013-1526279/ [Accessed: 21 September 2023].
5. Nelson, Jeff, 2021, 'Sinéad O'Connor remembers startling encounter with Prince: "The loneliness of fame was his undoing"' [online], *People*, available at https://people.com/music/sinead-oconnor-remembers-strange-night-prince/ [Accessed: 21 September 2023].
6. Hess, Amanda, 2021, 'Sinéad O'Connor remembers things differently' [online], *New York Times*, available at https://www.nytimes.com/2021/05/18/arts/music/sinead-oconnor-rememberings.html [Accessed: 21 September 2023].
7. Newman, Melinda, 2022, 'Why Prince's estate refused to allow "Nothing Compares 2 U" to be used in new Sinéad O'Connor documentary' [online], *Billboard*, available at https://www.billboard.com/pro/prince-sinead-o-connor-documentary-nothing-compares-2-u/ [Accessed: 21 September 2023].

23. Boycotting the Grammys (1991)

1. 1991, *The Arsenio Hall Show*, YouTube, available at https://www.youtube.com/watch?v=mAf7fGEeRQs&t=418s [Accessed: 15 September 2023].
2. 1991, 'The 33rd Annual Grammy Awards', *Variety*, available at https://books.google.co.uk/books?id=RxHbPxbBM1AC&pg=RA1-PA23&lpg=RA1-PA23&dq= [Accessed: 15 September 2023].
3. 2012, 'Sinéad O'Connor wins International Female presented by Paul Jones' [online], BRITs official Brit Awards account on *YouTube*, available at https://www.youtube.com/watch?v=_nr7x2ZnTJE [Accessed: 22 October 2023].

24. Saddam Hussein Incident on MTV (1991)

1. Sweeney, Ken, 2008, 'Nothing compares to you, Fachtna' [online], *Sunday Tribune*, available at https://www.sinead-oconnor.com/home/index.php/articles/273-nothing-compares-to-you-fachtna [Accessed: 22 October 2023].

25. *Am I Not Your Girl?* (1992)

1. Gardner, Elysa, 1992, '*Am I Not Your Girl?*' [online], *Rolling Stone*, available at https://www.rollingstone.com/music/music-album-reviews/am-i-not-your-girl-187171/ [Accessed: 17 October 2023].

2. Bernstein, Jonathan, 1992, 'Classic reviews: Sinéad O'Connor, *Am I Not Your Girl?*' [online], *SPIN*, available at https://www.spin.com/2023/07/classic-reviews-sinead-oconnor-am-i-not-your-girl/ [Accessed: 17 October 2023].

3. Sandow, Greg, 1992 [online], *Entertainment Weekly*, available at https://ew.com/article/1992/09/25/am-i-not-your-girl/ [Accessed: 17 October 2023].

26. Ripping Up the Pope (1992)

1. Hall, Jane, 1990, 'O'Connor won't sing on SNL in protest over Andrew Dice Clay' [online], *LA Times*, available at https://www.latimes.com/archives/la-xpm-1990-05-10-ca-1917-story.html [Accessed: 2 October 2023].

2. *Nothing Compares*, 2022, Director: Kathryn Ferguson, UK and Ireland, Paramount International.

3. Whatley, Jack, 2023, 'The infamous moment Sinéad O'Connor was banned from *Saturday Night Live* for calling out the Pope' [online], *Far Out*, available at https://faroutmagazine.co.uk/sinead-o-connor-banned-reason-snl-1992/ [Accessed: 2 October 2023].

4. Hutchinson, Sean, 2014, '10 People Banned from *SNL*' [online], *Mental Floss*, available at https://www.mentalfloss.com/article/55147/10-people-banned-snl [Accessed: 2 October 2023].

5. Specter, Emma, 2023, 'The world mocked and discarded Sinéad O'Connor. She deserved so much better' [online], *Vogue*, available at https://www.vogue.com/article/Sinéad-oconnor-deserved-better [Accessed: 12 September 2023].

6. Vassell, Nicole, 2023, 'Lawnmowers and ripped Pope pictures: Inside Sinéad O'Connor and Madonna's fraught history' [online], *Independent*, available at https://www.independent.co.uk/arts-entertainment/music/news/sinead-o-connor-madonna-feud-b2383538.html# [Accessed: 2 October 2023].

7. Cashin, Rory, 2023, 'Joe Pesci *SNL* rant on Sinéad O'Connor resurfaces following singer's death' [online], *Joe*, available at https://www.joe.ie/news/joe-pesci-sinead-oconnor-snl-778853 [Accessed: 2 October 2023].

8. Reilly, William M., 1992, 'Steamroller crushes Sinéad O'Connor recordings' [online], *UPI*, available at https://www.upi.com/Archives/1992/10/21/Steamroller-crushes-Sinead-OConnor-recordings/5284719640000/ [Accessed: 12 October 2023].

9. Vean, San, 2020, 'Madonna on Sinéad O'Connor *SNL* 1992' [online], *YouTube*, available at https://www.youtube.com/watch?v=nDtQdrb87Fs [Accessed: 2 October 2023].

10. 1992, 'Transcript: Interview: Camille Paglia' [online], *TVO Today*, available at https://www.tvo.org/transcript/008445/interview-camille-paglia [Accessed: 22 October 2023].

11. Kelly, Laura, 2023, 'How Sinéad O'Connor risked it all to speak truth to power – and inspired a new generation' [online], *Big Issue*, available at https://www.bigissue.com/culture/film/they-tried-to-bury-sinead-oconnor/ [Accessed: 23 October 2023].

12. Hess, Amanda, 2021, 'Sinéad O'Connor remembers things differently' [online], *New York Times*, available at https://www.nytimes.com/2021/05/18/arts/music/sinead-oconnor-rememberings.html [Accessed: 2 October 2023].

13. 2023, 'In Memoriam: Remembering Sinéad O'Connor's epic Saturday Night Live performance' [online], *DeadAnt*, available at https://deadant.co/in-memoriam-remembering-sinead-oconnors-epic-saturday-night-live-performance/ [Accessed: 2 October 2023].

14. Beaumont-Thomas, Ben, Cain, Sian and Snapes, Laura, 2023, '"She trembled with the truths she had to tell": Sinéad O'Connor by friends, fans and collaborators' [online], *Guardian*, available at https://www.theguardian.com/music/2023/jul/27/sinead-oconnor-tribute-by-friends-fans-and-collaborators [Accessed: 22 October 2023].

15. 2023, 'Novelist Colm Tóibín says Sinéad O'Connor sang with "sense of mission" against injustices' [online], ITV, available at https://www.itv.com/news/utv/2023-07-30/sinad-oconnor-sang-with-sense-of-mission-against-injustices-tibn-says [Accessed: 2 October 2023].

16. Holmes, David, 2023, 'Sinéad never, ever flinched from raising her head above the parapet, regardless of the flak awaiting her', *Hot Press*, Sinead O'Connor tribute issue 'Thank You for Hearing Me', p. 11.

27. The Bob Dylan 30th Anniversary Concert (1992)

1. 2023, '"I'm not down" – the day Sinéad O'Connor faced down the boos' [online], *Irish Examiner*, available at https://www.irishexaminer.com/news/arid-41192779.html [Accessed: 16 October 2023].

2. Stokes, Niall, 1992, 'Don't cry for me' [online], *Hot Press*, available at https://metro.co.uk/2019/01/20/sweet-story-emerges-infamous-sinead-oconnor-gig-people-cant-deal-8366567/ [Accessed: 16 October 2023].

3. Akingbade, Tobi, 2019, 'Sweet story emerges from infamous Sinead O'Connor gig and people can't deal with it' [online], *Metro*, available at https://metro.co.uk/2019/01/20/sweet-story-emerges-infamous-sinead-oconnor-gig-people-cant-deal-8366567/ [Accessed: 16 October 2023].

4. Stokes, Niall, 1992, 'Don't cry for me' [online], *Hot Press*, available at https://metro.co.uk/2019/01/20/sweet-story-emerges-infamous-sinead-oconnor-gig-people-cant-deal-8366567/ [Accessed: 16 October 2023].

5. 'Sinéad O'Connor slams old pal Kris Kristofferson for toxic masculinity' [online], *IrishCentral*, available at https://www.irishcentral.com/news/irishvoice/sinead-oconnor-kris-kristofferson-toxic-masculinity-twitter [Accessed: 16 October 2023].

6. De-Burca, Demelza, 2019, 'Sinéad O'Connor opens up about "sex" with actor Kris Kristoffersen – who's 30 years her senior' [online], *Irish Mirror*, available at https://www.irishmirror.ie/showbiz/irish-showbiz/sinead-oconnor-opens-up-sex-13888984# [Accessed: 16 October 2023].

29. Advert in *Irish Times* (1993)

1. O'Connor, Sinéad, 1993, 'Sinéad O'Connor's full-page *Irish Times* ad in 1993: "I deserve not to be treated like dirt. I deserve not to be hurt"' [online], *Irish Times*,

159

available at https://www.irishtimes.com/culture/music/2023/07/28/sinead-oconnors-full-page-irish-times-ad-in-1993-i-deserve-not-to-be-treated-like-dirt-i-deserve-not-to-be-hurt/ [Accessed: 23 October 2023].

2. Holmquist, Kate, 1993, 'Kate Holmquist on Sinéad O'Connor's full-page *Irish Times* ad: 'Like a poet, she has terrified us by speaking the truth' [online], *Irish Times*, available at https://www.irishtimes.com/culture/music/2023/07/28/kate-holmquist-on-sinead-oconnors-full-page-irish-times-ad-like-a-poet-she-has-terrified-us-by-speaking-the-truth/ [Accessed: 23 October 2023].

30. *Universal Mother* (1994)

1. Poulos, Maggie, 2013, '10 best Sinéad O'Connor songs' [online], *Diffuser*, available at https://diffuser.fm/best-sinead-oconnor-songs/ [Accessed: 23 October 2023].

2. Zacharek, Stephanie, 1994, '*Universal Mother*' [online], *Rolling Stone*, available at https://www.rollingstone.com/music/music-album-reviews/universal-mother-193409/ [Accessed: 23 October 2023].

31. Reconciling with U2 (1994)

1. Martin, Gavin, 1994, 'You've been framed!' [online], *NME*, available at https://www.flickr.com/photos/nothingelseon/53082247729/ [Accessed: 14 September 2023].

35. *Gospel Oak* (1997)

1. Foot, Tom, 2023, 'Sinéad O'Connor, her *Gospel Oak* album, and "the only person who was nice to me back then"' [online], *Camden New Journal*, available at https://www.camdennewjournal.co.uk/article/sinead-oconnor-her-gospel-oak-album-and-the-only-person-who-was-nice-to-me-back-then [Accessed: 16 October 2023].

2. 1997, 'Reviews: Singles' [online], *Music Week*, available at https://worldradiohistory.com/UK/Music-Week/1997/Music-Week-1997-04-26.pdf [Accessed: 16 October 2023].

3. Kot, Greg, 1997, '*Gospel Oak*' [online], *Rolling Stone*, available at https://www.rollingstone.com/music/music-album-reviews/gospel-oak-188562/ [Accessed: 16 October 2023].

4. Morse, Steve, 1997, 'Sinéad O'Connor shows gentler side' [online], *Tampa Bay Times*, available at https://www.tampabay.com/archive/1997/06/20/sinead-o-connor-shows-gentler-side/ [Accessed: 23 October 2023].

5. Sodomsky, Sam, 2023, 'Sinéad O'Connor was a voice of strength in the darkness' [online], *Pitchfork*, available at https://pitchfork.com/features/afterword/remembering-sinead-oconnor/ [Accessed: 16 October 2023].

38. Her First Suicide Attempt (1999)

1. Moreton, Cole, 2005, 'Sinéad O'Connor: talks exclusively about suicide and redemption' [online], *Independent*, available at https://www.independent.co.uk/arts-entertainment/music/features/sinead-o-connor-talks-exclusively-about-suicide-and-redemption-315633.html [Accessed: 13 October 2023].

2. Ibid.

39. Being Ordained as a Priest (1999)

1. Mullin, John, 1999, 'Now sinless Sinéad says Pope is nice' [online], *Guardian*, available at https://www.theguardian.com/uk/1999/apr/27/johnmullin [Accessed: 13 October 2023].
2. Ibid.
3. 1999, 'Sinéad O'Connor – *Late Late Show* 1999' [online], *YouTube*, available at https://www.youtube.com/watch?v=gsWL0uOyZkA [Accessed: 13 October 2023].
4. Sean O'Hagan, 2002, 'Mother superior' [online], *Observer*, available at https://www.theguardian.com/theobserver/2002/oct/06/features.review167 [Accessed: 29 October 2023].

40. Dating Dermott Hayes (1999)

1. Hayes, Dermott, 2023, 'A wild new year with my girlfriend Sinéad O'Connor' [online], *Sunday Times*, available at https://www.thetimes.co.uk/article/sinead-o-connor-death-ireland-church-abuse-son-shane-l8z7k9jmm [Accessed: 29 October 2023].

41. *Faith and Courage* (2000)

1. Pareles, Jon, 2023, '10 essential songs by Sinéad O'Connor' [online], *New York Times*, available at https://www.nytimes.com/2023/07/26/arts/music/10-essential-songs-by-sinead-oconnor.html [Accessed: 24 October 2023].
2. 2000 [online], *Metacritic*, available at https://www.metacritic.com/music/faith-and-courage/sinead-oconnor/critic-reviews [Accessed: 24 October 2023].
3. Walters, Barry, 2000, '*Faith and Courage*' [online], *Rolling Stone*, available at https://www.rollingstone.com/music/music-album-reviews/faith-and-courage-248624/ [Accessed: 24 October 2023].
4. Williamson, Nigel, 2000, 'Sinéad's journey of survival', *Music & Media*, Vol. 17, No. 25, p. 1 [online], available at https://www.worldradiohistory.com/UK/Music-and-Media/00s/2000/MM-2000-06-17.pdf [Accessed: 24 October 2023].

42. Saving Shane MacGowan (2000)

1. O'Hare, Mia, 2023, 'Sinéad O'Connor saved Shane MacGowan's life by calling the police on him' [online], *Mirror*, available at https://www.mirror.co.uk/3am/celebrity-news/sinead-oconnor-saved-shane-macgowans-31565299 [Accessed: 29 January 2024].

43. Coming Out … And Coming Back In (2000)

1. Anderson-Minshall, Diane, 2010, '*Curve*'s 20th Anniversary Retrospective: Sinéad O'Connor' [online], *Curve*, available at https://www.curvemag.com/blog/interviews/curves-20th-anniversary-retrospective-sinad-oconnor/ [Accessed: 22 October 2023].
2. Synon, Mary Ellen, 2000, 'God doesn't set limits, humans do' [online], *Irish Independent*, available at https://www.independent.ie/news/god-doesnt-set-limits-humans-do/26255133.html [Accessed: 22 October 2023].
3. Ibid.
4. Errico, Marcus, 2000, 'Sinéad O'Connor: I'm a lesbian' [online], *E! News*, available at https://www.eonline.com/news/39979/sinead-o-connor-i-m-a-lesbian [Accessed: 22 October 2023].

5. 2011, 'Sinéad O'Connor reveals sexual frustration on web' [online], *Reuters*, available at https://www.reuters.com/article/idINIndia-59078220110831 [Accessed: 22 October 2023].
6. Azzopardi, Chris, 2014, 'Q&A: Sinéad O'Connor On How Gays Changed Her Life & Getting Her "D*ck Hard"' [online], *Pride Source*, available at https://pridesource.com/article/67109-2 [Accessed: 22 October 2023].
7. Duffy, Nick, 2014, 'Sinéad O'Connor: I want to date women again, it isn't working with men' [online], *PinkNews*, available at https://www.thepinknews.com/2014/10/25/sinead-oconnor-i-want-to-date-women-again-it-isnt-working-with-men/ [Accessed: 22 October 2023].

44. Nursing Steve Fargnoli (2001)

1. Govan, Chloe, 2023, 'Janet Street-Porter recalls living with "unpredictable and enchanting" Sinéad O'Connor' [online], *Express*, available at https://www.express.co.uk/celebrity-news/1795781/Janet-Street-Porter-Sinead-O-Connor-living-together-unpredictable [Accessed: 22 October 2023].
2. Robinson, Stephen, 2001, 'Sinéad remembers Steve' [online], *Hot Press*, available at https://www.hotpress.com/music/sineacutead-remembers-steve-1525753 [Accessed: 22 October 2023].
3. Ibid.

45. Getting Married Again (2001)

1. 2001, 'Sinéad O'Connor reveals marriage to journalist' [online], *Irish Times*, available at https://www.irishtimes.com/news/sinead-o-connor-reveals-marriage-to-journalist-1.393459# [Accessed: 13 October 2023].
2. 2001, 'Sinéad O'Connor "to wed"' [online], *BBC News*, available at http://news.bbc.co.uk/1/hi/entertainment/1406579.stm [Accessed: 13 October 2023].
3. Ibid.
4. Flanagan, Pat, 2001, 'Sinéad and Nick wed in secret after an amazing three-month romance' [online], *Mirror*, available at https://www.thefreelibrary.com/Sinead+%26+Nick+wed+in+secret+after+an+amazing+3-month+romance%3B...-a077278807 [Accessed: 13 October 2023].
5. Hawken, Lydia, 2023, 'Sinéad O'Connor's tragic love life revealed' [online], *Daily Mail*, available at https://www.dailymail.co.uk/femail/article-12341539/Sinead-OConnors-tragic-love-life-revealed-late-Irish-musical-legend-married-four-times-bid-feel-normal-including-one-marriage-lasted-just-16-days.html [Accessed: 13 October 2023].
6. Quinitchett, Kevin, 2023, 'Nothing compares 2 him' [online], *US Sun*, available at https://www.the-sun.com/entertainment/8694771/sinead-oconnor-married-dating-history/# [Accessed: 13 October 2023].

46. *Sean-Nós Nua* (2002)

1. Miles, Milo, 2002, '*Sean-Nós Nua*' [online], *Rolling Stone*, available at https://www.rollingstone.com/music/music-album-reviews/sean-nos-nua-246119/ [Accessed: 16 October 2023].
2. Clarke, Betty, 2002, 'Sinéad O'Connor: *Sean-Nós Nua*' [online], *Guardian*, available at https://www.theguardian.com/music/2002/oct/04/popandrock.artsfeatures1 [Accessed: 16 October 2023].

3. Richardson, Mark, 2002, 'Sean-Nós Nua' [online], *Pitchfork*, available at https://pitchfork.com/reviews/albums/5942-sean-nos-nua/ [Accessed: 16 October 2023].

48. Early Retirement ... But Not for Long (2003)

1. 2003, 'Sinéad O'Connor retires from music' [online], *NME*, available at https://www.nme.com/news/music/osinead-connor-3-1384610 [Accessed: 29 October 2023].

50. Advert in *Irish Examiner* (2004)

1. Chrisafis, Angelique, 2004, 'Sinéad begs for mercy after nits joke' [online], *Guardian*, available at https://www.theguardian.com/uk/2004/sep/25/religion.artsnews [Accessed: 29 October 2023].

52. *Throw Down Your Arms* (2005)

1. Harvell, Jess, 2005, '*Throw Down Your Arms*' [online], *Pitchfork*, available at https://pitchfork.com/reviews/albums/5945-throw-down-your-arms/ [Accessed: 15 October 2023].
2. Spencer, Neil, 2005, 'Sinéad O'Connor, *Throw Down Your Arms*' [online], *Observer*, available at https://www.theguardian.com/lifeandstyle/2005/sep/18/shopping1 [Accessed: 15 October 2023].
3. Udell, Phil, 2005, '*Throw Down Your Arms*' [online], *Hot Press*, available at https://www.hotpress.com/music/throw-down-your-arms-2828771 [Accessed: 15 October 2023].
4. Robinson, Stephen, 2001, 'Sinéad remembers Steve' [online], *Hot Press*, available at https://www.hotpress.com/music/sineacutead-remembers-steve-1525753 [Accessed: 22 October 2023].

53. A Love Rivalry and Fourth Child (2006)

1. 2006, 'Sinéad O'Connor: NOT pregnant and smoking' [online], *People*, available at https://people.com/parents/sinead_oconnor_-2/ [Accessed: 14 October 2023].
2. Ibid.
3. 2006, 'Sinéad O'Connor expecting fourth child' [online], *People*, available at https://people.com/parents/sinead_oconnor__1/# [Accessed: 14 October 2023].
4. Ryan, Alexandra, 2012, 'Miracle at Mary's as Sinéad pops in for Christmas' [online], *Irish Mail on Sunday*, available at https://www.pressreader.com/ireland/the-irish-mail-on-sunday/20121202/281573762995333 [Accessed: 14 October 2023].
5. Harris, Anne, 2006, 'Why Sinéad O'Connor sent those toxic texts to Mary Coughlan' [online], *Irish Independent*, available at https://www.independent.ie/opinion/analysis/why-sinead-oconnor-sent-those-toxic-texts-to-mary-coughlan/26410126.html [Accessed: 14 October 2023].
6. Power, Ed, 2021, 'Mary Coughlan revisits her past' [online], *Irish Times*, available at https://www.irishtimes.com/culture/tv-radio-web/mary-coughlan-revisits-her-past-it-was-everywhere-bags-of-cocaine-champagne-and-tequila-1.4535006 [Accessed: 14 October 2023].
7. Harris, Anne, 2007, 'Sinéad and Bonadio split up: "There's no space for my needs"' [online], *Irish Independent*, available at https://www.independent.ie/opinion/analysis/sinead-and-bonadio-split-up-theres-no-space-for-my-needs/26284760.html [Accessed: 14 October 2023].

8. O'Toole, Jason, 2020, 'Mary Coughlan buries hatchet with Sinéad O'Connor and ex-husband after "realising own mistakes"' [online], *Irish Mirror*, available at https://www.irishmirror.ie/showbiz/irish-showbiz/mary-coughlan-buries-hatchet-sinead-23084505 [Accessed: 14 October 2023].
9. Gibson, Kelsie, 2023, 'All about Sinéad O'Connor's four children' [online], *People*, available at https://people.com/all-about-sinead-o-connor-children-7566003 [Accessed: 14 October 2023].

54. *Theology* (2007)

1. Murphy, Adrienne, 2007, '*Theology*' [online], *Hot Press*, https://www.hotpress.com/music/theology-2931459 [Accessed: 16 October 2023].
2. Spencer, Neil, 2007, 'Sinéad O'Connor, *Theology*' [online], *Observer*, available at https://www.theguardian.com/music/2007/jun/17/popandrock.features7 [Accessed: 16 October 2023].
3. Sheffield, Rob, 2007, '*Theology*' [online], *Rolling Stone*, available at https://www.rollingstone.com/music/music-album-reviews/theology-255470/ [Accessed: 16 October 2023].

56. Represented by O'Ceallaigh Again (2008)

1. Sweeney, Ken, 2008, 'Nothing compares to you, Fachtna' [online], *Sunday Tribune* available at https://www.sinead-oconnor.com/home/index.php/articles/273-nothing-compares-to-you-fachtna [Accessed: 22 October 2023].

57. Collaboration with Mary J. Blige (2009)

1. 2009, 'New version of "This Is to Mother You" with Sinéad and Mary J. Blige" [online], sinead-oconnor.com, https://www.sinead-oconnor.com/home/index.php/news/289-new-version-of-qthis-is-to-mother-youq-with-sinead-and-mary-j-blige [Accessed: 22 October 2023].
2. Ibid.
3. Petridis, Alexis, 2023, 'Controversy never drowned out the astonishing songcraft of Sinéad O'Connor' [online], *Guardian*, available at https://www.theguardian.com/music/2023/jul/26/controversy-never-drowned-out-the-astonishing-songcraft-of-sinead-oconnor [Accessed: 22 October 2023].

58. Song Used Without Permission on Real IRA Website (2009)

1. Lavery, Michael, 2009, 'Sinéad O'Connor song taken off Real IRA website' [online], *Belfast Telegraph*, available at https://www.belfasttelegraph.co.uk/news/sinead-oconnor-song-taken-off-real-ira-website/28497058.html [Accessed: 22 October 2023].
2. Ibid.
3. Ibid.

59. A Third Marriage (2010)

1. O'Sullivan, Claire, 2011, 'O'Connor "heartbroken" over Cooney split' [online], *Irish Examiner*, available at https://www.irishexaminer.com/news/arid-20151637.html [Accessed: 13 October 2023].
2. Dervan, Cathal, 2011, 'Sinéad O'Connor's third marriage breaks up' [online], *IrishCentral*, available at https://www.irishcentral.com/culture/entertainment/sinead-oconnors-third-marriage-breaks-up-119833684-237382011 [Accessed: 13 October 2023].

3. Sweeney, Ken, 2011, 'It's third time unlucky for Sinéad as she ends marriage' [online], *Irish Independent*, available at https://www.independent.ie/style/celebrity/its-third-time-unlucky-for-sinead-as-she-ends-marriage/26723348.html [Accessed: 13 October 2023].
4. Whitman, Sara, 2023, 'Sinéad O'Connor's husband: everything to know about her four marriages' [online], *Hollywood Life*, available at https://hollywoodlife.com/feature/sinead-oconnor-husband-5141723/# [Accessed: 13 October 2023].

60. Vindication (2010)

1. 2010, 'Pope apologises to Irish sex abuse victims' [online], *CBC News*, available at https://www.cbc.ca/news/world/pope-apologizes-to-irish-sex-abuse-victims-1.902607 [Accessed: 26 October 2023].

61. Looking for Love on Twitter (2011)

1. 2011, 'Sinéad O'Connor's internet sex quest' [online], *Stuff*, available at https://www.stuff.co.nz/ipad-big-picture/5543056/Sinead-O-Connors-internet-sex-quest [Accessed: 13 October 2023].
2. Vulliamy, Ed, 2012, 'Another tacky divorce, another album full of promise – nothing compares to Sinéad' [online], *Observer*, available at available at https://www.theguardian.com/music/2012/jan/01/sinead-oconnor-ireland-tabloids# [Accessed: 13 October 2023].
3. Buchanan, Kyle, 2011, 'The eleven best quotes from Sinéad O'Connor's online sex hunt' [online], *Vulture*, available at https://www.vulture.com/2011/08/sinead_oconnor_sex.html [Accessed: 13 October 2023].
4. DiGiacomo, Frank, 2014, '*Billboard* cover: Sinéad O'Connor on having no regrets, being "irregular" and resurrecting her career' [online], *Billboard*, available at https://www.billboard.com/music/music-news/billboard-cover-sinead-oconnor-on-having-no-regrets-being-irregular-and-6214061/ [Accessed: 24 October 2023].
5. Geraghty, Liam, 2011 [online], *YouTube*, @geraghtyliam, available at https://www.youtube.com/watch?v=h9m_nKmssQI [Accessed: 13 October 2023].

62. A Cry for Help (2011)

1. Finn, Natalie, 2011, 'Sinéad O'Connor's disturbing, suicidal tweets get the cops' attention' [online], *E! News*, available at https://www.eonline.com/news/264362/sinead-o-connor-s-disturbing-suicidal-tweets-get-the-cops-attention [Accessed: 13 October 2023].
2. 2011, 'Sinead O'Connor tweets for help after suicide attempt' [online], *Rolling Stone*, available at https://www.rollingstone.com/music/music-news/sinead-oconnor-tweets-for-help-after-suicide-attempt-120840/ [Accessed: 13 October 2023].
3. 2011, 'This week's uncut version of *Irish Sunday Independent* piece' [online], available at https://www.sinead-oconnor.com/home/index.php/news/330-this-weeks-un-cut-version-of-irish-sunday-independent-piece [Accessed: 13 October 2023].

63. A Fourth Marriage (2011)

1. Keneally, Tim, 2012, 'Sinéad O'Connor reunites with her husband for "mad lovemaking affair"' [online], *The Wrap*, available at https://www.thewrap.com/Sinead-oconnor-reunites-her-husband-mad-love-making-affair-34068/ [Accessed: 12 September 2023].

2. Goodwin, Harry, 2023, 'Sinéad O'Connor: Inside music legend's turbulent relationship history as star tragically dies aged just 56' [online], *The Sun*, available at available at https://www.thesun.co.uk/tvandshowbiz/23199967/Sinéad-oconnor-relationship-history-dies/ [Accessed: 12 September 2023].

3. Moylan, Brian, 2011, 'Sinéad O'Connor got married in Vegas in a pink cadillac' [online], *Gawker*, available at https://www.gawker.com/5866609/sinead-oconnor-got-married-in-vegas-in-a-pink-cadillac [Accessed: 15 September 2023].

4. Moylan, Brian, 2011, 'Sinéad O'Connor's wildly inappropriate wedding announcement' [online], *Gawker*, available at https://www.gawker.com/5866699/Sinéad-oconnors-wildly-inappropriate-wedding-announcement [Accessed: 9 September 2023].

5. 2011, 'Sinéad ends 16-day marriage' [online], *Sky News*, available at https://news.sky.com/story/sinead-ends-16-day-marriage-10482536 [Accessed: 15 September 2023].

6. Hardie, Beth, 2012, 'Sinéad O'Connor was "given crack" on her wedding night' [online], *Mirror*, available at https://www.mirror.co.uk/3am/celebrity-news/sinead-oconnor-was-given-crack-on-her-wedding-188368 [Accessed: 15 September 2023].

7. Michaels, Sean, 2012, 'Sinéad O'Connor seeks treatment for depression' [online], *Guardian*, https://www.theguardian.com/music/2012/jan/19/sinead-o-connor-depression [Accessed: 13 October 2023].

8. Hardie, Beth, 2012, 'Is she serious? Sinéad O'Connor says she's back with her husband AGAIN' [online], *Mirror*, available at https://www.mirror.co.uk/3am/celebrity-news/sinead-oconnor-tweets-that-she-is-back-with-her-husband-191086 [Accessed: 15 September 2023].

9. 'Sinéad O'Connor reunites with "cave man" hubby' [online], *NZ Herald*, available at https://www.nzherald.co.nz/entertainment/sinead-oconnor-reunites-with-cave-man-hubby/WFFQ2YRASVVFSITJKN7AELP2DU/ [Accessed: 15 September 2023].

10. Owoseje, Toyin, 2012, 'Sinéad O'Connor reunites with "cave-man" husband' [online], *International Business Times*, available at https://www.ibtimes.co.uk/Sinéad-o-connor-reunites-caveman-husband-night-276917 [Accessed: 12 September 2023].

11. Kiedis, Anthony, 2004, *Scar Tissue*, Time Warner Books.

12. 2012, 'Sinéad: I was never red hot for Chili Peppers frontman' [online], *Irish Independent*, available at https://www.independent.ie/life/sinead-i-was-never-red-hot-for-chili-peppers-frontman/26870977.html [Accessed: 15 September 2023].

13. Taysom, Joe, 2021, 'The Red Hot Chili Peppers song Anthony Kiedis wrote about Sinéad O'Connor' [online], *Far Out*, available at https://faroutmagazine.co.uk/the-red-hot-chili-peppers-song-anthony-kiedis-sinead-oconnor/ [Accessed: 15 September 2023].

14. 2014, 'I married the right man ... I'm renewing my marriage vows to Barry' [online], *Irish Independent*, available at https://www.independent.ie/style/celebrity/celebrity-news/i-married-the-right-man-im-renewing-my-marriage-vows-to-barry-sinead-oconnor/30026578.html [Accessed: 15 September 2023].

15. Hamilton, Sam, 2014, 'Sinéad O'Connor scraps plans to renew wedding plans with husband Barry Herridge' [online], *Irish Mirror*, available at https://www.irishmirror.ie/showbiz/irish-showbiz/sinead-oconnor-not-renew-wedding-3199599 [Accessed: 15 September 2023].

16. Lewis, John, 2013, 'An audience with ... Sinéad O'Connor' [online], *Uncut*, available at https://www.uncut.co.uk/features/an-audience-with-sinead-o-connor-17114/ [Accessed: 21 September 2023].

17. 2014, 'I wish I hadn't ever got married. Silly cow' [online], *Irish Independent*, available at https://www.independent.ie/style/celebrity/celebrity-news/i-wish-i-hadnt-ever-got-married-silly-cow-sinead-oconnor/30573038.html [Accessed: 15 September 2023].

64. *How About I Be Me (And You Be You)?* (2012)

1. Somaiya, Ravi, 2012, 'Engaging her public, seeking her peace' [online], *New York Times*, available at https://www.nytimes.com/2012/02/12/arts/music/sinead-oconnors-how-about-i-be-me-and-you-be-you.html [Accessed: 14 October 2023].

2. Ibid.

3. Hermes, Will, 2012, '*How About I Be Me (And You Be You)?*' [online], *Rolling Stone*, available at https://www.rollingstone.com/music/music-album-reviews/how-about-i-be-me-and-you-be-you-188354/ [Accessed: 14 October 2023].

4. Deusner, Stephen M, 2012, '*How About I Be Me (And You Be You)?*' [online], *Pitchfork*, available at https://pitchfork.com/reviews/albums/16339-how-about-i-be-me-and-you-be-you/ [Accessed: 14 October 2023].

5. 2012, 'Album review: Sinéad O'Connor, "*How About I Be Me (And You Be You)?*"' [online], *Billboard*, available at https://www.billboard.com/music/music-news/album-review-sinead-oconnor-how-about-i-be-me-and-you-be-you-1067098/ [Accessed: 14 October 2023].

6. Barker, Liz, 2012, 'New video: Sinéad O'Connor, "The Wolf Is Getting Married"' [online], MTV, available at https://www.mtv.com/news/0i2tgy/sinead-oconnor-the-wolf-is-getting-married-video [Accessed: 14 October 2023].

7. Empire, Kitty, 2012, 'Sinéad O'Connor: "*How About I Be Me (And You Be You)?*" – review' [online], *Guardian*, available at https://www.theguardian.com/music/2012/feb/26/sinead-oconnor-how-about-review [Accessed: 14 October 2023].

8. Deusner, Stephen M, 2012, 'How About I Be Me (And You Be You)?' [online], *Pitchfork*, available at https://pitchfork.com/reviews/albums/16339-how-about-i-be-me-and-you-be-you/ [Accessed: 14 October 2023].

9. Somaiya, Ravi, 2012, 'Engaging her public, seeking her peace' [online], *New York Times*, available at https://www.nytimes.com/2012/02/12/arts/music/sinead-oconnors-how-about-i-be-me-and-you-be-you.html [Accessed: 14 October 2023].

10. Lynch, Dónal, 2021, 'Singer/songwriter John Grant on sex, drugs, rock'n'roll and duetting with Sinéad O'Connor' [online], *Irish Independent*, available at https://www.independent.ie/entertainment/music/singersongwriter-john-grant-on-sex-drugs-rocknroll-and-duetting-with-sinead-oconnor/40577516.html [Accessed: 14 October 2023].

65. Splitting with O'Ceallaigh for the Third Time (2012)

1. Horan, Niamh, 2012, 'Sinéad O'Connor splits from her manager and former lover' [online], *Sunday Independent*, available at https://www.independent.ie/style/celebrity/sinead-oconnor-splits-from-her-manager-and-former-lover/26850527.html [Accessed: 23 October 2023].

2. Ibid.

66. A Very Candid Interview on Mental Health (2012)

1. Palmieri, Gaspare, 2012, 'The Psychiatrist and the Rock Star: interview with Sinéad O'Connor' [online], *State of Mind*, available at https://www.stateofmind.it/2012/10/Sinéad-oconnor-interview/ [Accessed: 9 September 2023].

67. An Argument with Miley Cyrus (2013)

1. Eells, Josh, 2013, 'Miley Cyrus on why she loves weed, went wild at the VMAs and much more' [online], *Rolling Stone*, available at https://www.rollingstone.com/music/music-news/miley-cyrus-on-why-she-loves-weed-went-wild-at-the-vmas-and-much-more-99493/ [Accessed: 19 September 2023].
2. 2013, 'Sinéad O'Connor warns Miley Cyrus against exploitation' [online], BBC, available at https://www.bbc.co.uk/news/entertainment-arts-24382051 [Accessed: 19 September 2023].
3. Danton, Eric R, 2013, 'Miley Cyrus mocks Sinéad O'Connor, who fires back in new letter' [online], *Rolling Stone*, available at https://www.rollingstone.com/music/music-news/miley-cyrus-mocks-sinead-oconnor-who-fires-back-in-new-letter-114019/ [Accessed: 19 September 2023].
4. Gibsone, Harriet and Jonze, Tim, 2013, 'Sinéad O'Connor threatens Miley Cyrus with legal action after mental illness tweet' [online], *Guardian*, available at https://www.theguardian.com/culture/2013/oct/04/sinead-oconnor-legal-action-miley-cyrus [Accessed: 19 September 2023].
5. Fetherstonhaugh, Neil, 2023, 'Miley Cyrus dedicates song to Sinéad O'Connor a decade after feud with Irish singer' [online], *Sunday World*, available at https://www.sundayworld.com/showbiz/music/miley-cyrus-dedicates-song-to-sinead-oconnor-a-decade-after-feud-with-irish-singer/a1218185716.html [Accessed: 19 September 2023].
6. 2013, 'Sinéad O'Connor demands apology from Miley Cyrus over mental illness taunt as she pens fourth letter' [online], *Daily Mail*, available at https://www.dailymail.co.uk/tvshowbiz/article-2449856/Sinead-OConnor-demands-apology-Miley-Cyrus-mental-illness-taunt-pens-FOURTH-letter.html [Accessed: 21 September 2023].
7. Cyrus, Miley, 2013 [online], *Twitter*, available at https://x.com/MileyCyrus/status/385917041452277760?s=20 [Accessed: 21 September 2023].
8. Cyrus, Miley, 2013 [online], *Twitter*, available at https://x.com/MileyCyrus/status/385917156141326337?s=20 [Accessed: 21 September 2023].
9. 2013, 'Amanda Palmer pens open letter to Sinéad O'Connor in support of Miley Cyrus' [online], *Fact*, available at https://www.factmag.com/2013/10/03/amanda-palmer-pens-open-letter-to-sinead-oconnor-in-support-of-miley-cyrus/ [Accessed: 21 September 2023].
10. Edmonds, Lizzie, 2023, 'Miley Cyrus says she was judged harshly as a child in the public eye' [online], *Evening Standard*, available at https://www.standard.co.uk/showbiz/miley-cyrus-british-vogue-child-star-judged-public-eye-b1082268.html# [Accessed: 21 September 2023].
11. Paul, Larisha, 2023, 'Miley Cyrus says she was unaware of Sinéad O'Connor's "fragile mental state" during "Wrecking Ball" dispute' [online], *Rolling Stone*, available at https://www.rollingstone.com/music/music-news/miley-cyrus-sinead-oconnor-wrecking-ball-dispute-revisited-1234812576/ [Accessed: 22 September 2023].

12. Bradshaw, Melissa, 2014, 'Sinéad O'Connor – don't assume Miley Cyrus is a victim' [online], *Guardian*, available athttps://www.theguardian.com/commentisfree/2013/oct/03/sinead-oconnor-miley-cyrus [Accessed: 22 October 2023].
13. Jones, Liz, 2013, 'Pop's poisonous princess: Glorying in drugs, guns and sleaze, Rihanna's toxic role model for her army of young fans' [online], *Daily Mail*, available at https://www.dailymail.co.uk/femail/article-2347680/Rihannas-toxic-role-model-army-young-fans-says-LIZ-JONES.html [Accessed: 14 September 2023].

68. Getting Face Tattoos (2013)

1. Coughlan, Maggie, 2013, 'Sinéad O'Connor debuts two new tattoos – on her face' [online], *People*, available at https://people.com/celebrity/sinad-oconnor-debuts-two-new-tattoos-on-her-face/ [Accessed: 30 October 2023].

69. Recognition of Misdiagnosis of Bipolar (2013)

1. Hamilton, Sam, 2013, 'Doctors tell Sinéad O'Connor: You're not bipolar' [online], *Irish Mirror*, available at https://www.irishmirror.ie/showbiz/irish-showbiz/doctors-tell-Sinéad-oconnor-youre-2344863 [Accessed: 9 September 2023].
2. Hattenstone, Simon, 2021, 'Sinéad O'Connor: "I'll always be a bit crazy, but that's OK"' [online], *Guardian*, available at https://www.theguardian.com/music/2021/may/29/Sinéad-oconnor-ill-always-be-a-bit-crazy-but-thats-ok- [Accessed: 14 September 2023].
3. Bozzatello, Paola; Rocca, Paola; Baldassarri, Lorenzo; Bosia, Marco; Bellino, Silvio; 2021, 'The Role of Trauma in Early Onset Borderline Personality Disorder: A Biopsychosocial Perspective' [online], *Frontiers in Psychiatry*, available at https://www.frontiersin.org/articles/10.3389/fpsyt.2021.721361/full#:~:text=In%2030%25%20up%20to%2090,disorders%20(13-15). [Accessed: 22 September 2023].
4. 'Borderline personality disorder' [online], NHS, available at https://www.nhs.uk/mental-health/conditions/borderline-personality-disorder/ [Accessed: 22 September 2023].
5. Cattane, Nadia; Rossi, Roberta; Lanfredi, Mariangela; Cattaneo, Annamaria; 2017, 'Borderline personality disorder and childhood trauma: exploring the affected biological systems and mechanisms' [online], *BMC Psychiatry*, available at https://bmcpsychiatry.biomedcentral.com/articles/10.1186/s12888-017-1383-2 [Accessed: 22 September 2023].

70. *I'm Not Bossy, I'm the Boss* (2014)

1. Reed, Ryan, 2014, 'Beyoncé wants you to stop saying "bossy"' [online], *Rolling Stone*, available at https://www.rollingstone.com/music/music-news/beyonce-wants-you-to-stop-saying-bossy-203689/ [Accessed: 22 October 2023].
2. Anderson, Christy, 2014, '"It's so stupid" – Joan Rivers isn't a fan of "Ban Bossy"' [online], *SiriusXm*, available at https://web.archive.org/web/20160304022624/http://blog.siriusxm.com/2014/03/25/its-so-stupid-joan-rivers-isnt-a-fan-of-ban-bossy/ [Accessed: 22 October 2023].
3. 2014, 'Sinéad O'Connor's new album inspired by Sandberg's "Ban Bossy" campaign' [online], *Guardian*, available at https://www.theguardian.com/music/2014/jun/03/sinead-oconnor-new-album-sheryl-sandberg-ban-bossy-campaign [Accessed: 22 October 2023].

72. Interest in Sinn Féin (2014)

1. 2023, 'Sinéad O'Connor's unusual relationship with Sinn Féin, from criticising Gerry Adams to querying partition policies' [online], *Belfast Telegraph*, available at https://www.belfasttelegraph.co.uk/entertainment/music/sinead-oconnors-unusual-relationship-with-sinn-fein-from-criticising-gerry-adams-to-querying-partition-policies/a697396364.html [Accessed: 22 October 2023].
2. Ibid.

73. Blasting *Rolling Stone* and Reality Shows (2015)

1. Strecker, Erin, 2015, 'Sinéad O'Connor blasts "Rolling Stone" Kim Kardashian cover: "Music has officially died"' [online], *Billboard*, available at https://www.billboard.com/music/music-news/sinead-oconnor-kim-kardashian-rolling-stone-cover-6633503/# [Accessed: 22 September 2023].
2. 2013, 'Simon Cowell asks Sinéad O'Connor to be a guest judge on The X Factor' [online], *IrishCentral*, available at https://www.irishcentral.com/culture/entertainment/simon-cowell-asks-sinead-oconnor-to-be-a-guest-judge-on-the-x-factor-227220461-237782551 [Accessed: 26 October 2023].
3. 2013, 'X Factor: Simon Cowell taunts Sinéad O'Connor with guest judge offer' [online], *Guardian*, available at https://www.theguardian.com/media/2013/oct/10/x-factor-simon-cowell-sinead-oconnor [Accessed: 22 September 2023].

74. Becoming a Grandmother (2015)

1. 2015, 'Sinéad O'Connor will be a granny: Singer reveals daughter-in-law is expecting' [online], *Irish Mirror*, available at https://www.irishmirror.ie/showbiz/irish-showbiz/sinead-oconnor-granny-singer-reveals-5255475 [Accessed: 22 September 2023].
2. 2015, '"I love you little rocker": Sinéad O'Connor, 48, becomes a grandmother after her son welcomes a baby boy' [online], *Daily Mail*, available at https://www.dailymail.co.uk/tvshowbiz/article-3165980/I-love-little-rocker-Sinead-O-Connor-48-grandmother-son-welcomes-baby-boy.html [Accessed: 22 September 2023].

75. Being Shafted by Her Agent (2015)

1. Kinsella, Carl, 2015, 'Sinéad O'Connor has been shafted out of money by her booking agent and she's venting her fury on Facebook' [online], *Joe*, available at https://www.joe.ie/news/pic-sinead-oconnor-has-been-shafted-out-of-money-by-her-booking-agent-and-shes-venting-her-fury-on-facebook-508514# [Accessed: 3 October 2023].

76. A Radical Hysterectomy (2015)

1. O'Donoghue, Anna, 2015, 'Sinéad O'Connor to undergo hysterectomy' [online], *Irish Examiner*, available at https://www.irishexaminer.com/lifestyle/celebrity/arid-30692475.html [Accessed: 3 October 2023].
2. Deerwester, Jayme, 2017, 'Sinéad O'Connor tells Dr. Phil her problems stemmed from being "flung into menopause"' [online], *USA Today*, available at https://eu.usatoday.com/story/life/tv/2017/09/12/sinead-oconnor-tells-dr-phil-her-problems-stemmed-being-flung-into-menopause/659140001/ [Accessed: 3 October 2023].

3. Nelson, Jeff, 2021, 'Sinead O'Connor on managing mental health after abusive childhood: "There was a lot of therapy"' [online], *People*, available at https://people.com/music/sinead-oconnor-finding-peace-after-childhood-trauma-managing-mental-health/ [Accessed: 3 October 2023].

77. Suicide Attempt (2015)

1. 2015, 'Sinead O'Connor angry suicide note ... my family betrayed me' [online], *TMZ*, available at https://www.tmz.com/2015/11/29/sinead-oconnor-suicide-note/ [Accessed: 3 October 2023].

78. Letters to Her Family (2016)

1. Hood, Bryan, 2016, 'Sinead O'Connor posts unhinged rant directed at family' [online], *Page Six*, available at https://pagesix.com/2016/05/17/sinead-oconnor-posts-unhinged-rant-directed-at-family/ [Accessed: 3 October 2023].
2. 2016, 'Sinead O'Connor missing, possibly "suicidal"' [online], *TMZ*, available at https://www.tmz.com/2016/05/16/sinead-oconnor-missing-suicidal/ [Accessed: 3 October 2023].
3. Hood, Bryan, 2016, 'Sinead O'Connor found safe after suicide scare' [online], *Page Six*, available at https://pagesix.com/2016/05/16/sinead-oconnor-found-safe-after-suicide-scare/ [Accessed: 3 October 2023].
4. Kaufman, Gil, 2016, 'Sinead O'Connor pens vicious open letter to ex-husband' [online], *Billboard*, available at https://www.billboard.com/music/music-news/sinead-oconnor-open-letter-7377317/ [Accessed: 3 October 2023].

79. Surgery and Complications (2016)

1. Sager, Jessica, 2015, 'Sinéad O'Connor details terrifying medical emergency' [online], *Page Six*, available at https://pagesix.com/2016/10/25/sinead-oconnor-details-terrifying-medical-emergency/ [Accessed: 15 September 2023].
2. Larkin, Mike, 2016, '"Liver all f***ed and killing me": Sinéad O'Connor reveals hospital dash as she was struggling to breathe due to agony following botched surgery' [online], *Daily Mail*, available at https://www.dailymail.co.uk/tvshowbiz/article-3869476/Sinead-O-Connor-reveals-hospital-dash-struggling-breathe-agony-following-surgery.html [Accessed: 15 September 2023].

80. Dispute with Arsenio Hall (2017)

1. Miller, Matt, 2016, 'Arsenio Hall has sued Sinead O'Connor for claiming he supplied Prince with drugs' [online], *Esquire*, available at https://www.esquire.com/entertainment/music/news/a44621/arsenio-hall-sinead-oconnor-prince-lawsuit/# [Accessed: 12 October 2023].
2. Spanos, Brittany, 2016, 'Arsenio Hall sues Sinead O'Connor for $5 million' [online], *Rolling Stone*, available at https://www.rollingstone.com/music/music-news/arsenio-hall-sues-sinead-oconnor-for-5-million-95310/ [Accessed: 12 October 2023].
3. Ibid.
4. Stone, Natalie, 2016, 'Sinead O'Connor responds to Arsenio Hall's defamation lawsuit' [online], *Hollywood Reporter*, available at https://www.hollywoodreporter.com/news/general-news/sinead-oconnor-responds-arsenio-halls-891653/ [Accessed: 12 October 2023].

5. Ax, Joseph, 2016, '"I'm more amused than I've ever dreamed a person could be" – Sinéad O'Connor dismisses Arsenio Hall lawsuit' [online], *Irish Independent*, available at https://www.independent.ie/world-news/im-more-amused-than-ive-ever-dreamed-a-person-could-be-sinead-oconnor-dismisses-arsenio-hall-lawsuit/34693074.html# [Accessed: 12 October 2023].
6. Goldstein, Danielle, 2016, '"Suck my dick" – Sinéad O'Connor responds to the Arsenio Hall lawsuit' [online], *NME*, available at https://www.nme.com/news/music/sinead-oconnor-5-1201721 [Accessed: 12 October 2023].
7. Minsker, Evan, 2017, 'Sinéad O'Connor apologises for saying Arsenio Hall gave Prince drugs' [online], *Pitchfork*, available at https://pitchfork.com/news/71821-sinead-oconnor-apologizes-for-saying-arsenio-hall-gave-prince-drugs/ [Accessed: 12 October 2023].
8. ABC News, 2017, 'Arsenio Hall to dismiss $5 million lawsuit against Sinéad O'Connor for Prince comments' [online], *ABC News*, available at https://abcnews.go.com/Entertainment/arsenio-hall-dismiss-15-million-lawsuit-sinead-oconnor/story?id=45676135# [Accessed: 12 October 2023].

81. Sued by O'Ceallaigh (2017)

1. O'Faolain, Aodhan, 2017, 'Sinéad O'Connor being sued for €500,000 by former manager' [online], *Irish Times*, available at https://www.irishtimes.com/news/crime-and-law/courts/high-court/sinead-o-connor-being-sued-for-500-000-by-former-manager-1.3168826 [Accessed: 22 October 2023].
2. Ibid.
3. Ibid.
4. O'Faolain, Aodhan, 2019, 'Sinéad O'Connor reaches "amicable" court settlement with former manager' [online], *Irish Times*, available at https://www.irishtimes.com/news/crime-and-law/courts/high-court/sinead-o-connor-reaches-amicable-court-settlement-with-former-manager-1.3877330 [Accessed: 22 October 2023].

82. Charity and Trans Rights (2017)

1. O'Donoghue, Anna, 2017, 'Sinéad O'Connor is donating "30 years" of clothes to Irish transgender youth' [online], *Irish Examiner*, available at https://www.irishexaminer.com/lifestyle/celebrity/arid-30789493.html# [Accessed: 12 October 2023].

83. Breakdown in Motel (2017)

1. 2017, 'Sinead O'Connor shares worrying video about being suicidal' [online], *YouTube*, available at https://www.youtube.com/watch?v=yg5Z-8FWEYE [Accessed: 26 October 2023].

84. Dr. Phil Interview (2017)

1. 2017, 'Dr. Phil Exclusive: The Sinéad O'Connor interview' [online], Dr. Phil on *YouTube*, available at https://www.youtube.com/watch?v=pxJeCpgNp7g [Accessed: 26 October 2023].
2. Ibid.
3. Lynch, Donal, 2017, 'Back from hell: the return of Sinéad O'Connor' [online], *Irish Independent*, available at https://www.independent.ie/entertainment/music/back-from-hell-the-return-of-sinead-oconnor/38273213.html [Accessed: 26 October 2023].

85. Change of Name (2017)

1. Kelly, Emma, 2017, 'Sinéad O'Connor changes her name to Magda Davitt to be "free of parental curses"' [online], *Metro*, available at https://metro.co.uk/2017/09/09/sinead-oconnor-changes-her-name-to-magda-davitt-to-be-free-of-parental-curses-6915108/ [Accessed: 12 October 2023].
2. Ibid.
3. Allday, Jasmine, 2023, 'Sinéad O'Connor's name changes over the years as she tragically dies at just 56' [online], *Mirror*, available at https://www.mirror.co.uk/3am/celebrity-news/sinead-oconnors-name-changes-over-30562407 [Accessed: 12 October 2023].

86. Conversion to Islam (2018)

1. Burke, David, 2009, 'Sinéad O'Connor: *Faith and Courage*' [online], *R2*, available at https://www.rocksbackpages.com/Library/Article/sinead-oconnor-faith-and-courage [Accessed: 16 October 2023].
2. Pasquini, Maria, 2018, 'Sinéad O'Connor reveals she's converted to Islam' [online], *People*, available at https://people.com/music/sinead-oconnor-converted-islam/ [Accessed: 16 October 2023].
3. Lane, Barnaby, 2023, 'Sinéad O'Connor converted to Islam in 2018 and changed her name to Shuhada' Sadaqat. Here is what she said about her Muslim faith' [online], *Insider*, available at https://www.insider.com/sinead-oconnor-islam-muslim-shuhada-sadaqat-explained-2023-7 [Accessed: 16 October 2023].
4. Bray, Allison, 2018, 'Nothing compares to Islam' [online], *Irish Independent*, available at https://www.independent.ie/regionals/herald/nothing-compares-to-islam-sineads-a-happy-old-hag-after-conversion/37460012.html [Accessed: 16 October 2023].
5. Butler, Alexander and Kholsa, Alanah, 2023, 'When did Sinéad O'Connor become a Muslim?' [online], *Daily Mail*, available at https://www.dailymail.co.uk/news/article-12346055/Sinead-OConnors-religious-journey-Irish-singers-troubled-relationship-Catholicism.html [Accessed: 16 October 2023].
6. Real, Evan, 2018, 'Sinéad O'Connor says she "never wants to spend time with white people again" [online], *Billboard*, available at https://www.billboard.com/music/music-news/sinead-oconnor-never-wants-to-spend-time-white-people-8483651/ [Accessed: 16 October 2023].
7. 2018, 'Sinéad O'Connor won't mix with "disgusting" white people after becoming a Muslim' [online], *Stuff*, available at https://www.stuff.co.nz/entertainment/celebrities/108413234/sinead-oconnor-wont-mix-with-disgusting-white-people-after-becoming-a-muslim [Accessed: 16 October 2023].
8. Shenton, Zoe and Gibb, Jessica, 2018, 'Sinéad O'Connor returns to Twitter with message for "white supremacists" after "disgusting white people" remark' [online], *Mirror*, available at https://www.mirror.co.uk/3am/celebrity-news/sinead-oconnor-returns-twitter-message-13592186 [Accessed: 16 October 2023].
9. Shepherd, Jack, 2018, 'Sinéad O'Connor says she "never wants to spend time with white people again" following conversion to Islam' [online], *Independent*, available at https://www.independent.co.uk/arts-entertainment/music/news/sinead-oconnor-islam-white-people-shuhada-davitt-muslim-a8620231.html [Accessed: 16 October 2023].
10. Robertson, Alexander, 2018, '"I love annoying supremacists": Sinéad O'Connor returns to Twitter in bizarre video explaining her "disgusting white people"

remark' [online], *Daily Mail*, available at https://www.dailymail.co.uk/news/article-6392317/Sinead-OConnor-returns-Twitter-explain-disgusting-white-people-remark.html [Accessed: 16 October 2023].

11. Harrington, Scheenagh, 2020, 'Sinéad O'Connor "absolutely thrilled" after scholarship named after her' [online], *Extra.ie*, available at https://extra.ie/2020/02/15/entertainment/celebrity/sinead-oconnor-bimm-scholarship [Accessed: 22 October 2023].

12. Tracy, Brianne, 2019, 'Sinéad O'Connor apologises for calling white people "disgusting", returns to stage after hiatus' [online], *People*, available at https://people.com/music/sinead-oconnor-apologizes-saying-white-people-disgusting/ *[Accessed: 28 October 2023].*

88. Performing Live Again (2019)

1. Sullivan, Caroline, 2019, 'Sinéad O'Connor review – radiant return for singer still seeking truth' [online], *Guardian*, available at https://www.theguardian.com/music/2019/dec/17/sinead-o-connor-review-shepherds-bush-empire-london [Accessed: 30 October 2023].

89. Studying Healthcare (2020)

1. Richards, Will, 2020, 'Sinéad O'Connor plans to become a healthcare assistant: "The COVID thing gave me more impetus"' [online], *NME*, available at https://www.nme.com/news/music/sinead-oconnor-plans-to-become-a-healthcare-assistant-the-covid-thing-gave-me-more-impetus-2679311 [Accessed: 2 October 2023].

90. 'Trouble of the World' (2020)

1. 2020, 'NEW MUSIC: Sinéad O'Connor "Trouble Of The World"' [online], available at https://heavenlyrecordings.com/new-music-sinead-oconnor-trouble-of-the-world/ [Accessed: 2 October 2023].

2. Daly, Rhian, 2020, 'Listen to Sinéad O'Connor's "Trouble Of The World" cover, her first release since 2016' [online], *NME*, available at https://www.nme.com/news/music/listen-sinead-oconnor-trouble-of-the-world-cover-first-release-2016-2768478 *[Accessed: 2 October 2023].*

3. Ehrlich, Brenna, 2020, 'Sinéad O'Connor drops Mahalia Jackson cover in honour of BLM, teases new album' [online], *Rolling Stone*, available at https://www.rollingstone.com/music/music-news/mahalia-jackson-sinead-o-conner-1066959/ [Accessed: 2 October 2023].

4. Segal, Victoria, 2020, 'Sinéad O'Connor Remembered: "I hope to God I'm not a pussy…"' [online], *MOJO*, available at https://www.mojo4music.com/articles/stories/sinead-oconnor-remembered/# [Accessed: 2 October 2023].

91. *Rememberings* (2021)

1. Masterson, Eugene, 2023, 'Eugene Masterson: "My run-ins and love-ins with Sinéad O'Connor"' [online], *Sunday World*, available at https://www.sundayworld.com/showbiz/irish-showbiz/eugene-masterson-my-run-ins-and-love-ins-with-sinead-oconnor/a1190801364.html [Accessed: 18 September 2023].

2. McCormick, Neil, 2021, 'Sinéad O'Connor hurled abuse at me – but now I understand why' [online], *Telegraph*, available at https://www.telegraph.co.uk/books/what-to-read/sinead-oconnor-hurled-abuse-now-understand/ [Accessed: 18 September 2023].

3. Hess, Amanda, 2021, 'Sinéad O'Connor remembers things differently' [online], *New York Times*, available at https://www.nytimes.com/2021/05/18/arts/music/sinead-oconnor-rememberings.html [Accessed: 18 September 2023].

92. A Retirement Announcement and Retraction (2021)

1. Cordero, Rosy, 2021, 'Sinéad O'Connor announces retirement' [online], *Entertainment Weekly*, available at https://ew.com/music/sinead-oconnor-announces-retirement/ [Accessed: 17 October 2023].
2. Reilly, Nick, 2021, 'Sinéad O'Connor to boycott Woman's Hour after "offensive and misogynistic" interview' [online], *NME*, available at https://www.nme.com/news/music/sinead-oconnor-to-boycott-womens-hour-after-offensive-and-misogynistic-interview-2953914
3. Snapes, Laura, 2021, 'Sinéad O'Connor retracts retirement announcement' [online], *Guardian*, available at https://www.theguardian.com/music/2021/jun/08/sinead-oconnor-retracts-retirement-announcement [Accessed: 17 October 2023].
4. Lloyd, Albertina, 2021, 'Sinéad O'Connor boycotts *Woman's Hour* after "offensive and misogynistic" interview' [online], *Yahoo! News*, available at https://uk.news.yahoo.com/sinead-o-connor-womans-hour-083003202.html [Accessed: 17 October 2023].
5. Pike, Molly, 2021, 'Sinéad O'Connor boycotts *Woman's Hour* after "offensive and misogynistic" interview' [online], *Mirror*, available at https://www.mirror.co.uk/3am/celebrity-news/sinead-oconnor-boycotts-bbc-womans-24229391 [Accessed: 17 October 2023].
6. 2021, 'Sinéad O'Connor reverses course, says she's not retiring from touring and recording' [online], *IMDB*, available at https://www.imdb.com/news/ni63319272/ [Accessed: 17 October 2023].
7. Ibid.
8. Heaney, Steven, 2021, '"I'm gonna keep being fabulous" – Sinéad O'Connor retracts retirement announcement' [online], *Irish Examiner*, available at https://www.irishexaminer.com/news/arid-40308401.html [Accessed: 17 October 2023].
9. Rice, Nicholas, 2021, 'Sinéad O'Connor backtracks and says she is not retiring from recording and touring: "I retract"' [online], *Yahoo!*, available at https://uk.sports.yahoo.com/news/sin-ad-oconnor-backtracks-says-155224688.html [Accessed: 17 October 2023].

93. Putting Her Own Stamp on the World (2021)

1. An Post official website, 2023, https://www.anpost.com/Shop/Products/Booklet-of-4-National-Stamps-(Irish-at-Glastonbury# [Accessed: 2 October 2023].

94. Shane (2022)

1. Skopeliti, Clea, 2022, 'Son of Sinéad O'Connor dies at age of 17 after going missing' [online], *Guardian*, available at https://www.theguardian.com/music/2022/jan/08/son-of-sinead-oconnor-dies-at-age-of-17-after-going-missing# [Accessed: 12 October 2023].
2. Gillespie, Tom, 2022, 'Sinéad O'Connor: "Please be at peace" – Irish singer's teenage son Shane dies after going missing' [online], *Sky News*, available at https://news.sky.com/story/sinead-oconnor-please-be-at-peace-irish-singers-teenage-son-shane-dies-after-going-missing-12511557 [Accessed: 12 October 2023].

3. Hamilton, Sophie, 2023, 'Sinéad O'Connor's son Shane: how singer tragically lost her 17-year-old son' [online], *Hello!*, available at https://www.hellomagazine.com/health andbeauty/mother-and-baby/498686/sinead-oconnor-son-shane-tragic-death/# [Accessed: 2 October 2023].

4. Allday, Jasmine, 2023, 'Sinéad O'Connor's heartbreaking final social media post before death at 56' [online], *BelfastLive*, available at https://www.belfastlive.co.uk/ news/northern-ireland/sinead-oconnors-heartbreaking-final-social-27404126 [Accessed: 12 October 2023].

5. Byrne, Kerry J., 2022, 'Sinéad O'Connor says teen son escaped suicide watch before being found dead' [online], *New York Post*, available at https://nypost.com/2022/01/ 08/sinead-oconnors-teen-son-escaped-suicide-watch-before-death/ [Accessed: 12 October 2023].

6. Roberts, Sam, 2022, 'Sinéad O'Connor pays heartbreaking tribute as "beautiful" son Shane dies aged 17' [online], *Irish Mirror*, available at https://www.irishmirror.ie/ news/irish-news/sinead-oconnor-pays-heartbreaking-tribute-25889499 [Accessed: 12 October 2023].

7. Sweeney, Ken, 2022, 'Sinéad O'Connor's teenage son dies as she pays tribute to "light of my life"' [online], *The Sun*, available at https://www.thesun.co.uk/tvandshowbiz/ 17258694/sinead-oconnor-teenage-son-shane-died-missing-person/ [Accessed: 12 October 2023].

8. Mallick, Dani, 2022, 'Sinéad O'Connor dedicates Bob Marley's "Ride Natty Ride" to late son' [online], *DanceHallMag*, available at https://www.dancehallmag.com/2022/ 01/09/news/sinead-oconnor-dedicates-bob-marleys-ride-natty-ride-to-late-son.html [Accessed: 12 October 2023].

9. Spence, Niamh, 2023, 'Sinéad O'Connor's vow to never sing again after tragic death of son as singer dies at age 56' [online], *Mirror*, available at https://www.mirror.co.uk/ 3am/celebrity-news/sinead-oconnors-vow-never-sing-30562322# [Accessed: 12 October 2023].

10. Khomami, Nadia, 2022, 'Sinéad O'Connor criticises Irish authorities after death of son Shane' [online], *Guardian*, available at https://www.theguardian.com/music/ 2022/jan/09/sinead-oconnor-criticises-irish-authorities-after-death-of-son-shane# [Accessed: 12 October 2023].

11. Donaghy, Gerard, 2022, 'Sinéad O'Connor criticises "evil" Irish state following son Shane's death' [online], *Irish Post*, available at https://www.irishpost.com/news/ sinead-oconnor-criticises-evil-irish-state-following-son-shanes-death-227693 [Accessed: 12 October 2023].

12. 2022, 'Sinéad O'Connor apologises to Tusla for "lashing out", slams Irish healthcare as "third world"' [online], *IrishCentral*, available at https://www.irishcentral.com/sinead-oconnor-apologizes-son-death [Accessed: 12 October 2023].

13. Ainsworth, Paul, 2023, 'Shane MacGowan and wife remember Sinéad O'Connor's "love and friendship" in emotional tribute' [online], *Irish News*, available at https://www.irishnews.com/news/2023/07/27/news/shane_macgowan_and_wife_ remember_sinead_o_connor_s_love_and_friendship_in_emotional_tribute-3476374/ [Accessed: 12 October 2023].

14. O'Riordan, Cáit, 2022 [online], *Twitter*, available at https://x.com/rockyoriordan/ status/1479634203151151105?s=20 [Accessed: 12 October 2023].

15. Mallon, Sandra, 2022, 'Devastated Sinéad O'Connor's message to son Shane's father in emotional social media post' [online], *Irish Mirror*, available at https://www.irishmirror.ie/showbiz/irish-showbiz/devastated-sinead-oconnors-message-son-25899844 [Accessed: 12 October 2023].
16. Shilliday, Beth, 2023, 'Sinéad O'Connor's heartbreaking last tweet before dying was about her son's death' [online], *Yahoo!*, available at https://www.yahoo.com/entertainment/sinead-o-connor-heartbreaking-last-171631770.html [Accessed: 12 October 2023].
17. Aizin, Rebecca, 2023, 'Sinéad O'Connor's Son: How She Mourned Shane After His Tragic Death at Age 17' [online], *People*, available at https://people.com/sinead-oconnor-son-what-she-said-after-tragic-death-7566094 [Accessed: 12 October 2023].
18. Goodwin, Harry, 2023, 'Sinéad O'Connor: Inside music legend's turbulent relationship history as star tragically dies aged just 56' [online], *The Sun*, available at https://www.thesun.co.uk/tvandshowbiz/23199967/Sinéad-oconnor-relationship-history-dies/ [Accessed: 12 September 2023].

95. *Nothing Compares* (2022)

1. Ferguson, Kathryn, 2023, "The film was a love letter to Sinéad", *Hot Press*, Sinéad O'Connor tribute issue 'Thank You for Hearing Me', p. 17.

96. Choice Music Prize (2023)

1. 2023, "'I wish you happiness" – Sinéad O'Connor dedicates Choice Music Prize to refugees' [online], *IrishCentral*, available at https://www.irishcentral.com/culture/entertainment/sinead-oconnor-choice-music-prize [Accessed: 2 October 2023].

97. Struggling with Grief (2023)

1. Goodwin, Harry, 2023, '"Love the life you have" Sinéad O'Connor's tragic final post revealed after legendary singer dies aged just 56' [online], *The Sun*, available at https://www.thesun.co.uk/tvandshowbiz/23199061/sinead-oconnors-tragic-final-post/ [Accessed: 2 October 2023].
2. Rodger, James, 2023, 'Sinéad O'Connor's tragic final post before death aged just 56' [online], *BirminghamLive*, available at https://www.birminghammail.co.uk/news/showbiz-tv/sinad-oconnors-tragic-final-post-27402607# [Accessed: 2 October 2023].
3. Anderson, Natasha, 2023, 'Sinéad O'Connor's anguished final Tweets: Star said she had been "living as an undead night creature" since her son, 17, took his own life last year' [online], *Daily Mail*, available at https://www.dailymail.co.uk/tvshowbiz/article-12341301/Sinead-OConnor-anguished-final-Tweets.html [Accessed: 12 October 2023].

99. Tributes (2023)

1. James, Rhiannon, 2023, '"Totally devastating news that is breaking": The moment Irish Radio 1 breaks listeners' hearts revealing Sinéad O'Connor had died – as the country's President leads tributes to "one of our most gifted performers of recent decades"' [online], *Daily Mail*, available at https://www.dailymail.co.uk/news/article-12341383/Ireland-mourns-Sinead-OConnor-Taoiseach-Leo-Varadkar-leads-tributes-saying-talent-unmatched-compare.html [Accessed: 15 September 2023].
2. Ibid.

3. Ibid.
4. Ibid.
5. Ibid.
6. Ibid.
7. Ibid.
8. Ibid.
9. Ibid.
10. Ibid.
11. Stubbs, David, 2023, *Twitter*, available at https://x.com/sendvictorious/status/1684262699339743238?s=20 [Accessed: 15 September 2023].
12. Martin Doyle, Conor Capplis, 2023, 'Sinéad O'Connor by Bono, Annie Lennox, Shane MacGowan and more: "The U2ers are heartbroken"' [online], *Irish Times*, available at https://www.irishtimes.com/culture/books/2023/07/28/sinead-oconnor-by-bono-annie-lennox-shane-macgowan-and-more-the-u2ers-are-heartbroken/ [Accessed: 2 October 2023].
13. Peter Gabriel, 2023, *Twitter*, available at https://x.com/itspetergabriel/status/1684525285847212032?s=20 [Accessed: 2 October 2023].
14. Kate Bush, 2023, 'Sinéad' [online], available at https://www.katebush.com/news/sinead [Accessed: 2 October 2023].
15. Amanda Palmer, 2023, 'Sinéad' [online], *Facebook*, available at https://www.facebook.com/story.php?story_fbid=pfbid0NUCggWot8hmob9us6yd YA43XPWkkgadz2g2zowBVKji7UC3tv9fgZmqzBZcnoha2l&id=100045146024077 &mc_cid=f5d342178c&mc_eid=f04cb52a3e [Accessed: 12 September 2023].
16. HIV Ireland, 2023, *Twitter*, available at https://x.com/HIVIreland/status/1684276941275254785?s=20 [Accessed: 15 September 2023].
17. Victoria Mary Clarke and Shane McGowan, 2023, *Twitter*, available at https://x.com/Victoriamary/status/1684316783400955909?s=20 [Accessed: 2 October 2023].
18. Naomi Clarke, 2023, 'Sinéad O'Connor sang with "sense of mission" against injustices, Toibin says' [online], *Evening Standard*, available at https://www.standard.co.uk/news/uk/catholic-church-ireland-sinead-o-connor-fiction-bbc-radio-b1097589.html [Accessed: 2 October 2023].
19. Caitlin Moran, 2023, *Twitter* [online], https://twitter.com/caitlinmoran/status/1684263831441113102? [Accessed: 2 October 2023].
20. Ingle, Rhiannon, 2023, 'Music legend Sinéad O'Connor has died aged 56' [online], *LadBible*, https://www.ladbible.com/entertainment/music/sinead-o-connor-dead-music-singer-240347-20230726 [Accessed: 2 October 2023].
21. Vassell, Nicole, 2023, '"She was a very good friend of mine": Bob Geldof recalls final texts with Sinéad O'Connor' [online], *Independent*, available at https://www.independent.co.uk/arts-entertainment/music/news/sinead-o-connor-final-texts-bob-geldof-b2389358.html [Accessed: 15 September 2023].
22. Stokes, Niall, 2023, 'Sinéad O'Connor 1966–2023', *Hot Press*, Sinead O'Connor tribute issue 'Thank You for Hearing Me', p. 3.

100. Pushback to Tributes (2023)

1. Lewchuk, Nikita, 2023, '"You hadn't the guts to support her when she was alive" says Morrissey in tribute to Sinéad O'Connor' [online], *Hot Press*, https://www.hotpress.com/culture/you-hadnt-the-guts-to-support-her-when-she-was-alive-says-morrissey-in-tribute-to-sinead-oconnor-22981883 [Accessed: 30 October 2023].

2. Geraghty, Hollie, 2023, 'Lily Allen "incensed" by "spineless" tributes to Sinéad O'Connor' [online], *NME*, https://www.nme.com/news/music/lily-allen-incensed-by-spineless-tributes-to-sinead-oconnor-3475673 [Accessed: 30 October 2023].

101. Pushback to Obituary (2023)

1. Sullivan, Caroline, 2023, 'Sinéad O'Connor obituary' [online], *Guardian*, https://www.theguardian.com/music/2023/jul/26/Sinéad-oconnor-obituary [Accessed: 9 September 2023].
2. Thorn, Tracey, 2023 [online], *Twitter*, https://x.com/tracey_thorn/status/1684266675011457026?s=20 [Accessed: 14 September 2023].
3. Ibid.
4. Ibid.
5. Ibid.
6. Ibid.
7. Ibid.

102. Funeral and Further Tributes

1. O'Carroll, Rory, 2023, 'Sinéad O'Connor tribute appears in Ireland as funeral plans announced' [online], *Guardian*, available at https://www.theguardian.com/music/2023/aug/06/sinead-oconnor-tribute-appears-in-ireland-as-funeral-plans-announced [Accessed: 2 October 2023].
2. Ibid.
3. BelongTo, 2023 [online], *Twitter*, available at https://x.com/Belong_To/status/1684533332145496064?s=20 [Accessed: 2 October 2023].
4. Hanley, Valerie, 2023, 'Sinéad O'Connor saved my life: Mother brutally raped by a business tycoon reveals how the Nothing Compares 2 U singer tracked her down and took her in' [online], *Daily Mail*, available at https://www.dailymail.co.uk/news/article-12352789/EXCLUSIVE-Sin-ad-OConnor-saved-life-mother-brutally-raped-business-tycoon-reveals-Irish-music-legend-tracked-took-in.html [Accessed: 2 October 2023].

103. Family Statement (2023)

1. Paul, Larisha, 2023, 'Sinéad O'Connor's children and family share appreciation for "outpouring of love" in statement' [online], *Rolling Stone*, available at https://www.rollingstone.com/music/music-news/sinead-oconnors-family-death-tributes-statement-1234813985/ [Accessed: 30 October 2023].

Dear Reader,

We hope you have enjoyed this book, but why not share your views on social media? You can also follow our pages to see more about our other products: facebook.com/penandswordbooks or follow us on Twitter @penswordbooks

You can also view our products at www.pen-and-sword.co.uk (UK and ROW) or www.penandswordbooks.com (North America).

To keep up to date with our latest releases and online catalogues, please sign up to our newsletter at: www.pen-and-sword.co.uk/newsletter

If you would like a printed catalogue with our latest books, then please email: enquiries@pen-and-sword.co.uk or telephone: 01226 734555 (UK and ROW) or email: Uspen-and-sword@casematepublishers.com or telephone: (610) 853-9131 (North America).

We respect your privacy and we will only use personal information to send you information about our products.

Thank you!